THE BOUNDARIES OF DEMOCRACY

This book provides a general theory of democratic inclusion for the present world. It presents an original contribution to our understanding of the democratic ideal by explaining how democratic inclusion can apply to individuals in a variety of contexts: the workplace, social clubs, religious institutions, the family, and, of course, the state. The book explores the problem of democratic inclusion, what it means to be subject to de facto authority, how this conception translates into legal systems, and the relationship between territorial claims by the state and law's claim to legitimate authority.

The volume will be of interest to scholars and researchers of politics, especially political theory and democracy.

Ludvig Beckman is Professor of Political Science at Stockholm University and research leader at the Institute for Futures Studies, Stockholm. His recent work includes books and articles on the boundary problem in democratic theory and on the idea of popular sovereignty in constitutional politics.

THE BOUNDARIES OF DEMOCRACY

A Theory of Inclusion

Ludvig Beckman

Cover image: Getty Images

First published 2023
by Routledge
4 Park Square, Milton Park, Abingdon, Oxon OX14 4RN

and by Routledge
605 Third Avenue, New York, NY 10158

Routledge is an imprint of the Taylor & Francis Group, an informa business

© 2023 Ludvig Beckman

The right of Ludvig Beckman to be identified as author of this work has been asserted in accordance with sections 77 and 78 of the Copyright, Designs and Patents Act 1988.

The Open Access version of this book, available at www.taylorfrancis.com, has been made available under a Creative Commons Attribution-Non Commercial-No Derivatives 4.0 license.

Trademark notice: Product or corporate names may be trademarks or registered trademarks, and are used only for identification and explanation without intent to infringe.

British Library Cataloguing-in-Publication Data
A catalogue record for this book is available from the British Library

ISBN: 978-1-032-15820-4 (hbk)
ISBN: 978-1-032-41810-0 (pbk)
ISBN: 978-1-003-35980-7 (ebk)

DOI: 10.4324/9781003359807

Typeset in Bembo
by SPi Technologies India Pvt Ltd (Straive)

CONTENTS

Acknowledgments   *viii*

1   The Unresolved Problem of Democratic Inclusion   1

    Including the Subjects 3
    Including Members 6
    What Is a Principle of Democratic Inclusion? 10
    A Brief Outline of The Book 14
    Notes 15

2   Democratic Inclusion in Associations   17

    Morally Binding Decisions 18
    The Moralized All-Subjected Principle 20
    Decisions That Claim to Be Binding 22
    Decisions and Authority 25
    Subject To De Facto Authority 27
    Notes 36

3   Democratic Inclusion and the State   38

    The State and The Law 38
    How The Law Binds 40
    The Brute Force Account 41
    The Moral Account 43
    The Authority Account 47
    Notes 49

4 Subject to Legal Authority   51

   Authority and Validity 53
   The People and The Internal Point of View 59
   Challenges to De Facto Legal Authority 61
   Notes 67

5 The Scope of Legal Authority   69

   The State-Based Argument 70
   The Substantive Account 72
   The Coercion Account 74
   The Legal Determination Account 77
   Notes 81

6 Authority and Extraterritorial Jurisdiction   82

   Jurisdiction and Authority 82
   The Limits of Territorial Authority 85
   Extraterritorial Jurisdiction 85
   Does Universal Law Claim Universal Authority? 87
   The Effects Doctrine 90
   Taxing People Abroad 93
   Notes 95

7 Authority and State Borders   97

   Borders and Border Regimes 98
   Territorial Borders and Nationalism 101
   The Demos in Border Decisions 103
   Notes 109

8 Does It Matter That State Borders Are Arbitrary?   111

   Contingent Borders 113
   Contingent Peoples 114
   Moral Arbitrariness 117
   Historical Injustice 119
   Global Injustice 124
   Notes 127

9 End Discussion: The Limits of Democratic Inclusion   129

   Social Norms 130
   Epistemic Authority 132
   Private Decisions 134
   Failures of De Facto Authority 137
   Notes 140

References   *141*
Index   *156*

ACKNOWLEDGEMENTS

This book has benefitted from generous and instructive comments from colleagues in seminars where I had the opportunity to present drafts of individual chapters at various stages in the process. In particular, I am grateful to the participants in the *Cevipof* weekly seminar in Paris (March, 2019); the *Political Theory* seminar at Université de Louvain-la-Neuve (April, 2019); the *Nordic Network in Political Theory* in Oslo (October, 2019); the workshops arranged by the *Boundary Problem in Democratic Theory* project hosted by the Institute for Futures Studies in Stockholm (2019–2021); the *Political Theory* working seminar at the Department of Political Science, Stockholm University (2019–2022); the *GOODPOL* research project in Oslo (2020–2022); the higher seminar at the Department of Law, Stockholm University (October, 2019); and the *Geneva Colloquium in Political Theory*, University of Geneva (May, 2019). In addition, I wish to extend my thanks to Kim Angell, Gustaf Arrhenius, Vuko Andric, Samantha Besson, Keith Dowding, Jakob Elster, Eva Erman, Andreas Föllesdal, Axel Gosseries, Cathrine Holst, Robert Huseby, Annabelle Lever, Mats Lundström, David Miller, Ulf Mörkenstam, Naghmeh Nasiritousi, Valeria Ottonelli, Jonas Hultin Rosenberg, Ben Saunders, Torben Spaak, and Jan Teorell.

Finally, the research and publication of this work benefitted from financial support from: The Swedish Research Council, *The Boundary Problem in Democratic Theory* (Grant agreement ID: 2015-01588); The Swedish Research Council, *Who are 'We, the People'? A Study of National and Indigenous Peoples' Constitutions* (Grant agreement ID: 2015-01000); Horizon 2020, Coordination and Support Action (CSA): *Reconstructing Democracy in Times of Crisis: A Voter-Centred Perspective* (REDEM) (Grant agreement ID: 870996).

1
THE UNRESOLVED PROBLEM OF DEMOCRATIC INCLUSION

This book seeks to answer one of the most basic and yet elusive questions about the democratic ideal: who are the people? 'The people' is here used to mean the group that is entitled to participate in an association that strives to realize the democratic ideal. The people thus correspond to what in contemporary writings is also termed 'the demos', in veneration of the ancient origin of this idea in Greek practices of 'demo-cracy'.[1] In contemporary states, the people or the demos is equal to the electorate: the demos signifies all individuals with the right to vote in national elections. In other associations that aspire to be governed by democratic standards, but that are not ruled by elected representatives, the demos signifies the group of people with the exclusive right to participate in the decision-making process. The demos is, in short, the group that is fully included in the decision-making process of an association that is or aspires to be democratic.[2]

The point at issue, however, is not who *is* entitled to vote or participate but who *should* be so entitled. The question asked is normative, not descriptive. The correct answer is of immense practical import. In order to determine if an association that pretends to be democratic is, in fact, democratic, whether that is a state or some other entity, a standard is needed for judgments about who *should* be included in the demos. No association is fully democratic unless it grants the right to vote or participate to all who should be able to vote or participate according to the principle of inclusion stipulated by the democratic ideal. Thus, the normative question about the demos is the more basic one and is answered only by identifying the principle for demos membership that should govern access to participation in any prospective democratic association.

Now, some readers might be skeptical about the need to engage with this topic as they might for good reason believe that we already do know a great deal about it. Surely we have learnt a few things about acceptable and unacceptable electoral exclusions from the many 'waves' of democratization that have swept the world since its modern revival? Indeed, the struggle for equal and universal suffrage used to be the first step in the process of democratization, as indicated by early mobilization against electoral exclusions based on income, social status, gender, ethnicity and race (e.g., Keyssar 2000; Przeworski 2009). Equal-treatment norms in the distribution of voting rights has since been almost universally accepted, albeit belatedly in some places. Today, democracy is – as is frequently acknowledged – a theory of inclusion that mandates political participation and voting on an equal basis (Taylor 1998).

Though the ideal of equal voting rights raises issues worthy of attention, questions about whom to include in democratic decision-making cannot be fully answered by recourse to norms of equal treatment. In fact, the claim that inclusion should be equal leaves undetermined the group to which this requirement applies. To take a very simple example; the proposition that men and women should be equally entitled to the vote, is not usually taken to mean that to *all* men and women should be equally entitled to vote in the elections of a particular political system. Rather, the norm of equal treatment with respect to sex or gender is presumed to apply to the subset of men and women of the *relevant* group.

In contemporary democratic states, the relevant group is almost everywhere defined in terms of citizenship. In nearly every state citizenship is a necessary precondition for demos membership. Obviously, this is not to say that citizenship is sufficient for voting rights. Many citizens remain excluded from the vote, particularly people with mental disabilities, in prison, residing abroad, and, most obviously, children (Beckman 2009).[3] The point is, however, that irrespective of whether these exclusions are justified or not, the judgment that they are *exclusions* presupposes that they are members of the relevant group. Children and others are excluded from the electorate only because they are citizens and because citizenship is otherwise considered the relevant currency for demos membership in the democratic state. Arguments about the extent of the suffrage in contemporary democracies are consequently indebted to more fundamental assumptions about the defining characteristics of the group to which norms of equal treatment apply.

Now, as already mentioned, citizenship is the almost universally accepted currency of demos membership in the present world. But the fact that citizenship *is* necessary for membership in the demos is no reason to conclude that it *should* be. Indeed, as I will argue in a moment, there is reason to think that citizenship is not the relevant condition for membership in the demos. Consequently, the topic of this book is to explore what this condition should be. As it turns out, centuries of democratic thought have as yet failed to produce a convincing answer to this question – no doubt a dizzying insight.

One reason that democratic theory has been unsuccessful in addressing the boundary problem is due to the exclusive focus on the state and the conditions for political democracy. Attending to the state is of course warranted for many reasons. The state remains the most powerful entity of social organization, with the capacity to influence and coercively determine virtually every aspect of society. However, for purposes of advancing our understanding of the conditions for demos membership, exclusive attention to the state can lead us astray.

A variety of entities below and above the state claim to be democratic. Democracy is a percept of local and regional public authority as well as of transnational structures of governance and, potentially, of future global authority. Moreover, democracy is practiced in a variety of associations that are not vested with public authority: voluntary associations, social clubs, and organizations for sports, both at national and international levels. Any association can be democratic, and it must be inclusive in order to be that. This point is well captured by Robert Dahl's observation that democratic criteria apply to 'associations whether or not they constitute a state' (Dahl 1989: 107). Inclusion is a requirement of any democratic association and political democracy is just a special case of a more general phenomenon.

This point is methodologically significant as it implies that an adequate account of the demos must not only explain the grounds for demos membership in the state. A theory of democratic inclusion should be able to tell us who should be included in all democratic associations. This is of course not to deny that participation and voting may be more important in some associations than in others. The harm suffered from exclusion from the demos of the state is likely to be considerably greater than the harm suffered from exclusion from the demos of many other associations. But that is due to the immense normative significance of the state, not because the conditions for demos membership are different.

The lesson to be drawn is that an adequate theory of democratic inclusion must not derive the conditions of inclusion from the specific relationship that obtains between the state and its citizens. Reasons for democratic inclusion must be sought in the nature of the relationship that obtains between individuals and associations generally.

Including the Subjects

The account advanced here is that demos membership should be understood in terms of subjection to binding decisions. The 'subject' is someone for whom a decision is made and who is expected to comply with the decision. This notion is familiar in the literature as the 'all-subjected principle' articulated already in the work of the eminent political scientist Robert Dahl in the 1980s. But the concept of 'subjection' that Dahl used was limited in scope and insufficiently differentiated.

Dahl's view is limited in scope as he defined the 'subjects' exclusively in relation to the state. For Dahl, the principle of democratic inclusion is one that applies to the 'subjects to a government and its laws' (Dahl 1989: 124). If subjection to 'government' is a necessary attribute of the demos, there can be no demos in non-governmental associations. This state-centered perspective is reproduced in the bulk of subsequent writings on the all-subjected principle. The notion that democracy calls for all subjects to be included is said to apply to the subjects of the 'authority of the state' (Parvu 2015), 'political rule' (Näsström 2011), the 'government's dominion' (Miklosi 2012), 'the system of law and institutions' (Pavel 2018), 'the legal system' (Miller 2009), 'laws and legal obligations' (Erman 2022), and the 'laws and binding decisions of the state' (Lopéz-Guerra 2005). Just like Dahl, these accounts proceed to define the 'subject' in relation to the state and the law and are consequently ill-equipped to explain what constitutes the demos in associations distinct from the state.

Furthermore, Dahl's account of subjection is not differentiated enough to help distinguish between separate instances of its meaning.[4] On some occasions, Dahl says that people are subject to the laws of the state to the extent that they are 'compelled to obey' (Dahl 1989: 96). More frequently, he defines subjection in relation to 'the rules of the demos', 'binding collective decisions', or even to the 'authority' of the state.[5] These statements invite a variety of conflicting accounts of what it means to be a subject. Is a person a subject in the relevant sense only if she is compelled to obey? Is subjection to rules sufficient, or must these rules also be 'binding'? If so, in virtue of what are rules 'binding'? Alternatively, a person is subject to a decision only if the decision is made by an authority. That hypothesis raises further questions, however. What makes a body an 'authority' and how far does the authority of that body extend? Dahl's account of the all-subjected principle apparently lacks the recourses to distinguish between different senses of what it means to be a subject to decisions.

The idea introduced in this book is that the principle of democratic inclusion depends on an account of what it means to be subject to rules. The laws of the state are rules and the decisions made by states are based on rules. That is true also for non-state associations. An association is a rule-governed entity that make decisions according to rules. The idea that democratic inclusion depends on subjection to rules thus helps explain how the ideal of democracy applies both to the state and to associations generally. The account of 'rules' that informs this account is informed by H.L.A Hart's seminal contributions to legal theory. The insight of Hart is that decisions about rules are dependent on a system of rules, or what is otherwise termed a 'normative system'. The normative power to make decisions about rules originates from rule-dependent normative powers. The subjects of rules are consequently subject to powers of rule-making that are established by systems of rules.

This is just a preliminary and incomplete statement of the all-subjected principle to be advanced here. The general idea is that the subjects of decisions can be identified only in relation to normative systems. This account narrows down the settings that are judged relevant to democratic decision-making compared to, for example, the idea that any decision 'affecting' others is generating a claim for inclusion. On the other hand, there is a great variety of normative systems in operation. The legal system of the state is just a particular instantiation of the general attempt to regulate conduct by a system of rules. The United Nations is another example and so is the International Chess Federation, the local scout club, and numerous other local, national, and international associations. Accordingly, the sites available for democratic inclusion are, in the view proposed here, considerably more expansive than imagined by the state-based conception.

But from the acknowledgment that these associations are normative systems with the capacity to make decisions, no particular view follows about the scope of their decisions. Who is subject to the decisions made by the Security Council of the United Nations, the executive board of the International Chess Federation, the Parliament and government of the state of Sweden, or the local scout club?

This question prompts a long-lasting issue in the philosophy of law that arguably has significant, and thus far overlooked, implications for democratic theory. In the case that the extent of democratic participation is conditioned by subjection to systems of rules, it appears that the full meaning of the democratic ideal hinges on who is regulated by such systems and the decisions authorized by them.

The account of subjection to rules developed in this book is informed by the influential theory of authority of Joseph Raz. The starting point is that normative systems claim the legitimate authority to regulate conduct. Decisions made by normative powers conferred by normative systems are accordingly premised on the claimed authority to create morally binding rules for conduct. The decisions made are intended to regulate how people or entities should behave. The extent of subjection to rules therefore depends on the extent of the authority claimed by the normative system.

The all-subjected principle, so construed, applies to all associations: the authority to regulate conduct is claimed equally by international organizations, legal systems, humanitarian associations, corporations, unions, employers' associations, voluntary associations, and so on. All of them make decisions by rules that intend to regulate conduct. The extent to which others are subject to normative systems depend on the scope of their claimed authority. Thus, the principle of democratic inclusion is designed to track the claimed authority of normative systems. Democracy is the ideal that normative systems that claim to regulate conduct by rules are governed by the agents they intend to regulate.

The account of the all-subjected principle introduced in this book provides an appendage to the prevailing understanding of procedural democracy. Standardly, the democratic ideal is explicated in terms of criteria for the making of collective decisions. Democracy is a particular 'method' for the organization of decision-making procedures. This 'procedural' account is not entirely uncontroversial, for sure, and is challenged by those who believe that democracy is better understood as criteria for *what* decisions should be made (e.g., Dworkin 2012).

The relevant point though, is that it remains unclear *to what* the procedural conception of democracy applies. Presumably, it does not apply to just about anything called 'a decision'. The answer supplied by the all-subjected principle is that democratic procedure is a property only of decisions that claim the authority to regulate the conduct of others. Procedural democracy is the ideal of empowering the subjects of rules that claim to be binding for them. The democratic method of decision-making is to include everyone whose conduct the decision claims to regulate.

Since the all-subjected principle has implications for our understanding of procedural democracy, it turns out that more is at stake in the problem of democratic inclusion than who should be entitled to participate and to vote. The emerging understanding of the democratic ideal is that of a particular method for the regulation of behavior. Democracy applies to the decisions made by rule-governed powers in normative systems.

Hence, 'democracy' is not concerned with decisions that are affecting people.[6] Nor is it concerned with decisions that are either coercive or dominating. The heart of the democratic aspiration is instead that people should be able to collectively determine the rules that seek to regulate them on the basis of the authority claimed by normative systems. Accordingly, debates about the boundaries of the demos are not just about the criteria for membership in the demos but also, and perhaps more fundamentally, debates about the nature of the democratic ideal. At stake is the 'nature' of the decisions that can meaningfully be described as democratic and therefore evaluated by democratic standards.

If the aim of this book would be to justify the all-subjected principle, a systematic engagement with rival conceptions would have been necessary. However, my aim here is *explicative*, not justificatory. Explication is a species of 'conceptual re-engineering' that seeks to render a concept more precise in order to make it fruitful with respect to the target theory (Brun 2016). An explication of the all-subjected principle thus aims for an account of subjection that is informative from the vantage point of democratic theory. In that regard, it is worth emphasizing that the boundaries of the demos pertain only to whom should participate in the process of determining decisions that are potentially binding. The boundaries of the demos do not settle the interests and needs that such decisions should take into consideration. Hence, from the fact that some agents should be excluded from the demos it does not follow that their interests or needs can legitimately be ignored. The moral demands placed on democratic decision-making are not exhausted by an account of the demos.

Including Members

The conventional understanding of democratic inclusion is that it applies to the members of the association. An association is organized for the purpose of advancing the goals and interest of the members and the mark of a democratic association is that it includes all members in its internal decision-making process. Membership is the necessary prerequisite for the right to participate in the decisions by a democratic association: 'Democratic inclusion in the internal governance of organizations in all domains requires that all those who are formal members [...] should have a voice and vote.' (Bader 2018).

In the context of the state, this view is mirrored both in current state practices and the widely accepted understanding that the right to vote is the privilege of the citizen of the state. When applied to the state, the idea of democratic association implies that the demos should include only citizens because only citizens are recognized as members of the state.

The significance of membership is downplayed by the all-subjected principle. The state is democratic with respect to inclusion only if it extends voting rights to all subject to claims for compliance with the decisions by the state. It may be that only the members of the state are subject to the state in that sense. If so, only citizens should be included in the demos according to the all-subjected principle. But as we shall see, that is rarely the case. Non-citizens are often subject to the authority claimed by the state and it is often the case that many citizens are not subject to its authority. Citizenship status is of no intrinsic importance to the democratic character of the state.

But why is the conventional view of inclusion mistaken? What is wrong with the claim that citizenship is necessary for democratic inclusion? Before explaining why, tribute should first be paid to the inclusive tendencies prompted by the historical alliance between citizenship and the democratic ideal. This alliance traces its modern roots to the revival of the democratic ideal ignited by the French revolution (Brubaker 1992). The image of a demos premised on citizenship carried a strong inclusive message in societies where political participation had for long been the prerogative of collectives (the estates) to which access was conditioned by social standing and inherited privilege. For a century or more, the idea that democracy is the rule by the citizens of the state propelled the expansion of suffrage rights to workers, women, and to ethnic and religious minorities (Shaw 2017).

The exclusionary implications of citizenship-based inclusion were recognized only later, following increased cross-border travel and migration. The assumption that states are populated by the citizens of that state is becoming outdated in a world where the citizens of one state are able to relocate into the territory of another state. As a result of this process, the formerly inclusive connotations of the principle that citizenship is both necessary and sufficient for democratic rights evaporates. Instead, the message now is that resident non-citizens should be excluded from the repertoire of participatory rights in the democratic state (Neuman 1992; Beckman 2006).

The main issue with citizenship as the standard for democratic inclusion is that it does not provide a *principled* solution to the democratic boundary problem. If a principled solution is one that provides a normative standard by which political decisions can be evaluated, the citizenship-based view is not a principled standard. The critical potential of the democratic ideal is lost if it is accepted that citizenship status exhausts the conditions for democratic rights to participation.

This is realized once it is appreciated that citizenship is a legal status that is granted in accordance with the laws of citizenship. The laws of citizenship are decided by the government. Hence, the claim that democratic inclusion is premised on citizenship-status is equivalent to the claim that democratic inclusion is up to the government to decide. The notion that the demos should depend on citizenship is ultimately a political rather than a principled account of demos membership.

Moreover, not too distant historical records offer terrifying examples of the consequences of the citizenship-based conception. The first to mention is the Nüremberg Laws (*Die Nürnberger Gesetze*) introduced by the national socialist government in Germany in 1935. The Nüremberg Laws deprived Jews, Roma, and colored Germans of their citizenship status and turned them into 'Reich subjects', deprived of the rights associated with legal citizenship including the right to vote. The point is that while the law can be condemned as racist and discriminatory, it is not clear that it can be condemned as contrary to democracy as construed by the citizenship-based account. Despite the fact that the Nüremberg Laws disenfranchised Jews, Roma, and colored people, the German state remained as inclusive as before with respect to its citizenry. The Nüremberg Laws made no difference in terms of the requirement that only citizens are presumptively entitled to political rights.

An additional illustration of this point is from apartheid South Africa before 1994. As is well known, the apartheid system enforced not just systematic segregation between whites and blacks in social and economic life, it also deprived the black population of political rights, including the right to vote. As the black population comprised a large majority of the residents in the country, the result was that the white minority retained the right to unilaterally decide the political future of the nation. And yet, the state of South Africa could still insist that it respected the spirit of the democratic ideal. How could this be? The explanation is to be found in the South African law of citizenship of 1970.[7] According to this law, no black person is a citizen of South Africa. Black residents were instead forced to be citizens of 'Bantustans'; small, semi-autonomous regions, purposely created by the government on its own territory. Irrespective of where in South Africa a black person lived, she was from that point a citizen of one of the Bantustans and not a citizen of South Africa. Again, even though the law effectively deprived millions of black residents of the right to vote in South Africa, it remained as true as before that the citizens of South Africa could vote (Le Roux 2015).

However, the point that citizenship laws are arbitrary does not fully close the door for a citizenship-based account of the demos. In case citizenship is grounded in a normative theory, rather than in the laws of citizenship, a principled account of the demos can be formulated that remains centered on citizenship. Precisely this route is taken by Rainer Bauböck who in a series of publications has defended what he calls the 'citizenship stakeholder principle'. According to this view, individuals have an interest in membership in a polity in so far as their autonomy and well-being depends on it (Bauböck 2018a). Since citizenship is the currency for membership in a polity, and citizenship includes democratic rights to participation, Bauböck's argument for a right to membership is also an argument for democratic inclusion.

Evidently, the citizenship stakeholder principle can explain what is wrong both with the Nüremberg Laws and the denaturalization policy pursued by the apartheid regime in South Africa. These policies were not just excluding people from political rights. They also attacked people's critical interest in recognition as members of the society where they lived and on which their autonomy and well-being depended.

But in avoiding one problem, the normative account of citizenship is caught in another. The price to be paid for making democratic inclusion incumbent on a normative theory of citizenship is to conflate reasons for membership with reasons for democratic inclusion. The right to membership taps a broad set of concerns and interests that are not necessarily co-extensive with the concerns and interests that pertain to the right to democratic participation. The moral right to membership is grounded in individual interest of autonomy and well-being, but also in shared interests in stable political community. According to Bauböck, the laws of citizenship must be consistent with the ability of democracy to reproduce over time. The rules governing access to the membership must therefore be such that a sufficient number of existing members can recognize them as legitimate (Bauböck 2018b: 72). A similar concern with the 'instrumental conditions' for democratic stability are voiced by David Miller and Sarah Song. In their estimate, the boundaries of the demos must be shaped with the aim of creating a 'relatively stable' group. A democratic community that is to rule itself coherently cannot afford too large shifts in the composition of the demos. Only a group with continuity over time is conducive to the shared sense of solidarity among the members that is necessary for decisions that adjudicate between their short and long-term interests (Song 2012; Miller 2018, 2020).

The interests and values highlighted by Bauböck, Miller, and Song may be relevant in deciding the rules for membership in the state. However, this is not to imply that every concern that is relevant in the allocation of citizenship is also relevant in deciding the rules that should govern demos membership in a democracy. Reasons for citizenship are not necessarily reasons for demos membership. Conversely, reasons against citizenship are not necessarily reasons against demos membership. No contradiction is involved either in the judgment that some citizens of the state *should not* be entitled to participate in elections or in the judgment that some non-citizens *should* be entitled to participate in elections.

Moreover, by fusing together collective and individual interests to be preserved by rules allocating citizenship, potential conflicts between them are obscured.[8] Reasons that pertain to the stability of the demos may be in tension with reasons that pertain to the extent of democratic inclusion. The value of stable community is a reason to be cautious about extending citizenship to groups who either lack knowledge about the ends of the association or explicitly reject them. But these reasons may conflict with the democratic ideal. This conflict can be discerned only if a distinction is made between the conditions for democratic inclusion and the conditions for political stability.

An account of the demos should provide a yardstick for demos membership that aligns with the ideal of procedural democracy. Of course, reasons that are not concerned with procedural democracy may in the end be normatively relevant to judgments about how to regulate the right to vote. But other normative reasons must be distinguishable from democratic reasons. There is accordingly good reason to avoid the 'broad strategy' (Miller 2020: 7) according to which standards for democratic inclusion are inferred from the totality of desirable features of the people in a democratic state.

Not even these remarks may be sufficient to categorically reject the claim that demos membership should be the privilege of citizens, however. If the moral right to citizenship is grounded exclusively in a concern with democratic inclusion, the members of the state will effectively coincide with the demos as defined by democratic criteria. Citizenship is on that account limited to the circle that should be members of the demos. Such an account does not exhibit any defects that pertain to democratic inclusion. Yet, it is unclear that reasons for membership in the state are fully reducible to reasons for democratic inclusion.

What Is a Principle of Democratic Inclusion?

I have so far written rather carelessly about 'principles' of democratic inclusion and said that the aim of this book is to offer an account of the all-subjected *principle*. In this I conform to established usage in democratic theory according to which the conditions for demos membership are based on reasons that are normatively relevant. However, even though it is widely accepted that principles should determine membership in the demos, it is frequently unclear what a principle of democratic inclusion is.

Normative principles are reasons that are *basic* as they serve to identify the aims for an inquiry or practice. In that regard, democratic principles are no different either from the principles of mechanics or from the principles of good parenthood. These principles are normative reasons that are meant to guide participants of the relevant practice. Moreover, principles are *general* such that they apply widely, not just in specific situations or to particular actions (List and Valentini 2016). Normative principles are reasons that should guide all or most actions undertaken by the participants in the relevant practice.

However, the notion that normative principles are basic and general reasons does not tell us much about their *strength* when invoked as the basis for claims in particular situations. In fact, there is a tendency to assume that principles of democratic inclusion provide conclusive reasons for membership in the demos. Given that a person meets the conditions stipulated by the principle, he or she should be included in the demos, no matter what. The principle of democratic inclusion is consequently meant to provide 'all-things considered' reasons; it offers reasons that are indefeasible and that remain valid even in the face of countervailing considerations. This is the image on which the debate on rival principles of democratic inclusion largely proceeds. The all-subjected principle is accordingly pictured as a bid for all things considered reasons for voting rights. The fact that a person is subject to binding decisions, is considered a final, or indefeasible, reason for inclusion in the demos.

This assumption about the justificatory force of principles of democratic inclusion has important ramifications for how to evaluate them. Counter-intuitive implications are instantly judged as proof of a *reductio ad absurdum*, that is, reasons to conclude that the principle should be rejected because it is absurd. For instance, a frequent complaint about the all-subjected principle is that transients and tourists appear to satisfy the conditions it stipulates (Arrhenius 2018; Angell 2020). Now, if transients and tourists are subjected to the state in a sense that is relevant from the viewpoint of the principle of democratic inclusion, it evidently follows that they too should be included in the demos. Arguably, this is an absurd conclusion. But only on the further assumption that the all-subjected principle does indeed provide conclusive reasons is that a valid inference.

A more promising view is that principles of democratic inclusion are *conditional presumptions*. They are conditional as they are reasons for including the subjects of decisions only if there are ulterior reasons justifying the claim that these decisions should indeed be democratic. They are presumptions in the sense that they are strong albeit defeasible reasons for including the subjects of decisions. Before I proceed to explain what this means, I will consider two alternative understandings of what democratic principles are.

The first alternative is to imagine democratic principles as conceptual stipulations and not as normative reasons. On this understanding, the all-subjected principle (or any of its rivals) is not offering *reasons* for either inclusion or exclusion. Principles of inclusion propose to describe a specific element of the ideal-typical meaning of democracy (Cf. Ross 1952). So conceived, the all-subjected principle is not really a 'principle' since it does not impart reasons that intend to guide democratic practices. It does provide, however, a standard for operating the concept of democracy in regard to matters of inclusion. The principle defines the descriptive meaning of the demos in a democracy. Accordingly, the proposition that the demos correspond to the subjects of binding decisions is not a claim about who should be a member of the demos. It is instead meant to report the meaning of 'the people' in democratic discourse.

The conceptual approach offers the basis for a response to the objection that the all-subjected principle has counter-intuitive implications. Against the charge that it is absurd to extend the vote to tourists and transients, the reply is that it does not follow from the all-subjected principle that members of these categories should be granted voting rights. No inference about who *should* be included in the demos can be made from claims about the meaning of 'the demos'.

Though I have previously been tempted by the conceptual view (Beckman 2009), I currently believe that it fails to account for the fact that principles for democratic inclusion are designed to articulate *reasons* for inclusion. Whether standards for democratic inclusion are explicated in terms of being affected by decisions, subject to coercion, or subject to binding rules, the purpose is to offer *reasons* of normative import. Principles of democratic inclusion are meant to guide judgments on social practices and not just to clarify the terms used in describing them.

Another attempt to skirt the objection that the principle has counter-intuitive implications is to insist that democracy is a *partial* normative ideal (Arrhenius 2018; Erman 2022). Democratic principles are normative reasons in favor of a particular mode of collective decision-making. But there may be other normative reasons that pertain to the organization of collective decision-making that we should attend to. Hence, principles of democratic inclusion are not necessarily 'all things considered' judgments about who should be included in the demos. On this view, the all-subjected principle should be read as an attempt to capture democratic normative reasons for demos membership. But since democracy is a partial normative ideal, it is conceivable that other normative reasons also apply that negate some of the implications of the all-subjected principle.

The notion that democracy is a partial normative ideal elegantly disposes of the claim that principles of democratic inclusion convey reasons that apply all things considered. Nevertheless, it is doubtful that this strategy adequately reflects the relationship between the democratic ideal and other normative ideals. As defined by Arrhenius and Erman, partial normative ideals are *pro tanto* reasons and principles of democratic inclusion are consequently pro tanto reasons for demos membership. The implication is that – following the all-subjected principle – there is always a pro tanto reason to include anyone subjected to binding rules. But that claim overlooks a prior question: should the decision be democratic at all? In fact, people subject to binding rules are to be included in the process of rulemaking only if it should be democratic. No pro tanto reason for including the subjects of rules exists in associations that for good reason should not be organized by democratic principles. Though democracy is a partial normative ideal, it appears unwarranted to conclude that reasons for democratic inclusion must therefore be pro tanto reasons.

A better alternative is to consider democratic inclusion as a *conditional principle*.[9] The claim that the subjects of binding rules should be included is a reason that is conditioned by *other* reasons to believe that the association should be governed by democratic procedures. The all-subjected principle supplies reasons to believe that the subjects of binding rules ought to be included in the demos in associations that should be democratic – it does not supply reasons to believe that associations should be democratic.

Now, reasons that follow from conditional principles may still be valid either all-things considered or pro tanto. Reasons for demos membership are either conditional for all things considered reasons or conditional for pro tanto reasons. Reading them as pro tanto reasons is attractive on the assumption that democracy is a partial normative ideal. But the notion that the principle of democratic inclusion offers only pro tanto reasons for demos membership belittles the normative significance of inclusion for democracy. Pro tanto reasons are not necessarily strong reasons. A reason that is valid 'pro tanto' is a consideration that is so far undefeated by other considerations. This seems too weak, given that inclusion is of critical importance to democracy. Reasons for democratic inclusion are not easily defeasible.

Hence, the principle of inclusion should be understood as strong – albeit not indefeasible – reasons for including the subjects in associations that should be democratic. The problem then is that the strength of the reasons for democratic inclusion are not adequately reflected either by the formula that they are pro tanto reasons or that they are all-considered reasons. The challenge is to articulate the strength of the reasons that follow from the principle of democratic inclusion while avoiding the Scylla of all things considered reasons and the Charybdis of pro tanto reasons.

The formula that best reflects these dual concerns, I contend, is that the principle of democratic inclusion is providing a *presumptive* reason for inclusion. A presumption is a reason that applies *as if* some particular fact is true (Ullman-Margalit 1977; Mendonca 1998). The relevant 'truth' in this case, is not a matter of fact, of course, but a normative conclusion. The presumption is that a person should be included in demos, provided that she is subject to decisions. Now, presumptions are defeasible and not conclusive reasons. Yet, they are not just pro tanto reasons either. A presumption is an instruction to proceed 'as if' the conditions specified by the principle are valid even in case of uncertainty or countervailing considerations. A presumption is intended to hold in the absence of sufficient reasons to the contrary. Thus, the all-subjected principle urges the critical observer to proceed *as if* anyone subjected to decisions that are binding should be included in the demos *unless there is sufficient reason to the contrary*.

A further observation is that the presumption in favor of inclusion in the demos, is valid only on condition that democracy is justified. This is consistent with – but does not depend on – the view that democracy is one of several normative ideals to be pursued. Indeed, the presumptive and conditional nature of the principle of inclusion is not dependent on reasons to believe that any particular association should be democratic. This makes sense, I submit, since democracy is an ideal about collective decision-making that can be employed in a range of different social, economic and political contexts. Though there are good reasons to believe that the state should be democratic, and while there may be good reasons to believe that many other associations should also be democratic, it is not clear that all associations must be. The point then is that the principle of democratic inclusion is presumption for including the subjects that is conditioned by compelling reasons for democracy. The principle of democratic inclusion applies only *if* democracy is justified and, in so far as it is, we shall proceed as if all subjects should be included.

★★★

A final point to consider about the principle of democratic inclusion is whether it conveys sufficient or also necessary conditions for the presumption of inclusion. In case the principle identifies the sufficient but not the necessary conditions, it appears that it is permissible to include also non-subjects. The all-subjected principle is, in that event, equivalent to the claim that all subject to binding decisions should presumptively be included. Whether non-subjects should be included is left undecided. Alternatively, the all-subjected principle identifies the sufficient *and* necessary conditions for inclusion. The all-subjected principle is, in that event, equivalent to the claim that all *and only all* subject to binding decisions should presumptively be included. Extending the demos to non-subjects would then be contrary to the democratic principle of inclusion.

Given that the significance of democratic inclusion derives from its value as an instrument to influence and determine the outcome of a decision-making processes, it follows that inclusion is a rival good. Rival goods are less valuable the more they are consumed. Hence, the larger the number of people that are included, the less valuable inclusion is to others. This puts pressure on the notion that it is permissible to include non-subjects. By including non-subjects, the value of inclusion to subjects decreases. There is accordingly something to be said against interpreting the all-subjected principle as merely sufficient conditions for inclusion. If inclusion is of instrumental importance to individuals, we should ensure that inclusion is reserved to those who are entitled to be included. In order to include only those who are entitled to be included, the principle of democratic inclusion should be read as specifying the necessary and sufficient conditions for inclusion. The idea then is not just that the subject of binding decisions should presumptively be included, but also that those *not* subject to binding decisions should presumptively *not* be included. However, since presumptions are strong but defeasible reasons, this reading of the all-subjected principle leaves open the possibility of including non-subjects in the event that reasons in favor of that conclusion are strong enough to rebut the presumption to the contrary.

A Brief Outline of The Book

The plan for the following eight chapters is as follows. First, I advance a general interpretation of the all-subjected principle that explains the 'subject' in terms of decisions that claim to be binding. A decision is binding, on this account, neither because it is morally binding, nor because it is coercive, but because of the claimed legitimate authority of the normative system that creates the normative power to make the decision. An important feature of this account is that it is general: it applies to all normative systems. Furthermore, it applies only to normative systems with *de facto* authority. The main thesis of this chapter is accordingly that the all-subjected principle should be understood as the claim that the subjects of decisions made by de facto authorities should presumptively be included in the decision-making process.

In the third chapter, I address how the decisions of the state can be binding. The claim defended is that the state pretends to have the authority to make binding rules by virtue of the authority claimed by the legal system. The genesis of the binding decisions of the state is thus its claimed legal authority, neither moral legitimacy nor brute force. The fourth chapter digs deeper into the legal authority claimed by the state by surveying different views on how the state achieves de facto legal authority. The conundrum is that de facto authority depends on widespread recognition of authority. But how can the general population recognize the legal authority claimed by the state if legal authority also depends on complex criteria for legal validity provided by the legal system?

Chapter five proceeds to explore the *scope* of the authority claimed by the state. I am here trying to rebut two specific theories of the scope of the law: the thesis that its scope depends on the substantive meaning of legal norms and the thesis that its scope depends on the reach of coercive enforcement. Instead, I defend the view that the scope of the authority claimed by the state is conditioned by the ability of legal institutions to determine valid and exclusive claims to compliance.

Chapter six goes on to develop the implications of this view for the scope of the authority claimed by the state. Specifically, the question is if a person or other entity can be a subject of the state's claimed authority beyond its territorial borders. In addressing this question, I am engaging with current practices of extraterritorial law, universal jurisdiction, and international taxation, which all appear to be premised on the state possessing the authority to regulate behavior abroad. Yet, the view advocated for is that the legal system is unable to determine the validity of exclusive claims to authority beyond territorial borders. Given present configurations of the international state-system, the scope of the all-subjected principle is circumvented by state borders.

Arguably, this makes the all-subjected principle controversial since state borders are often disputed, contingent historical constructs, morally arbitrary and potentially morally illegitimate. These issues are in focus in chapters seven and eight. The argument examined is that the all-subjected principle is unable to explain who should be a member of the demos in democratic decisions about border disputes. The reply is that no state has the authority to regulate its own borders and that, therefore, states cannot democratically regulate international borders anyway. Chapter eight responds to the objection that state borders are contingent, morally arbitrary, or illegitimate. The claim defended is that reasons to include the subjects of the state remain even in the event that territorial borders are morally arbitrary and illegitimate. The ninth and final chapter of the book proceeds to clarify the limitations of the all-subjected principle. Four situations are identified to which the all-subjected principle does not seem to apply: social norms, private decisions, epistemic decisions, and decisions made by tyrannical political entities.

Notes

1 Although 'demos' is Greek for 'the people' and was used by the Athenians in the same way as today to mean the whole of the citizen body (Ober 1989: 3), the Athenians also used the 'demos' to variously designate the state as a whole, the constitution of the state, the democratic assembly or just the 'common people' (Hansen 2010: 502f.).
2 In the following I will speak interchangeably about the demos as equal to the people included, the people with rights to participate and the people entitled to vote, despite the fact that venues for consultation and participation regularly remain open also for non-members of the demos and the fact that the demos need not be defined in terms of voting rights at all.
3 The only country that currently allows non-citizens to vote in national elections is New Zealand where one year of residence is sufficient for the right to vote. Moreover, citizens are not guaranteed voting rights in all existing democracies. For example, Puerto Ricans are US citizens though not entitled vote in US general elections (Bauböck 2018b: 71). Also, citizens that reside in some territories are not entitled to vote in local elections unless qualified as 'belongers' (British citizens in the Falkland Islands can vote in the Falkland Islands only subject to special conditions, for example). See Harmer (2020).
4 On differentiation as a criterion of concept formation, see Gerring (1999: 375f.).
5 See Dahl (1989: 122, 120, and 98 respectively).
6 The all-affected principle is perhaps the most popular account of democratic inclusion in contemporary democratic theory, notwithstanding a range of familiar difficulties that have been widely debated (e.g., Goodin 2007; Owen 2011; Miklosi 2012). Although no systematic evaluation of these principles is offered here, the all-subjected principle is at least better equipped to handle the objection against the all-affected principle that it ignores the 'institutional context' (Gould 2018: 390); the 'constitutional framework' necessary for democratic participation (Beitz 2011); pays insufficient attention to the 'constitutive force of social mediations' Fraser (2010: 292) and denigrates the normative significance of 'ongoing social relations' (Kolodny 2014: 223).
7 *Bantu Homelands Citizenship Act*, 1970 (Act No. 26 of 1970), repealed by the Interim Constitution of South Africa in 1994.

8 The argument is analogous to the criticism directed against early attempts to measure democratic political regimes empirically. Many of these studies defined democracy in terms of 'stable democracy'. As soon pointed out by others, this measurement strategy made the results difficult to interpret. By fusing together stability and democracy into a single measure, a range of possible and potentially important questions about the relationship between stability and democracy were excluded from the research agenda (Bollen and Jackman 1989).

9 Southwood (2019: 543) elaborates the distinction between conditional and unconditional principles, albeit in a somewhat different sense.

2
DEMOCRATIC INCLUSION IN ASSOCIATIONS

The view to be considered is that only the subjects of decisions should be included in democratic associations. The basic idea is that the subjects are those for whom decisions are binding. A decision is binding only if it should be complied with; it is intended to provide reasons for action that others should act on. A preliminary specification of the all-subjected principle is thus that only the subjects of binding decisions should be entitled to participate in the democratic process: the demos should presumptively include all and only all for whom decisions are or claim to be binding. A prerequisite for democracy, on this view, is that people determine together the decisions to which they are subjected.

Clearly however, the all-subjected principle is virtually meaningless in the absence of an account of binding decisions. Since democracy is an ideal that applies to all kinds of associations, the account of binding decisions should be applicable to all kinds of associations. The relevant understanding of subjection to binding decisions must not, therefore, be extracted from the specific conditions that obtain between the citizen and the state.

One suggestion is that 'binding' refers to reasons for compliance that are morally justified. Binding decisions are morally required reasons for action. On this view, the subjects are morally required to do as decided. I term this view the *moralized* account of democratic inclusion: people should be included in collective decisions if, and only if, they are morally required to comply with them. I examine and ultimately reject the moralized account of the all-subjected principle in the first sections of this chapter.

Alternatively, decisions are 'binding' even if they are not morally required reasons for action. The claim that a decision is binding does not mean to convey that there is a moral obligation to comply. Instead, the idea is that, under certain conditions, a decision-making body is able to claim the legitimate authority to make decisions that are binding. The authority claimed is the presumed moral right to determine

DOI: 10.4324/9781003359807-2

how others should act, though the decision-making body may not possess any actual moral right to that effect. The point is that decisions need not be morally binding in order for people to be subject to a decision that claims to be morally binding. A person is accordingly subject in the relevant sense only in relation to a body with the claimed authority to make binding decisions.

Not just anybody is able to claim legitimate authority, however. In order to make decisions that are binding in the relevant sense, the decision-maker must possess the *potential* for legitimate authority. The conditions for potential legitimate authority correspond to what Joseph Raz and others have termed 'de facto authority'. The notion of de facto authority is applicable to all kinds of associations. States can be de facto authorities, just as voluntary associations can be. Whenever people are subject to de facto authority, they are ipso facto subjected to claimed legitimate authority. Hence, the all-subjected principle applies to all de facto authorities and to them only, given that only de facto authorities make decisions that claim to be binding. The account defended here thus provides a rationale for the notion that people should be able to participate in the process of deciding norms that purport to be binding for them. Inclusion is a precondition for democracy because it is necessary for the ideal of collective self-regulation.

The first two sections of this chapter explore the moralized version of the all-subjected principle and argue that it fails to provide a plausible account of democratic inclusion. Subsequent sections outline the non-moral account of binding decisions that is based on the claimed right to compliance by de facto authorities. Indeed, the reader less interested in the defects of the moralized view and more interested in the conception of the all-subjected principle defended can jump directly to the third section.

Morally Binding Decisions

The claim that the members of an association are morally obligated to comply can be explained in several ways. One influential view is that the obligation to comply derives from consent. The starting point is that people are generally equipped with the normative power to impose moral obligations on themselves by means of consent. This power is practiced in, for example, promise-making and in contractual relationships. A promise is typically a moral reason to do as promised just as a contract is typically a moral reason to do as agreed. It is, of course, much more controversial that consent is sufficient to justify moral obligations to comply with the laws of the state. The state is a coercive organization that leaves the individual with few and more costly exit-options. In case consent generates moral reason for compliance only on condition that it is free and uncoerced, it is uncertain that consent can generate a moral obligation to comply with the state (Klosko 1991).

However, not every association is coercive. In the context of voluntary associations, exit is virtually costless and the extent of coercion available to the association very limited. Associational membership may therefore be free and uncoerced such that members consent to comply with rules and decisions. Membership is in that case akin to contractual obligations acquired by signing the 'terms of agreement'.

The thesis then would be that members are morally bound to comply with the decisions made by an association on the premise that they have freely consented to subjugate their will to it. Harry Beran provides one of the clearest summaries of this view: 'in accepting membership in an association, be it a state or some other association, one agrees to obey the rules of that association; and in agreeing to obey the rules of the state, one puts oneself under an obligation to obey its rules and gives it authority to govern. (Beran 1977: 262). For Beran, the decisions made by an association are morally binding for members because they have consented to obey the association.

Though consent represents a well-known basis for moral obligations, it is not evident that consent (even if free and uncoerced) is sufficient. Consent is often described as 'morally transformative' or even as 'moral magic' as it allows individuals to change the normative situation merely by changing their mental state (Alexander 2014; Hurd 2018).[1] The 'moral magic' of consent is not unlimited, however. Arguably, the magic that transforms the mental state of consent to a moral obligation to obey is conditioned by the requirements of morality. It is questionable that individuals have the normative power to create moral obligations to do what is morally wrongful (Green 1989: 809). A consenting recruit of the Nazi party is not under a moral obligation to comply with the Nazi party's decision to engage in the persecution of political opponents, minorities, and others. As explained by Kleinig (2009: 21), the moral magic of consent does not work in case the background conditions are 'morally bankrupt'.[2]

The claim that consent is a source of moral obligations gains intuitive force from the practice of promising. Promises are voluntary and undertaken with the intention of creating obligations to perform particular actions. The promisor is usually considered to be under a moral obligation to the promisee for no other reason than having so promised. Now, consent appears relevantly similar to promising in the sense that it represents an exercise of the normative power to impose obligations on self. A possibility is accordingly that members are morally bound to comply with decisions because they have promised to.[3] The members *should* comply because they have so promised.

Yet, even if consent is akin to a promise, it is unclear that consent is sufficient to establish obligations to comply. The normative power to consent does not necessarily impose obligations to self. Consent might as well establish a permission for others, that does not incur obligations to compliance for anyone (Hurd 2018). For example, my consent to you entering my house is not creating any obligation for anyone. All that follows from my consent is that you are permitted to enter my house. The normative work performed by consent in this context is to extinguish a pre-existing moral obligation on your part not to enter my house.

In this interpretation, the normative consequences of consent appear in a different light. Through consent, members grant the association permission to make decisions for them. Consenting members allow the association to make decisions for them but do not acquire obligations to obey as the fact that a decision is permitted is not premised on the fact that anyone is obligated to do as decided. It is consequently uncertain that consent can do the normative work required to conclude that consenting members are subject to morally binding decisions.

Of course, the moral obligations of the members of associations can also be defended by different arguments. One view is that the moral obligations of compliance derive from the value of communal relationships. Samuel Scheffler (2018) offers a vivid defense of this view. The idea is that membership enables 'social bonds' between members that are non-instrumentally valuable. The social bond provides 'relationship-dependent reasons' to care for other members that justify moral obligations. The members of associations are morally bound to comply in order to preserve the non-instrumental value of associational membership.[4]

These so-called 'associative obligations' are unlikely to extend to all members of an association, however. It is at the heart of Scheffler's argument that membership generates moral obligations only if membership is of non-instrumental value. But the social bond that is non-instrumentally valuable may not materialize for all members. Perhaps the social bond does not emerge among members who join the association solely with the intention to acquire extrinsic membership-benefits. For example, one person may join the stamp club only because it gives a rebate on the entrance ticket to the next national stamp exhibition; another person may join the union only to gain favorable terms for home insurance. In neither case does it seem plausible to say that membership has generated a social bond that justifies moral obligations for relationship-dependent reasons. Indeed, for some types of associations, such as corporations, it may well be that no-one is obligated to comply for such reasons.

The Moralized All-subjected Principle

Both the argument from consent and the argument from associative obligations are controversial. However, the relevant question in this context is not *if* the decisions made by associations are morally binding but if the all-subjected principle of democratic inclusion can plausibly be based on such an account *provided* that the decisions made by associations are morally binding. The consequent account would be something like this: a democratic association is one that grants members the right to participate in the decision-making process because they are morally bound to comply. The resulting interpretation of the all-subjected principle is *moralized* in the sense that grounds to conclude that a person is subject in the relevant sense depend on moral considerations. Democratic inclusion applies only to members who are morally obligated to comply.

Is the moralized version of the all-subjected principle plausible? As clarified above, it should be assessed on its own terms, without disputing the tenet that members can be morally obligated to comply. On the other hand, as already mentioned, it is unlikely that all members are subject to morally binding decisions on either account. Hence, if the presumption for democratic inclusion applies only to members who are subject to morally binding decisions, the all-subjected principle implies that a democratic association should be inclusive only with respect to *some* members; a democratic association need include only the subset of members that are subject to morally binding decisions. The scope of the demos that follows from the moralized version of the all-subjected principle is consequently considerably narrower than the scope of the demos that follows from the standard view, according to which *all* members should be included in democratic associations.

A further implication of the moralized account is that it applies only to associations that do make decisions that are morally binding. The claim to democratic inclusion finds no application in associations that do not. An association that is unable to make morally binding decisions can be neither democratic nor undemocratic in terms of inclusion. It cannot be undemocratic as it is unable to exclude anyone subject to morally binding decisions. It cannot be democratic as it is unable to include anyone subject to morally binding decisions. Associations that fail to make morally binding decisions are not candidates for democratic decision-making at all.

The observation that some associations may be neither democratic nor undemocratic following the moralized version of the all-subjected principle is perplexing but not necessarily damning. Every principle of democratic inclusion is premised on some account of the kind of decisions that are relevant for democratic participation. The account defended in this book is no exception. Even on the version of the all-subjected principle developed in due course, there are associations to which claims for democratic inclusion do not apply because they do not make decisions that are 'binding' in the relevant sense.

The main defect of the moralized view lies elsewhere and is becoming clearer once we consider the relationship between principles of justice and the criteria for democratic inclusion. Consider, to begin, the implications of the moralized account of the all-subjected principle when applied to decisions that are contrary to justice. To see the problem, it is helpful to recall that decisions are morally binding only if members are morally obligated to comply and that such obligations obtain only with respect to morally justified decisions. Assuming, plausibly, that unjust decisions are not morally justified, it follows that unjust decisions are not morally binding. Hence, the moralized version of the all-subjected principle offers no valid claim for democratic participation by the members of associations that are either unjust or that make unjust decisions. Members are not morally required to comply with unjust decisions and therefore not subject to them. Since only subjects should be included, no-one should be included in decisions that are unjust.

That conclusion is problematic as it contravenes the precept that democratic participation is instrumental to justice. In voluntary associations as well as in states, it is commonly and often rightfully believed that policies are more likely to be just if the people concerned participate in deciding them. This is illustrated by historical experience where political agitation for the right to vote and inclusive participation is a frequent response to injustice. But the tenet that democratic participation is instrumental to justice is negated by the moralized view. If democratic inclusion is premised on being subject to decisions that are morally binding and unjust decisions are never morally binding, it follows that claims to democratic inclusion are never valid where they are most needed. Predominant justifications of democracy and participatory rights are thus inconsistent with the moralized account.

Moreover, it appears that the moralized account is also inconsistent with the claim that democratic participation is a requirement of justice. According to principles of 'political fairness', people should be able to participate in the 'institutional provisions that govern political participation' (Beitz 1989: 229). In this view, it is contrary to political fairness to exclude people from decisions that apply to them. Yet, it now appears that the principle of political fairness is inconsistent with the moralized account of the all-subjected principle. This is realized once these principles are brought together. The conjunction of the principle of political fairness and the moralized all-subjected principle is that inclusion is required only for people subjected to just decisions and that decisions are just only if they are inclusive. But this statement makes no sense. In case justice requires that decisions are inclusive, the fact that decisions are just already entails that they are inclusive. Hence, in the event that we accept the principle of political fairness, the moralized account of the all-subject principle must be rejected. Conversely, the claim that inclusion applies only to just decisions implies the rejection of political fairness as a requirement of justice. If you believe that only members with moral obligations to comply are subjected to decisions and that only decisions that are just can give rise to moral obligations, you are committed to believe that decisions can be just independently of the extent to which they are inclusive. To believe *that* is effectively to deny the principle of political fairness.

This section has surveyed the moralized version of the all-subjected principle according to which democratic inclusion is premised on subjection to morally binding decisions. In the process, I have identified various justifications of this principle but, most importantly, focused on its implications. The conclusion is that the moralized view should be abandoned and we should try to identify a non-moralized account of subjection to binding decisions.

Decisions That Claim to Be Binding

The challenge is how to make sense of the claim that a decision can be binding and yet not morally binding. The first thing to remember is that a binding decision is predicated on reasons for compliance. Reasons for compliance are normative in the sense that they are reasons that should be acted on. Thus, a person is 'subject' to a decision only if the decision is associated with a normative claim for compliance.

One immediate implication of this understanding is that the extent to which decisions are binding does not depend on the extent to which they are coercive. A coercive threat does not establish normative reasons for compliance. The fact that you will be punished unless you comply is no reason to conclude that you *should* comply. Coercion consequently does not explain how decisions can be binding.

Though more will be said about the place of coercion and sanctions in coming chapters, I will for now proceed on the assumption that the all-subjected principle is fully captured by an account of binding decisions. Decisions need not be coercive in order to be binding and decisions are binding if there is a sense in which people 'should' comply with them.

The initial step toward a non-moral understanding of binding decisions is to separate prudential and normative reasons for action. Consider a group of terrorists communicating their decision to blast a bomb in an unknown location unless their demands are met. Their decision is undoubtedly a reason for both the authorities and the general public to take action. The decision made by the terrorists is a reason for the authorities to evacuate people from relevant locations and for trying to capture the terrorists. The decision is also a reason for the general public to take necessary precautions. Accordingly, the decision made by the terrorists generates a variety of *prudential* reasons for action.

Compare this scenario with a decision taken by the local stamp collectors' club. Assume that the association decides that members should meet only on Tuesdays. The decision claims to be *normative* as it seeks to establish reasons that members should be acting on. Of course, members that have an interest in attending the meetings of the association also have prudential reasons to act because meetings are now expected to take place on Tuesdays only. But these prudential reasons depend on the incentives created by *the fact* that meetings can now be expected to take place only on Tuesdays. Prudential reasons are generated by the consequences of decisions.

Though a decision can generate reasons for action that are both normative and prudential, only normative reasons are determined by the decision. This is illustrated by the fact that prudential reasons to attend the meeting of the stamp club remain the same even in the event that no decision is made that makes a normative claim. Assume for example that the association is forced to arrange meetings on Tuesdays – perhaps the local thugs compel the chairman of the stamp club to organize meetings on that day. In that case, members with an interest to attend do have prudential reasons that are basically the same as if the association had decided to meet on Tuesdays. But the fact that the association has not decided to meet on Tuesdays implies that members now lack normative reasons to attend the meeting. It is not the case that members *should* meet on Tuesdays just because they have incentives to that effect. 'Brute facts' do not elicit norms that should be complied with (Hage 2018).

The distinction between normative and prudential reasons for action is further illustrated by the distinction between invitations and decisions. A person who is invited to attend a meeting may have prudential reasons to accept the invitation, but is not given an obligatory reason to comply with. Invitations are not claims for compliance. By contrast, the decision that members should meet only on Tuesdays intends to communicate an 'ought' that is addressed to members and that they *should* act on. Decisions aim to establish reasons for compliance that are normative and not merely prudential.

Finally, the distinction between prudential and normative reasons for action aligns with the distinction between compliance and conformity. A person who complies with a decision is acting because of the decision, taking the decision as reason for action. This is distinct from mere conformity with a decision. A person conforms to a decision when acting because of the incentives created by the decision (Brennan et al. 2013: 218; Sevel 2018: 197).[5]

To illustrate, consider Jane, who for prudential reasons halts at a pedestrian crossing when the lights turn red. Perhaps she found it prudent not to cross the road when the pedestrian light turned red as the traffic happened to intensify at that moment. Assume, further, that there is a rule such that pedestrians should stop when the lights turn red. Apparently, Jane is fulfilling the behavioral requirements stipulated by the rule. Yet, since this is a mere coincidence, we should say that she conforms to the rule rather than complying with it. Compliance entails recognition that the rule is normatively significant and a source of practical reason.

Now, the tenet that decisions can be reasons that should be complied with corresponds neatly to the notion of binding reasons for action. Decisions do not just purport to be reasons for action; decisions purport to be reasons that *should* be acted on (Raz 1975: 490f.). Another way to put this is to say that decisions are binding to the extent that they are reasons *not* to act on other reasons. A binding decision is providing a reason for the agent to exclude other reasons for action. Raz famously captured this idea by the notion of 'exclusionary reasons'.[6] Exclusionary reasons are reasons of higher order, not weightier reasons, which preclude the subject from acting on other reasons than that identified by the decision (Raz 1999: 39f.; see also Edmundson 1993: 330; Essert 2012: 53).[7] The notion of binding decisions can thus be specified as decisions that provide exclusionary reasons for action.

It can be objected that although *reasons* for action can be binding it is mysterious how *decisions* can. What a person should do depends on the balance of reasons. If there is a reason for why A should do X rather than Y, this is because the balance of reasons is speaking in favor of X. But if what A *should* do depends only on the balance of reasons, it follows that the decision that A should do X is binding only if the balance of reasons speaks in favor of X. The fact that A so decided is no longer relevant.

One response is to point out that a decision is intended to reflect the balance of reasons for and against the relevant alternatives. When A is deciding X, A is engaged in balancing the reasons for and against X and Y on the basis of the relevant considerations. The decision to pursue X rather than Y is the endpoint of a process where the relevant reasons are compared and weighed (Raz 1975: 490). A decision is a kind of frozen picture of the course of action that should be pursued on the balance of reasons. Hence, a decision is binding if it reflects a conclusion about what should be done once all relevant reasons have been adequately considered in accordance with their weight. Hence, it is not so mysterious how a decision can be binding after all.

This is most clearly seen when we consider agents who are making decisions about their own conduct. Agents who deny that their decisions are binding for them are basically professing that 'although I have decided to do X, I have no reason to do X'. But if decisions summarize judgments on the balance of reasons, not treating the decision as binding is irrational as it implies that 'we can act contrary to the balance of reason without thereby acting contrary to reason' (Green 1988: 37).[8] Agents who refuse to consider their decisions as binding are effectively denying that they are decisions (Raz 1999: 66).

The conclusion is that decisions can be associated with claims for compliance that are not contingent on them being morally binding. Decisions that claim to be binding are intended to provide the subject with exclusionary reasons for action. This conclusion represents a basic component in a non-moralized conception of the all-subjected principle. People are subject to decisions in the sense relevant for democratic inclusion only if they are subject to decisions that claim to be binding. Hence, associations are democratic to the extent that they presumptively include all and only all for whom they claim to make decisions that are binding. Of course, not just any claim to make a binding decision establishes that others are subjected in the relevant sense. Some decisions, such as in the terrorist example, are merely intended to be threats. So far, we have shown that binding decisions can be made but not yet ascertained how they are to be separated from other decisions. More is to be expected from an account of the subjects of decisions that claim to be binding.

Decisions and Authority

One obvious way in which decisions can be understood as binding in a non-moral sense is when people accept decisions as binding for them. The decision made by an association are binding if the members perceive themselves as morally bound to comply. But it is questionable that this view offers a plausible account of when people are subject to binding decisions. A decision that is 'binding' only if the subject *accepts* the decision as normative in practical deliberation does not seem particularly binding at all. As noted by Westlund (2013), the binding force of a decision is largely forgone if the subject can simply choose not to be bound by it; the notion that a person can choose to accept a decision as binding virtually dissolves its binding force. In order to say that a decision is binding it should be possible to say that individuals *ought* to comply with the decision even when they do not.

One possibility is that the conditions for binding decisions can be explained on the basis of an account of practical reason. If binding decisions are by definition practical reasons that the agent should comply with, it seems that the conditions for being subject to binding decisions depend on what constitutes a practical reason. Since the nature of practical reason is controversial, the answer depends on the specific account invoked. Let us briefly try this out by appeal to two contrasting views of practical reason: the psychologist and the realist account (Alexy 1992; Wiland 2002; Chang 2010).[9]

In both the psychologist and the realist view, decisions are practical reasons only if they are relevant. A relevant practical reason is one that is 'personal' in the sense of being pertinent to the goals or circumstances of a person (Alvarez 2010: 19; Bongiovanni 2018: 19). If a practical reason speaks to the goals or circumstances of a person, it is relevant and therefore regulative. If A decides that B should X, the decision is binding for B only if it provides reasons that speak either to the goals or circumstances of B. The realist and psychologist view offer different accounts of what the relevant goals and circumstances of a person are, however.

On the realist account, practical reasons are binding only if they represent reasons that are relevant to the deliberations of the agent given the particular situation. Hence, decisions are binding only if they speak to the relevant facts. The mental state of the agent for whom a decision purports to represent a binding practical reason is of no significance. In this view, it is perfectly consistent to assert that a decision is binding for agents even if they ignore it or are oblivious to its normative force.

The alternative is to envisage practical reasons in psychological terms. A practical reason is binding for a person only if it is accepted as relevant by the person. Individuals should comply with a practical reason only if they do in fact recognize it as a consideration that speaks to them. The fact that members ignore what the association decides is consequently evidence to conclude that the association has failed to provide them with reasons for action that are binding. Agents are bound by a decision only if the decision provides practical reasons that are operative in the mental state of the agent such that it provides a motivation to act.

The question 'Can a decision be binding for someone who does not comply?' is answered in radically differently terms by the realist and psychologist accounts. In the realist view, the decision is binding only if relevant to the circumstances. No-one is bound to comply with a practical reason that makes no difference to their choice-situation. Conversely, if the decision represents a practical reason that is relevant to that situation, the fact that individuals do not comply is no reason to deny that it is binding for them.

By comparison, the psychologist account would say that individuals who do not comply with a decision have either rejected the decision as relevant to them or are unaware of it. If people are bound to comply with decisions only if reasons for compliance are relevant to them, and if 'relevant' means that they accept them, then individuals are never bound to comply with decisions that they do not accept as relevant to them. Decisions are binding only if they are grounded in reasons that the subject recognizes as a source of normativity.

The realist and psychologist views of practical reason are divergent accounts of normativity. Yet, reasons to comply with decisions cannot be fully explained by the nature of practical reasons since reasons for compliance also depend on the standing of the decision-maker. Consider the colleague who advises me to give a lecture next week. In the realist account we are bound to conclude that the colleague's advice is a practical reason that I should act on only if the reason is relevant to me. But that conclusion abjures the distinction between advising someone and deciding for someone. In the event that my employer *decides* that I should give a lecture next week, I am not simply provided with a practical reason that I should comply with if it is relevant. The employer's decision is intended to be authoritative in a way that the advice offered by my colleague is not.

The nature of a decision that claim to be binding cannot be explained by reference to the nature of practical reason as such. What is missing is an account of *authority*. Advising for another is different from deciding for another. Authority is invoked only when deciding for another and is therefore key to understand the relevant sense in which decisions can be binding.

Authority is a relationship between agents such that one is entitled to make decisions that others have duties to comply with. Hence, if the capacity to make binding decisions depends on the authority of the decision-maker, decisions are binding only if they are taken by bodies with the right to make them and for people who have duties to comply with them. This is why the decision by my employer is very different from the advice offered by my colleague. My employer, but not my colleague, claims the authority to decide what I should do. The answer to the question: 'Can a decision be binding for a subject who does not comply?' must accordingly be sought in the conditions for practical authority. It turns out that if the all-subjected principle applies only to persons who are subject to decisions that are or claim to be binding, the conditions for democratic inclusion identified by that principle ultimately depends on an account of practical authority. The all-subjected principle is the claim that democratic rights to participation are triggered by exercises of practical authority.

Subject To De Facto Authority

Authority is the capacity to make binding decisions. The subjects of authority ought to do as decided for no other reason than that the authority so decided.[10] In the case that A is a practical authority for B, A's decision is binding for B irrespective of what A decided. Authority is the capacity to make decisions that provide exclusionary reasons that are 'content-independent' (Hart 1962; Raz 1986; Valentini 2018). The notion of content-independent reasons captures the essential meaning of acting on reasons provided by an authority; an entity is an authority only if able to make decisions that are binding for others independently of what is being decided. By contrast, the notion of exclusionary reasons explains what it means for decisions by an authority to be binding. But it does not follow that only an authority can establish binding reasons for action. For example, I have exclusionary reasons but not content-independent reasons to do as I promised. Reasons for action that are both content-independent and exclusionary are 'protected reasons' in the terminology of Raz (1986: 18).

Authority is a normative concept. An association is vested with authority only if it satisfies the normative conditions for authority. However these conditions are understood, authority is an attribute only of bodies with legitimate authority. Given the normative character of authority, it follows that people are *subject* to decisions in the sense relevant for democratic inclusion if, and only if, they are subject to legitimate authority.

The notion that democratic inclusion is premised on subjection to legitimate authority is nevertheless problematic. Legitimacy is a moral concept, meaning that authority is possessed by bodies only to the extent that they are morally legitimate. The idea that the subject of a binding decision is necessarily subject to legitimate authority is therefore yet another version of the moralized understanding of the all-subjected principle. For reasons given earlier, a moralized understanding of binding decisions is an unlikely candidate for the all-subjected principle.

In fact, as argued by Robert Wolff (1990: 25) it is possible that 'all claims to authority may be wrong'. In case no authority is legitimate, it follows that no-one is subject to a body with the capacity to make decisions that are binding for them. But if the principle of democratic inclusion only applies to the subjects of binding decisions, the implication is that no-one is entitled to democratic inclusion. Such an account of democratic inclusion would be practically useless.

Now, an association need not *possess* legitimate authority in order to *claim* legitimate authority. Political parties, sport clubs, and so on, behave 'as if' they had the legitimate authority to make decisions that are binding for members. Moreover, it is conceivable that members believe that the authority claimed is legitimate. In that event, they are subject to decisions that claim to be authoritative and that they also believe are authoritative. From the combination of claimed legitimate authority and belief in legitimate authority a particular relationship materializes between the association and its members. The association becomes a 'de facto authority'.

The notion of de facto authority forms the basis of yet another hypothesis about the meaning of the all-subjected principle. The hypothesis is that a person is subject to decisions in the sense relevant for democratic inclusion to the extent that they are subject to de facto authority. The all-subjected principle embodies the claim that the subjects of de facto authorities should presumptively be included in order for them to be democratic. Of course, an association with de facto authority is not rendered legitimate just because it claims to be. The decisions made by an association that claims legitimate authority are not necessarily morally binding. But if it is a de facto authority, it follows that at least some people do perceive themselves as morally bound to comply. The decisions made by de facto authorities claim to be normative and are understood as normative. In the following, the conditions for de facto authority are explored further.

The Idea of De Facto Authority

The notion that de facto authority should take the center stage in democratic theory is not commonly appreciated. More common is the conviction that authority exists only in so far as it is morally legitimate and that decisions without legitimate authority are mere exercises of coercion. David Estlund notably endorses this view. According to him, people are subject to authority only if decisions tend to coincide with their moral requirements. In the case that no such tendency can be established, people are subject only to 'brute power' (Estlund 2007: 2).

The distinction between legitimate authority and brute power is nevertheless too crude. It fails to properly differentiate between cases where people comply with decisions because they believe that they are subject to legitimate authority, and cases where people are subject only to either coercive pressure or compelling incentives.

To illustrate, consider the difference between the members who comply with the decisions made by an association and a group of people who do as they are told by a gang of terrorists. In both cases, there is a body making decisions and others that act in accordance with them. But only the members of the association are complying with decisions. They comply because they believe that the body making decisions has legitimate authority and that they are consequently under an obligation to obey. To make sense of this, we must recognize that 'naked power' is not the same as de facto authority (Nowell-Smith 1976).

A further difference between de facto authority and brute power is that only the former *claims* legitimate authority to regulate behavior. A group of terrorists, or a gang of bank robbers, do not pretend to be morally entitled to compliance (though they might conceivably believe that their actions are morally justified). The defining attributes of de facto authority thus include both the claim to legitimate authority and belief in legitimate authority among at least some subjects. Together, these properties are sufficient to distinguish between de facto authority and exercises of brute power (Raz 1990: 3; Raz 2009b: 128).

The defining attributes of de facto authority are nevertheless ambiguous. According to Raz, a body with de facto authority '*either* claims to be legitimate *or* is believed to be so' (Raz 1994: 215). Raz thus identifies two conditions for de facto authority that are both sufficient. By implication, a decision-making body qualifies as a de facto authority in so far as it claims legitimate authority, even if not believed to be legitimate. Also, a decision-making body qualifies as a de facto authority in so far as it is believed legitimate, even if it does not claim legitimate authority. Though this would leave us with two very different accounts of the subjects of de facto authority, I believe there is reason to think that both conditions are in fact necessary and only jointly sufficient.

Consider an association that does not claim legitimate authority despite being widely considered a legitimate authority. Since subjects believe they are subject to legitimate authority, they are predisposed to accept its decisions as binding. The situation can be illustrated by a person asking a shopkeeper why the shop is not open on Sundays. The shopkeeper mistakenly believes that the person is a public official who requests that the shop should be open on Sundays. The shopkeeper therefore believes that there is a moral obligation to keep the shop open on Sundays and accordingly replies that the shop will be open.

If perceived legitimate authority were sufficient for de facto authority, the shopkeeper would indeed be subject to the de facto authority of the person. But *is* that enough? It appears more plausible to assume that exercises of authority are conditioned also by the intention to exercise authority. Just as a promise cannot be made unintentionally, authority cannot be exercise by coincidence. A necessary precondition for authority is the intention to give reasons for action that others should comply with (Enoch 2014: 302). Another way of expounding this point is by observing that individuals cannot comply *with* authority unless there is an antecedent intention that they should comply. There is consequently reason to conclude that claimed authority is necessary for subjection to de facto authority and that perceived authority is not sufficient to that end.

Consider next, bodies that claim legitimate authority but that are not believed to have it. Imagine, for example, an employer who claims legitimate authority to regulate the workplace but whom no employee perceives as a legitimate authority. In the event that perceived authority is not required for de facto authority, we should conclude that the employer is nevertheless a de facto authority by virtue of her to legitimate authority.

What is wrong with the notion of de facto authority premised exclusively on claimed legitimate authority? The problem is that authority is presumed to be effective in regulating behavior, at least to some extent (Raz 1979: 9). Hence, de facto authority must be effective in order to be a species of authority. But a body that claims legitimate authority while being completely ignored by others is not effective in regulating behavior. Claims for compliance are effective only if at least some people accept them as binding. This is why de facto authority depends on 'belief by some that the person concerned has legitimate authority' (Raz 1979: 29).

The conclusion is that de facto authority is premised both on claims to legitimate authority *and* belief in legitimate authority. This is consistent with Dagger's (2018: 5) observation that de facto authority is characterized by some degree of acceptance on the part of subjects.[11] Decisions by an association with de facto authority are *taken as binding* by those who believe that the authority it claims is justified. People who believe that they are subjected to legitimate authority do consider themselves as morally bound to comply.

Again, the fact that authority is believed legitimate does not mean that it *is* legitimate. The legitimacy of the authority that is claimed depends on reasons unrelated to the extent to which it enjoys de facto authority. An association with de facto authority that lacks legitimate authority is claiming to be what it is not. An association with de facto authority that does possess legitimate authority is claiming to be what it is. In any case, since effective authority is a precondition for any version of legitimate authority, only associations that are de facto authorities can be legitimate. Legitimate authority requires the ability to regulate behavior and only de facto authorities do in fact regulate behavior. Thus, de facto authorities both claim legitimate authority and are believed to be legitimate by at least some subjects. The upshot is that principles of democratic inclusion apply to the subjects of de facto authorities by virtue of their claim to legitimate authority. The principle of democratic inclusion is that everyone subjected to claimed legitimate authority should presumptively be included.

Now, this account still leaves undecided who the subjects of de facto authorities really are. It appears that there are two possibilities. The first is that anyone for whom a de facto authority *claims* legitimate authority is a subject in the relevant sense. On that account, the all-subjected principle applies to anyone who is intended to comply with the decisions made. The second is that only those who perceive themselves as morally bound to comply are subject in the relevant sense. The all-subjected principle does in that case apply only to people who accept the authority claimed by a de facto authority. There are consequently two potential readings of the all-subjected principle. Either the principle only applies to the subjects of *claimed* legitimate authority, or the principle only applies to the subjects of claimed legitimate authority that also *believe* they are bound to comply. In what follows, I argue in favor of the former and against the latter understanding of the all-subjected principle.

The Subjects of De Facto Authority

The proposal here is that the all-subjected principle applies only to the subjects of de facto authority. A characteristic of a body with de facto authority is that some believe they are bound to comply with it. But it is unclear if the subjects of de facto authority include only those that so believe. In untying this knot, it is helpful to distinguish between the conditions for *subjection* to de facto authority and the conditions for the *existence* of de facto authority. The conditions for the existence of de facto authority are not the same as the conditions for subjection to de facto authority.

The distinction helps make sense of the possibility that the subjects of de facto authority may not all comply. Individuals who do not comply with a decision do not accept the decision as binding for them. But there is a difference between refusing to comply with a decision that does *not* claim legitimate authority and refusing to comply with a decision that *does* claim legitimate authority. As a matter of fact, only the latter is a case of refusal to comply. No person can fail to comply with a decision that is not intended to be binding for them. Hence, the very notion of non-compliance presupposes that people can be subject to decisions that they should comply with.

Consider for example a membership-based association that claims the right to make decisions that are binding for all members. Of course, only members that do accept the authority of the association as legitimate will consider themselves bound to comply. Members who do not accept the authority of the association have no reason to comply. But non-compliance is premised on subjection to claims for compliance. Hence, non-compliers are subject to decisions even though they do not comply.

Thus, the argument is that democratic associations should presumptively include everyone subject to *claims* for compliance. Only de facto authorities make claims for compliance grounded in the pretense of legitimate authority. Furthermore, de facto authorities necessarily depend on some degree of recognition of their claimed authority. But the authority claimed is not limited to those who believe they are legitimate. Hence, a democratic association is one that presumptively includes not just those who consider themselves as bound by decisions but everyone for whom the association claims to possess legitimate authority. The all-subjected principle should thus be read as follows: *A presumption for democratic inclusion applies to the subjects of de facto authority*.

Rulemaking and De Facto Authority

De facto authorities make decisions that some perceive 'as if' morally binding. They comply because they consider that the authority is legitimate. The basis for belief in legitimate authority is of course varied. The authority claimed by Pope Francis is perhaps accepted for religious reasons by many members of the Catholic Church. The authority claimed by Liz Truss as leader of the Tory party is perhaps accepted by many of its members for ideological reasons. The authority claimed by the president of the chess club is perhaps accepted by the members because of her irresistible charm.

Nevertheless, divergent reasons to accept legitimate authority do have one thing in common: they are contingent on reasons to believe that the powers claimed are *authorized*. In all associations, the claimed right to decide is conditioned by *rules* that confer the normative power to decide by virtue of a person's position. Pope Francis would not be able to claim legitimate authority as Pope unless he had been appointed in accordance with the rules of the Catholic Church. Similarly, Liz Truss's authority as the Tory party leader depends on her being elected to that position by the relevant procedures, and the same goes for the president of the chess club. However charming, competent, or powerful people are, they are unable to exercise the authority of an association unless authorized to that effect by the normative system.

Here then is an important clue to what must be accepted in order for de facto authority to exist. An entity that claims legitimate authority is a de facto authority only if validated by rules. The claim to legitimate authority is premised on rules that *confer* the normative powers that it claims to possess. Rules that confer normative powers were famously termed 'secondary norms' by H.L.A. Hart (1962). Secondary rules are 'rules about rules' that allocate the normative power to make decisions that determine the rights, duties, and other normative relationships of members. A defining feature of a normative system is that the normative power to make decisions is determined by secondary norms.[12] That is why the claim to legitimate authority by a normative system is conditioned by the possession of the normative powers that are conferred by the secondary norms of that system (Hohfeld 1917; Halpin 1996).[13]

The implication is that subjection to de facto authority depends on belief in the *validity* of the normative powers that it claims to possess. In order for an association to achieve de facto authority, its claim to legitimate authority must be recognized in the sense of being legitimately authorized by the rules of the relevant system of norms. Though this is considerably more complicated in the context of the state, this precondition for de facto authority is more straightforwardly illustrated in other associations.

Every association represents a normative system such that the powers exercised by officials are defined and regulated by secondary norms. These norms are typically documented in the so-called 'bylaws.' The bylaws of associations perform basically the same role as the constitutional frameworks of political and legal systems. Analogous to the constitution that empowers the legislature and other public institutions, bylaws empower the representatives of the association to make decisions. The bylaws *authorize* decisions by specifying the conditions for the legitimate exercise of normative power. The authority claimed by representatives are valid only if authorized by the rules of the association. The implication is that the belief in the authority of an association that is a condition for its de facto authority cannot be completely separated from the rules of the normative system that grounds the authority claimed.

It is worth noting that claims to legitimate authority are feasible also in loosely organized groups that do not include formalized power-conferring norms. Though the all-subjected principle applies only to 'normative systems', the rules that confer the normative power to make decisions need not be formalized. Unwritten rules embedded in shared social understandings or entrenched social practices may be sufficient for the existence of a normative system. The point is that de facto authority can be attributed also to informal normative systems. Accordingly, the all-subjected principle applies to the subjects of decisions made by de facto authorities, whether they are formalized or not.

As an illustration, consider a group of friends who agree to make decisions on some specific set of issues. As they agree to comply with the decisions made, they effectively recognize the legitimate authority of certain power-conferring rules. The group is transformed from a network of individuals into a rule-governed body with the capacity to make decisions that regulate conduct. For this collective to be democratic, the opportunity to participate in decisions should extend to all subject to the authority it claims. In the end, democracy turns out to be a species of 'rule-governed relations' (Ceva and Ottonelli, forthcoming).

The Idea of Democratic Association Revisited

The standard view of democratic association is that members should be included and that non-members either should not be included or are permissibly excluded. In either view, granting the right to participation to all members is sufficient for a democratic association to be inclusive. By contrast, the all-subjected principle holds that a democratic association should include all subject to claims of legitimate authority. Membership is of no intrinsic importance to democratic inclusion following the all-subjected principle.

Despite these differences, the practical implications of the all-subjected principle and the standard view might coincide. To illustrate this possibility, consider a chess club where membership is obtained by payment of the annual membership fee. According to the standard view, the chess club is democratic to the extent that all paying members are entitled to participate in the decisions of the association. Though this is the wrong reason for democratic inclusion according to the all-subjected principle, the prescriptions of that principle are identical in a case where only paying members are subject to the authority claimed by the club.

However, the extent of inclusion required by the all-subjected principle diverges from the standard view if one of either two conditions obtains. The first is if the association claims legitimate authority to regulate the actions of non-members. In thiscase, non-members should be included according to the all-subjected principle, though the standard view would still maintain that only members should be included. The second is when the association does not claim legitimate authority for all members. In that case, the standard view is more inclusive than the all-subjected principle. Of course, these conditions are not mutually exclusive; it is conceivable that an association claims legitimate authority for certain non-members while at the same time *not* claiming legitimate authority for all members.

How is it possible for an association to regulate the actions of non-members? A good illustration is housing associations that accept as members only registered owners of the property, but where not all residents are registered owners. Some residents are tenants who pay rent to the association. Yet, the housing association claims the authority to regulate the whereabouts of all residents, whether they are owners or not. Since only owners are members, the association effectively claims legitimate authority also for non-members. The housing association should extend rights of participation to tenants and owners alike in order to be democratic according to the all-subjected principle.

Now, what about the possibility of an association that does not claim the authority to regulate the conduct of all members? This is less obvious as we usually assume that an association would insist on the authority to make decisions for all members. To identify the relevant situation it is important to recall that claims to legitimate authority are contingent on de facto authority. In order for an association to claim legitimate authority, it must be widely recognized as vested with the right to make decisions that are binding. Consequently, an association that is not a de facto authority for all members would be unable to claim legitimate authority. To illustrate, imagine a conflict at an annual general meeting where a minority establishes their candidates on the board only by violating the rules as defined in the bylaws of the association. In so far as other members are concerned, a coup d'état has just taken place. To them, the board is illegitimate and has no authority to make decisions for all members.

The fact that some members consider the new executive board as illegitimate does not necessarily imply that the association is no longer a de facto authority. Other members might deplore what happened and hesitate for a moment about the legitimacy of the association, only to conclude that they still accept the association's claim to legitimate authority. In that case, the association retains de facto authority for all members.

However, in the case where a sufficient number of the members conclude that the association is no longer legitimate, it follows that the association has forfeited its de facto authority. As the association is no longer recognized as a source of binding decisions it now lacks the capacity to regulate how members should act by means of authoritative decisions. Members no longer consider themselves as bound by the decisions made. The implication is that the association is not a de facto authority that claims legitimate authority for members. The presumption that the members of the association should be included because they are subject to claims of legitimate authority no longer holds true.

The account defended here contrasts with the notion that a democratic association includes all and only all the *members*. Though associations typically claim the authority to make decisions for members, they sometimes claim the authority to make decisions also for non-members. The relevant criterion for democratic inclusion is not formal membership but the extent to which you are subject to decisions that are intended to regulate your behavior. A democratic association is ruled by those subject to its claimed authority.

Democracy in Non-Member Associations

Not every association is membership-based. Who are, for example, the members of business corporations? According to Ciepley (2020), the corporation is not membership-based at all. In his estimate, corporations are legal entities that are independent of the individuals that own and operate them. A corporation is not constituted by membership but by the bundle of legal rights conferred by the law. This view is controversial, for sure. Others insist that the owners of the corporation are its only true members (Robé 2011). On that understanding, the standard view of democratic association implies that only the owners of the corporation – which often does not include employees – should be included in a corporation that is ruled democratically. There is a third alternative, however, according to which membership in the corporation extends to all active participants in the organizational structure, including both employees and owners (Deakin 2021). The fact that most employees tend to be excluded from participation in corporate decision-making is testimony to their undemocratic character in the standard view of democratic association.

The conclusion is very different on the basis of the all-subjected principle. According to Dahl (1985: 113) corporations are relevantly similar to governments in that they 'make decisions that apply uniformly to all workers or a category of workers'. The decisions of the state and the corporation are similar in that they claim the authority to regulate the behavior of others. Just like states, corporations are norm-governed entities that claim the authority to regulate the conduct of employees (Singer 2018: 133). If the corporation is also generally perceived as legitimate by the employees, they are subject to decisions that are binding in the sense relevant for the principle of democratic inclusion to apply. Corporations that aspire to be democratic, or that should be, are hence inclusive in the democratic sense only if they include all employees in the decision-making process. The extent of membership in the corporation turns out to be irrelevant.[14]

This chapter has advanced an account of the all-subjected principle that explains the grounds for democratic inclusion in general. Following the all-subjected principle, presumptions for democratic inclusion apply to the subjects of decisions. Individuals are subject to decisions to the extent that the decisions are made by a body that claims legitimate authority to regulate their conduct. As only de facto authorities can claim legitimate authority, the present account of democratic inclusion applies only to de facto authorities.

Notes

1 In opposition to the received view, Alexander (2014) argues that consent is a mental state that is not conditioned by express performative action.
2 Yet, this is controversial as some defend the notion that a subject of legitimate authority can be morally obligated to comply with morally wrongful decisions. For a critical discussion, see Venezia (2020).
3 See Sheinman (2011) for an overview of debates on the nature of promising.
4 A similar but distinctive view is that the moral obligation to obey is owed to other members given that the association constitutes a 'genuine community' (Dworkin 1986). See Christiano (2004) for a critical summary of associative obligations.
5 This particular theory of norms is assuming that norms can be reasons for action. An alternative view is that norms are reasons for action only to the extent that they provide incentives, such as punishments or rewards. The latter view is represented by Axelrod (1986: 1097) and much work in economics. For a critical appraisal of the contrast between normative and economic paradigms of norms, see Kornhauser (1999).
6 Hart's term is 'peremptory'. Raz later substituted 'exclusionary' for 'pre-emptive' reasons (Raz 1986, chap. 1).
7 Some argue that exclusionary reasons serve to exclude *deliberation* on contrary reasons for action – in contrast to excluding *actions* on contrary reasons for action (Gans 1986: 390; Enoch 2014: 321). This version of exclusionary reasons is associated with Hart and is sometimes considered more problematic than the version defended by Raz (Himma 2018: 204).
8 The alleged irrationality of accepting decisions as reasons for action is pressed by Hurd (2018: 94) and further discussed in Simmons (2016: 25) and in Brennan et al. (2013: 212). See Raz (2009a, chap. 1) for a reply.
9 A third influential view is the Aristotelian or Kantian account according to which practical reasons are given by the practical identity of a person such that only reasons that are relevantly connected to a person's identity can be practical reasons for her (e.g., Korsgaard 2008). A virtue of the Aristotelian/Kantian view is that reasons that are 'relevant' are inherently motivating (which they may not be in the realist account) while at the same time potentially mistaken (which they cannot be in the psychologist account).
10 Hershovitz (2012) believes that we commonly mistake obligations to obey grounded in the moral legitimacy of authority with obligations to obey grounded in the moral legitimacy of the content of decisions. The latter is sufficient for moral obligations to comply with the decision, while insufficient for moral obligations to comply because of the authority of the decision-maker.
11 The prefix 'de facto' is sometimes used to belittle the status of an authority, such as when a president is said to be in office 'merely de facto' and, implicitly, therefore illegitimately. However, a president that assumes power by illegitimate means may still *claim* legitimate authority and be widely recognized as legitimate. In that case, the president holds de facto authority even if there are independent reasons to conclude that the president is a usurper. On the other hand, if the president illegitimately assumes power and is able to remain in office only by brutal oppression of opposing voices, we shall conclude that the president is not just a usurper but also devoid of authority. The point is that brute power, de facto authority, and legitimate authority are distinct.
12 The concept of normative power can be specified either broadly as the capacity to change the normative position (of self or others), or more narrowly as the capacity to change the normative position (of self or others) by invoking *a power-conferring norm*. The broad conception applies to changes in the normative position of an agent that are not authorised by decisions made in accordance with power-conferring norms. To illustrate, a convict who successfully escapes from prison is exercising a normative power in the broad view but not in the narrow view. The escape changes the normative position of the convict, albeit not by invoking a power-conferring norm. For a discussion, see Kurki (2017).

13 Secondary norms include power-conferring norms as well as immunities. Norms that confer immunity to A with regard to S in relation to B, are denying B the power to change the normative situation of A in regard to S. For example, members of an association may enjoy the right not to be excluded from the association unless certain conditions are met. Such a right equals an immunity that denies the association the normative power to deprive members of membership in the absence of a decision taken by the required procedures. An immunity that denies someone the normative power to make a particular decision should not be confused with a claim-right that implies a duty not to exercise normative powers to particular ends. See Kramer (2005: 79); cf. Himma (2005).
14 A distinct though potentially relevant question is whether corporations and other associations are themselves subject to binding decisions and therefore entitled to participate (and to vote) in a democratic state (Beckman 2018).

3
DEMOCRATIC INCLUSION AND THE STATE

According to the all-subjected principle, all subject to authority should presumptively be included in the decision-making process. A democratic association is one that is ruled by the subjects of decisions that intend to provide binding reasons for action. This model should now be applied to the state. To the extent that the state claims legitimate authority, the implications of the all-subjected principle are the same as for associations generally. A democratic state should be ruled by the subjects of decisions that claim to represent binding reasons for action.

The question then is how the state claims legitimate authority. The purpose of this chapter is to answer this question by arguing that the authority claimed by the state depends on features inherent in the legal system. The authority claimed by the state is thus a species of legal authority; the state makes a claim for compliance that is conditioned by the authority of the legal system. The subjects of the state are ultimately subjected to claims for compliance with the *law*.

The state's claim for compliance with the law is not just a *legal* claim. Legal systems seek to provide subjects with moral reasons for compliance. The notion that people are subjected to the state consequently pushes us into an inquiry about the basis for the claimed moral authority of the law. In the context of the state, the all-subjected principle depends on an account of law's pretense of moral authority.

The State and The Law

The first step is to clarify *what* people are subjected to, when subjected to the state. This is by no means a trivial task as 'the state' is a 'polysemic' term that lends itself to multiple definitions (O'Beirne 2011). For present purposes, however, it is sufficient while also essential to acknowledge the dual nature of the state. Whatever states are doing and however they are organized, states are entities with causal as well as normative powers. This understanding is reflected in the remark that the state possesses

DOI: 10.4324/9781003359807-3

both normative power and 'power-in-fact' (MacCormick 1998: 495); in the theory of the 'two sides' of the state (Lepsius 2020: 6) and in the point that 'norm and power' are two sides of the same coin in the context of the state (Bobbio 1998: 448). The state is at once a social institution with causal power and a legal institution with normative power.

The causal powers of the state are reflected in exercises of coercion and in attempts by public authorities to monitor and penetrate the social, economic, and physical environment. These features correspond to what sociologist Michael Mann influentially termed the 'despotic' and 'infrastructural' powers of the state (Mann 1984; Soifer 2008). The state wields causal power to the extent it possesses the capacity to effect changes in the world by structuring the behavioral incentives of others, or enforcing its aims by brute force.

The dual nature of the state implies that it is not merely a vehicle of causal power, however. The state is also vested with normative powers by which standards of conduct are created that are intended to guide and direct the behavior of people and other entities. The state is a manufacturer of normative relationships that are intended to serve as standards of conduct which should be complied with.

The normative powers of the state are incomprehensible unless it is recognized that the state is intimately related to the legal system. The normative powers of the state derive from the legal system that defines and empowers the 'system of offices and roles' embodied by public agents and institutions (Copp 1999: 7; Waldron 2006: 180). The normative powers of the state are 'creatures of the law' that are distinct from the causal powers of the state.

The legal system defines the normative powers of the state both through regulative norms and power-conferring norms. Norms that are regulative identify normative standards for behavior, whereas power-conferring norms allocate rights to create, revise, and abolish regulative norms. Together, regulative and power-conferring norms represent the basic ingredients of the legal system. In Hart's influential terminology, the legal system is a 'union' of primary (regulative) and secondary (power-conferring) norms. Though regulative norms are the most obvious, the secondary norms are more fundamental. The secondary norms of legal systems are what separates them from mere social norms and make possible decisions about regulative norms; they constitute 'manuals' for 'creation and variation' in the law (Hart 1962: 79).

Of course, states always remain social institutions with causal powers. But public officials and public institutions do not just wield causal powers. They also claim the normative power to define reasons that others should comply with by virtue of the authority vested in them by the legal system. The precise relationship between the state as a sociological entity with causal power, and the state as a legal entity with normative power, is subject to debate. Did the legal system emerge before the sociological entity called the state, or is the opposite true, such that the coercive apparatus of the state is the outcome of the legal system (Troper 2020: 47)? However that may be, the duality of causal and normative power remains an inescapable fact about the state well captured by the notion that the state is an 'institutional normative order' (MacCormick 1997; Raz 2009a: 150).

Based on these observations, we can give a preliminary account of the all-subjected principle in the context of the state: the presumption for democratic inclusion applies to all for whom the laws of the state claim to be binding. This position inevitably raises issues about the nature of 'the law'. The claim that the laws of the state are binding is plausible only if the laws of the state *can* be binding. But if the laws of the state can be binding, why not simply say that the subjects of the state are those for whom the laws *are in fact* binding? Thus, it is necessary to explain both how the laws of the state can be binding, and why the subjects of the state are not better understood in terms of binding legal norms. The remainder of this chapter seeks to answer these questions and to explain what it means to be 'subject' to the state in the sense relevant for democratic rights to participation as understood by the all-subjected principle.

How The Law Binds

The term 'law' figures in a variety of contexts that are distinct from that of the state. There are laws of physics, laws of economics, and laws whenever there are 'rules of some permanence and generality, giving rise to one kind of necessity or another' (Raz 2004). Of course, claims to democratic inclusion do not arise whenever a person is subject to 'laws' in this general sense: it would be awkward to insist that the subjects of the laws of gravity and the subjects of the laws of economics are entitled to democratic inclusion because they are subjected to 'laws'. Democratic participation is concerned with participation in the making of decisions about rules that set normative standards for behavior. A characteristic of the laws relevant to democratic participation is that they are rules of conduct, or norms, not mere regularities of the natural or social world.

The laws of the state *are* norms (or most of them, in any case) for the regulation of conduct (Kelsen 1945; Hart 1962: 82; see also Bobbio 1998; Yankah 2008). Decisions made by states are thus normative, at least in the sense that they are 'norms' of the legal system – 'legal oughts'. The directives and laws decided are *legally* binding regardless of the moral quality of the legal system, or 'automatically' as explained by Lyons (1993: 98). The subjects of the state should legally speaking comply with the law. They are subject to legal oughts that are independent of moral oughts (Martin 2003; Spaak 2003; Himma 2013b: 25).

The preliminary conclusion is that the laws of the state are always binding in a *legal* sense. People are subject to laws that provide *legal reasons* for compliance whenever there is a legal system in force that identifies legal rights and duties. For example, if the law requires that income should be taxed, it necessarily follows that there is a 'legal ought' such that income taxes should be paid.

However, the claim that legal norms are legally binding is a statement about the meaning of law, not a statement about the extent to which the law provides *reasons* for action. Therefore, the fact that people are subject to legally binding norms – 'legal oughts' – is not evidence to conclude that they are subject to reasons for compliance. To see this, consider that no contradiction is involved in accepting that there is a legal reason such that A should pay taxes while A may have no *reason* to pay taxes. In fact, it is conceivable that legal norms do not provide reasons for action at all. For them to provide reasons for action, legal rules must be practical reasons.

But in the case that legal rules are imperatives expressed in deontic form, they are but 'commands' or 'musts'. Imperatives are not reasons for action, they are exhortatives *that* others act. If all legal norms are imperatives and if only reasons for action can be binding, it evidently follows that no legal norm is ever binding.[1]

Yet, the view that legal norms are just imperatives is not currently very fashionable and I will therefore proceed on the assumption that legal norms are, or at least intend to be, practical reasons. Legal norms cannot be mere imperatives if they are to provide reasons for action. Instead, legal norms are to be read as 'it is the rule that one ought'. Rules are facts that provide reasons for action (Raz 1999: 79).[2]

The notion that legal norms are reasons for action is necessary for the thesis that legal systems claim legitimate authority to hold. Authority is the right to give others reasons for action that they should comply with. The claim to legitimate authority entails the presumed moral right to establish binding reasons for action. If the laws of the state were but imperatives, the very idea of authority in the realm of law and the state would make no sense.

The question then is whether the legal system of the state does provide binding reasons for action. Practical reasons are binding only if they are conclusive such that the action required should be performed. Practical reasons are either prudential or moral reasons for action. They are prudential reasons if grounded in the self-interest of the agent.[3] They are moral reasons if grounded in moral requirements that apply to the agent. Legal norms are consequently reasons for action only if they are either prudential or moral reasons that the agent should act on.

The trouble is that neither prudential nor moral reasons for action offer a plausible basis for the all-subjected principle of democratic inclusion. In fact, prudential reasons to do what is required by the law is not to be bound by the law at all. From the fact that an agent has prudential reasons to perform the action identified as required by the law it does not follow that the law is binding for the agent. The moral account fares better in this regard: laws that are morally legitimate *are* reasons that the agent *should* comply with. In the case that the law provides moral reason for action, the law is morally binding. The difficulty with this view is that it proposes the wrong connection between the fact of being subject to binding decisions and democratic inclusion. As I will explain below, the moral account does not offer a plausible basis for the claim that the subjects of binding decisions should be able to participate in their making. In the end, I am proposing a different view. The view proposed is analogous to the position defended in chapter two: the all-subjected principle applies to the subjects of claimed legitimate authority. The subjects of claimed legitimate authority are intended to comply with decisions. Since the legal system of the state does claim legitimate authority, the subjects of the state are subject to claims for compliance with the decisions of the state.

The Brute Force Account

Well-functioning states have the capacity to engage in coercion, physical force, and to impose sanctions for non-compliance. Based on this fact, it is frequently implied that the laws of the state can be fully accounted for in terms of coercion.

The defining characteristic of populations in territories controlled by states is that they are joined into a 'coercively imposed political community' (Nagel 2005: 133). The subjects of the state are subject to physical force or threats of physical force (Abizadeh 2008: 57; Blake 2016).

The coercive powers of the state are obvious. As testified in the canonical works of political theory, the state is an organization with extant coercive power at its disposal that insists on monopolizing legitimate uses of coercion.[4] The state is clearly not the sole agent with the capacity to engage in coercion, though the state is usually able to mobilize greater coercive power than any other agent. The defining mark of the state is that it claims to be the only agent entitled to legitimate coercive power and therefore equipped with the right to regulate the coercive actions of everyone else.

A virtue of this account is that it provides a clear basis for the distinction between the legal system of the state and other normative systems. The legal system of the state is not the only normative system around. A variety of normative systems exist in the realm of religion, including canonical law, Jewish law, Islamic law, and Hindu law (Lindahl 2001; Raz 2017; Tuori 2018). In addition, there exist multiple indigenous systems of law, practiced by peoples independently of the state since time immemorial (e.g., Zion and Yazzie 1997). But the brute force account does explain why normative systems associated with the state are different. The subjects of the laws of the state are vulnerable to the vast repressive machinery of the state; only the laws of the state are enforced by an organization that insists on monopoly on legitimate coercion.[5]

However, the observation that the state is coercive is not sufficient to establish that coercion is a defining element of subjection to the state. The notion that subjection to the state is fully accounted for in terms of coercion is premised on a particular theory of what both the law and the state *is*. Hence, to say that the subjects of the law are but subjects to coercion, is to deny that the normative powers of the state are relevant in characterizing the relationship to the state. No normative claim such that the laws of the state *should* be complied with is required in order to explain what it means to be subject to the coercive powers of the state. In the following, I shall term this the 'brute force account' of subjection to the laws of the state.

The first point, then, is that the coercive powers of the state do not engender claims for compliance. Fear of sanctions can be sufficient for conformity with legal directives, of course. But fear of sanctions is no different from reasons to avoid other unpleasant and potentially harmful experiences. Torrential rain, hot weather, and ice storms frequently do induce people to abstain from doing what they would otherwise have done. Sanctions issued by the state are in one sense just like fluctuations in the weather. They are 'brute facts' that may be coercive but that do not intend to be binding. The fact that breaking the law is associated with the risk that you will suffer from the sanctions imposed by the state is no reason to conclude that you *ought* to comply with the law; just as the fact that unpleasant or dangerous weather is no reason to conclude that you *ought* not to leave the house.

Hence, the brute force account is unable to recognize the law as a source of normativity. If the laws of the state are simply instructions for coercion, no 'claim for compliance' is associated with the laws of the state. The notion that the subjects of the state should comply with the law is falling out of the picture if the only reason to comply with the law is that of avoiding the coercive sanctions that the state has at its disposal. To say that the laws of the state are 'binding' could mean no more than that people usually have prudential reason to conform to legal requirements.

A good illustration of why the brute force theory of law is unable to establish that the laws of the state are *binding* is found in the work of John Austin. Following Austin, the laws of the state are ultimately the commands that are communicated by the sovereign. The sovereign is a person or body that is 'habitually obeyed' by the 'bulk' of the population while at the same time not being subordinated to any other body. The commands of the sovereign are laws in the sense that they are injunctions for action conditioned by coercive sanctions (Tapper 1965; Mindus 2013).

If the laws of the state are but 'commands' supported by coercive sanctions, legal norms do not provide practical reasons for compliance. Commands are requests and just as the robber who requests your money does not provide you with a reason for compliance, the requests communicated by the law are not reasons for compliance. The sole reason for obedience with the law, according to this theory, is, instead, that the subject has incentives to avoid the 'evils or pains' imposed by the sovereign (Bix 2001). Hence, in Austin's view, the assertion that I am 'bound' by the law could only mean that I have prudential reasons to consider the risk that I will suffer from sanctions unless I do as required by the law. Prudential reasons for conformity with the law are not reasons to act because of the law but reasons to act out of self-interest. The conclusion is that the laws of the state, in Austin's view, are never norms that ought to be complied but, at best, incentives for conformity (Yankah 2008: 1205). This is the gist of Hart's influential critique of Austin's command theory of law. A theory of law built on fear of sanctions does not admit of the legal system of the state as a source of normative power (Hart 1962: 79ff.; Postema 1998; Lamond 2001; Spaak 2003: 480; cf. Schauer 2015).

The brute force account is unable to explain how the subject of the laws of the state can be subject to binding legal norms. Indeed, the brute force account does not even recognize that the laws of the state *claim* to be binding. In the brute force account, the only claim that the state can make is that people usually have reason to do as requested by the law because of the incentives provided by the coercive institutions of the state. We need to look elsewhere to vindicate the claim that the subjects of the laws of the state should presumptively be included because they are subjected to laws that claim to be binding.

The Moral Account

The alternative is to identify moral reasons for compliance. Moral reasons for action are reasons that should be complied with; they are morally binding reasons. If the laws of the state are moral reasons for action – if they are *moral laws* – it follows that the subject of the state is morally bound to comply with the laws of the state. The notion that the laws of the state are binding would then be predicated on the fact that legal norms are also moral norms.

The laws of the state are, of course, not always moral reasons for action. There is a constant possibility that the substance of many laws deviates from justified moral reasons for action. Hence, if the laws of the state are binding only if they are morally binding, it remains an open question to what extent the actual laws of the state are indeed binding. Moreover, even if all the laws of the state were morally justified, it would not be enough to conclude that subjects are bound to comply with the directives of public officials or with the laws of the state. The state does not merely pretend to make decisions that are morally justified. More importantly, the state pretends to be morally entitled to decide how people should act because of its legitimate authority. The point is that the laws of the state are morally binding only if it is true that the state wields morally legitimate authority.

Legitimate authority is explained by Raz as the capacity to make decisions that morally apply anyway. The 'anyway' signals that the *reasons* provided are such that the subject should have acted on them even if the decision had not been made. The consequent claim is that authority is legitimate only when '*the alleged subject is likely better to comply with reasons which apply to him if he accepts the directives of the alleged authority as authoritatively binding*' (Raz 1986: 53 emphasis in original). There is reason to comply with the decisions made by a legitimate authority because compliance with legitimate authority is instrumental in making the subject comply with the demands of morality. For the state to wield legitimate authority, it must consequently be true that compliance with the legal norms of the state is what subjects morally ought to do.

The claim that the legal system of the state wields legitimate authority is to insist that it has the ability to supply reasons for action that apply to the subject anyway. For decisions to depend on reasons that apply anyway, the decision must correctly reflect the balance of reasons that apply to the subject. Hence, it would be a mistake for the subjects of legitimate authority to perceive the decision as just one reason for action that should be balanced against other reasons for action. It would be a mistake since the decision *already* encapsulates the correct balance of all relevant reasons that apply to the situation (Raz 1985; Shapiro 2005; Ehrenberg 2011).[6] The decisions by a morally legitimate authority are binding irrespective of their content.[7]

The question now is whether the moral account of binding decisions is helpful for the purpose of explicating the all-subjected principle. The principle holds that a presumption for inclusion applies to the subjects of binding decisions. If subjects are bound to comply only with the laws of legitimate authority, it follows that the presumption for inclusion only applies if the state is a legitimate authority. This view is reminiscent of the moralized conception of the all-subjected principle discussed in chapter two. As explained there, the moralized version of the all-subjected principle is problematic both in terms of scope and in terms of consistency with standard justifications of democratic rights.

The concern with scope is evident from the fact that few existing legal systems are likely to pass the test of morally legitimate authority. Hence, if subjects are bound by decisions only if the state is a legitimate authority, and if subjection to binding decisions is necessary for democratic inclusion, the conditions for democratic inclusion rarely obtains. Indeed, if *no* state wields legitimate authority, the conditions for the right to democratic participation stipulated by the all-subjected principle do not obtain anywhere. That makes an odd account of democratic inclusion.

A first attempt to rescue the moralized account is to dispel the assumption that legitimate authority applies to legal systems and to insist that it applies to individuated legal norms. In that case, we are likely to discover that at least *some* legal norms are legitimate and should therefore be recognized as authoritative. Indeed, this appears to be the view endorsed by Joseph Raz: legitimate authority is 'piecemeal' as it 'depends on the person over whom authority is supposed to be exercised' (Raz 1986: 73). For instance, a significant portion of criminal law is likely to coincide with moral requirements such that the law's claim to authority with respect to behavior that is harmful to others is morally legitimate. In situations where criminal law applies, we are likely to comply better with moral reasons that already apply to us by complying with the criminal law. If some legal norms are legitimate, it evidently follows that some legal norms are morally binding. Critics describe this as the 'patchwork' theory of legitimate authority (Regan 1990; Mian 2002: 112).

However, not much is gained for our purposes by conceding that *some* legal norms may be morally binding. The conjunction of the claim that *some* laws are morally binding and the principle that only subjects of binding laws should be included in the demos, is that democratic inclusion applies only in relation to some laws. If the law is morally binding only in 'some states some of the time' (Christiano 2004) and democratic inclusion applies only to the subjects of morally binding law, it appears that the preconditions for democratic inclusion obtain only in 'some states some of the time'. The result is to reactivate the concern with the scope of the moralized conception of the all-subjected principle already addressed.

A distinct issue with the patchwork theory of legal authority is that it runs counter to the authority claimed by the legal system. To recognize 'the law' as authoritative, is to grant the existence of reasons for compliance with the legal order and not just for individuated norms of that order. But this notion of 'systemic authority' evaporates if it is accepted that authority is attached to some legal norms, but perhaps not to others, depending on their moral merit.

A second attempt to rescue the moralized view is by introducing an alternative theory of *what* makes the laws of the state legitimate. Raz's account is that legitimate authority hinges on the ability to make decisions that depend on reasons that would apply to subjects anyway. Moral reasons that apply to the subject in a given situation (such as 'it is wrong to murder') are substantive reasons – they are reasons about what is morally right or wrong to do. But this account overlooks the procedural sources of legitimate authority. For an entity to wield legitimate authority, it is not enough that it has the capacity to produce morally justified decisions. A further requirement is that it makes decisions by procedures that are morally justified.

How decisions are made is as pertinent to legitimate authority as *what* decisions are made. Accordingly, we could envisage a distinct version of the moral account such that legitimate authority depends on the procedures followed in the making of collective decisions. Instead of saying that the laws of the state are legitimate if, and only if, they depend on reasons that apply to the subject anyway, we should say that the laws of the state are legitimate only if enacted by procedures that are morally required for independent reasons.

The consequent objection against Raz is well known in the literature (Shapiro 2002; Hershovitz 2003; Christiano 2004; Marmor 2005). Perhaps the most compelling version of it is Daniel Viehoff's (2011) according to which Raz mistakenly assumes that morally justified obligations depend exclusively on the substance of law. The thesis is that the law helps subjects to comply with reasons that apply to them anyway only if the law is created by procedures that are morally justified. Arguably, the democratic ideal, properly specified, is an account of morally justified procedures of law-making. Consequently, democratic procedures of law-making are either sufficient or necessary for the legitimate authority of the legal system. In the view spelled out by Viehoff, democratic law-making secures moral reasons for compliance with the law by virtue of the moral qualities of the procedures.

Viehoff effectively demonstrates that a moral account of the authority of law can be 'source-based'. If there is moral reason to accept the sources of law, any norm that derives from these sources should be complied with. Putatively, there are moral reasons to accept democratic procedures as a source of moral obligation. Hence, the laws of the state are morally binding if they are generated by democratic procedures; the laws of the state are legitimate by virtue of their democratic provenance.[8]

Does the democratic account of legitimate authority save the moralized conception of the all-subjected principle? In fact, it seems that the scope problem associated with moralized conceptions of the all-subjected principle is reappearing. How the problem plays out depends, however, on how the democratic version of the moralized view is specified. Are democratic procedures sufficient for legitimate authority, or are democratic procedures necessary though insufficient for legitimate authority?[9] In the latter case, the laws of the state represent legitimate authority only if it is true both that the laws are morally justified and are enacted by democratic procedures. That account would raise the bar for legitimate authority even further with the result that its scope is more limited. In the former case, the laws of the state represent legitimate authority *only* if it is true that the law is enacted by democratic procedures. This account is more permissive. If democratic procedures are sufficient for legitimate authority, we should be able to say that the subjects of any democratic state are subject to morally binding laws. The claim that only the subjects of morally binding decisions are presumptively entitled to inclusion does in that event apply to the subjects of all democratic states.

Yet, the second objection against the moralized conception still applies. The problem is that a conception of inclusion is meant to be among the conceptual requirements of a democratic process. But democratic inclusion cannot both be a defining attribute of democratic procedures and a precondition for subjection to the law in the sense required by the principle of democratic inclusion. It makes little sense to say that only the subjects of democratic states are presumptively entitled to democratic inclusion. Subjection to laws made by democratic procedures cannot be preconditions for the right to participate in the making of the law. We should consequently reject as irrelevant the suggestion that law is morally binding only if the sources of law are democratic.

The Authority Account

The account to be defended proceeds on the assumption that the state wields normative power based on the claimed legitimate authority of the legal system. Every legal system claims legitimate authority, according to Joseph Raz: the laws of the state claim compliance grounded in the pretense of legitimate authority (Raz 1979: 30).

The claim to legitimate authority is what separates legal systems from mere coercion. The claim that subjects ought to comply is a normative quality that is not present either in imperatives that something is done, or in advice that doing something would be good. Moreover, the laws of the state differ fundamentally from the requests that are supported by coercive threats; 'the law – unlike the threats of the highwayman – claims to itself legitimacy. The law presents itself as justified" (Raz 2009a: 158).[10] The distinctive mark of the legal system is the insistence that it represents reasons for action that should be complied with.

The view that the laws of the state claim legitimate authority suggests that something important is missing in the conventional picture that subjects are either morally bound to comply with the law or not bound by the law at all. Instead, we should recognize that subjects are targeted with claims for compliance. Of course, the fact that the laws of the state *claim* to be binding does not warrant the conclusion that subjects are morally obligated to comply with the law. The legal system may not qualify as morally justified authority, indeed few if any legal systems are likely to do that. But, following Raz, the claimed authority to regulate behavior is made by every legal system; 'though a legal system may not be a legitimate authority, or though its legitimate authority may not be as extensive as it claims, every legal system claims that it possesses legitimate authority' (Raz 1994: 215).

The consequent 'authority thesis' is not all uncontroversial. With regard to the *nature* of the claim, some object that legal systems typically make a different claim – they make claims of justice (Soper 1996). Others have questioned the assertion that an abstract entity such as 'the legal system' is able to claim anything at all (Himma 2001a). Instead, the suggestion is that the claim to legitimate authority is more plausibly attributed either to the lawmakers (MacCormick 2007) or to public officials (Roughan 2018).[11]

I do not believe these disputes matter for present purposes. Our aim is to explicate the claim that democratic inclusion applies to the subjects of the laws of the state, where the subjects are defined in terms of legal norms that are binding. The upshot of the authority thesis is that a necessary and sufficient condition for subjection to the laws of the state is subjection to claims to legitimate authority: the subject of the law equals the people for whom the legal system claims to provide binding legal norms. It is of no immediate interest whether that claim is made by the legal system as such, by legal officials, or by the lawmakers. It does matter, however, *that* a claim to legitimate authority is made. For Raz, institutional normative orders inevitably make such claims. The legal system of the state claims legitimate authority because it is an institutional normative order. An entity that does not claim for itself legitimate authority is not a legal system. An entity that claims to be 'legal' but not 'legitimate' can be little else than a coercive apparatus.

This point is leaving the door open for a distinct objection against the authority thesis. The objection is that it represents an implausibly rigid requirement for the existence of the legal system of the state. Why should we deny that states that do not pretend to be legitimate are still legal systems to which people are subjected (Kramer 1999: 391)?

Raz's reply is that the legal system of the state must be *capable* of legitimate authority in order to claim legitimate authority.[12] If the state and the legal system could be just about anything, its claim to legitimate authority would be indistinguishable from the 'highway man'. Of course, this reply is unlikely to convince someone who believes that even the most arbitrary and evil regime could be legal.[13] They might willingly jettison the notion that claims to legitimate authority are worth taking seriously. Pushing the challenge a bit further, there seems to be two last-ditch defenses of the position that only entities capable of legitimate authority can pretend to wield legitimate authority.

The first is phenomenological: the legal system of the state claims legitimate authority because legal practices are similar to moral practices. Legal language is akin to moral language as evinced by the fact that basic legal concepts – 'rights', 'duties', 'powers', and 'immunities' – are the same (Green and Adams 2003). The language of law and morality both intend to provide reasons for action that should be complied with. Law is not just an attempt to induce conformity by means of coercion or force since it 'presents itself' as endowed with the moral authority to establish binding reasons for action (Raz 2009a: 158).

The second defense of the authority thesis is pragmatic. The idea that legal systems necessarily claim legitimate authority is not an empirical claim about existing states. It is a conceptual stipulation that allows for a distinction between exercises of brute force and legal authority (Gardner 2012). No such distinction is possible in the absence of the authority thesis. Now, this point could certainly be rejected out of hand as dependent on an arbitrary definition of 'law'. If the authority thesis is just a conceptual stipulation, we might equally well define 'law' in terms of coercion.

Nonetheless, the possibility of defining the law differently is no reason to deny the authority thesis. A definition is not an arbitrary semantic stipulation. A definition implies claims about the nature of the world as described by language. The way the world is described is not arbitrary but a reflection of reasons about how the world is best understood.[14] The authority thesis depends on reasons to believe that normative power is an essential feature of legal systems. Though the authority thesis may be mistaken, it is mistaken only if there is reason to deny that normative power is a significant property of legal systems. The observation that law 'can' be defined differently is no such reason.

Notes

1. See Bertea (2021) for a good overview of the contrast between the view that legal norms are imperatives and the view that they are practical reasons.
2. This is not to say that all legal norms are reasons for action. Specifically, secondary norms are not. This is the point made by Raz (1970) in his criticism of Kelsen's attempt to reconstruct law as a strict hierarchical system of norms. Cf. Kramer (1999: 381ff.) denying that all primary norms are practical reasons and that at least some of them are imperatives.
3. The nature of prudential reason and how they are to be separated from moral reasons is philosophically controversial. For an overview and an argument to the effect that prudential reasons are reducible to 'conative states' (mental representations of goals for the person) see Worsnip (2018).
4. See, among others, John Rawls (1993: 136), 'government alone has the authority to use force in upholding its laws', and Max Weber, the state 'claims the monopoly of the legitimate use of physical force within a given territory'. An instructive criticism of these accounts is found in Morris (2012).
5. The coercive capacity of the state is also fundamental to the distinction between the laws of the state and international law. For a discussion of this claim, see Roponi (2016).
6. As noted by Marmor (2011: 126) not all decisions by a legitimate authority are binding. There is no obligation to comply with legitimate decisions that provide only hypothetical reasons (e.g., 'you must register a bank account in order to receive tax refunds').
7. The reasoning here follows Raz in assuming that legitimate authority grounds moral obligations. On a distinct account, legitimate authority does not ground moral obligations but only moral rights *to rule*. The implication of that account is that the subjects of a morally legitimate authority are not obligated to comply though they have duties not to interfere with the operations of the authority. A third alternative is that legitimate authority does establish *moral liabilities* such that they have obligations to accept as binding the normative relations established by the authority. See Perry (2005) for a helpful discussion.
8. See also Hampton 1994.
9. Though Viehoff explicitly attacks only the 'exclusive' (2011: 249) concern with outcomes in contrast to procedures, it is not clear that a moral account of binding law can accommodate both.
10. Cf. Ripstein (2004) who argues that law claims for itself both the legitimate authority to create binding norms and the legitimate authority to enforce them by means of coercion. See also Edmundson (2010: 180) for the view that legal authority consists in the (purported) moral power to place us under obligations to obey its commands, particularly its laws.
11. The difference between these versions of the authority thesis and Raz's original formulation may in the end prove illusory if true that the best interpretation of Raz is that law's claims to legitimate authority is 'inferred from the behaviour of officials in their activities as officials to law as a whole' (Himma 2007: 22).
12. Himma (2001b) refers to this claim as the 'instantiation thesis'; law cannot sincerely claim authority unless it is capable of instantiating authority. In order not to complicate things unnecessarily, I am in the following assuming that the instantiation thesis is encapsulated by the authority thesis.
13. Lon Fuller's influential reply to this challenge is that only states that comply with norms of 'formal legality' qualify as legal systems. For a discussion, see Waldron (2006: 197).

14 A conceptual claim is not simply a claim about linguistic meaning. A conceptual claim seeks to separate objects in the world from other objects on the basis of theoretically motivated interest. So, Raz does not pretend that law's claim to legitimate authority is a feature of the linguistic meaning of 'law'. His point is that it is a characteristic of 'our' legal systems. See, on this point, Spector (2019: 27f.).

4
SUBJECT TO LEGAL AUTHORITY

Claimed authority is not actual authority. Though every state with a legal system claims to possess legitimate authority, it is far from clear that every state with a legal system is in fact legitimate. Indeed, it is an incontrovertible possibility that no existing legal system is fully endowed with legitimate authority. Is the implication that the subjects of the state are only subject to inherently doubtful claims of authority?

Not so. The authority claimed by legal systems is not made out of thin air. It is made on the premise that the legal system holds *de facto authority*. Only states with de facto authority are able to claim legitimate authority (Raz 2009a: 9; Raz 1994: 215). Anyone subject to the claimed authority of the legal system is necessarily also subject to a legal system with de facto authority. Hence, if subjection to the legal system of the state is premised on its claimed authority, and if only a state with de facto authority can claim legitimate authority, only the subjects of a legal system with de facto authority are subjects of the state in the relevant sense.

De facto authority is the capacity to act authoritatively such that others accept the authority claimed. The mark of legal systems with de facto authority is that they are effective in regulating conduct on the basis of perceived legitimacy (Raz 2009a: 7). Therefore, for the state to achieve de facto authority, it must be the case that sufficiently large segments of the population recognize the authority claimed by the state. States with de facto authority behave as if they are legitimate authorities and are perceived as legitimate authorities by a significant part of the population. The laws enacted by a state with de facto authority are presented 'as if' imbued with legitimate authority and widely recognized as so imbued (Alexander 1990; Roughan 2018). The point is that the subjects of a state that claims legitimate authority are not merely subject to a *claim*, they are also subject to laws that are widely recognized as authoritative and legitimate.

DOI: 10.4324/9781003359807-4

The fact that the authority thesis applies only to de facto authorities has immediate implications for the all-subjected principle.[1] If people are subjects in the sense relevant for principles of democratic inclusion to apply only if they are subject to claims of legitimate authority, and if such claims are made only by de facto authorities, it follows that people are subject in the sense relevant for democratic inclusion only in relation to states with de facto authority. The subjects of a legal system with de facto authority are subject to claims for compliance by a body that claims legitimate authority and that is widely recognized as legitimate.[2]

Based on these considerations, the all-subjected principle can be specified in greater detail. The all-subjected principle is the idea that people should be able to participate in the making of decisions that they are expected to comply with. The expectation for compliance is premised on claimed legitimate authority. Hence, subjection to the state is premised on the state's claimed legitimate authority. As only states with de facto authority are able to claim legitimate authority, the principle of democratic inclusion applies only to the subjects of states with de facto authority.

Now, one issue is that the legal system of the state achieves de facto authority only if the authority it claims is generally accepted. However, it is not clear how the population can recognize the authority claimed by legal systems. A legal system includes all norms that are validated by the sources of law. Hence, for the people at large to accept the legal system as authoritative, they must be able to validate the law by relevant sources of the law; ordinary citizens need some standard for legal validation. Without a firm understanding of the sources of law, valid legal claims cannot be separated from invalid legal claims. But the 'sources of the law' are likely to be fuzzy to most people. The challenge is to explain how the legal system of the state achieves de facto authority.

A further issue with this account is the scope of de facto authority. Not *every member* of society needs accept the legal system as legitimate authority in order for it to achieve de facto authority. It is enough that 'sufficiently many' accept the legal system as authoritative. But is everyone subject to the law, in a case where only some accept the authority of law? Should we conclude that people who either reject or ignore the law's claimed authority are not subjects of the state? That conclusion would unsettle the all-subjected principle. If the all-subjected principle applies only to the portion of society that accepts the state's claim to legitimate authority, the principle is not very inclusive at all.

The aim of this chapter is to address these dual concerns. In the first section, I explain the urgency of legal validity to the de facto authority of the legal system. I then proceed, in the second section, to examine alternative ways of bridging the gap between the conditions for de facto authority and legally valid authority. The view defended is that the law is accepted as binding among citizens in general when a sufficient number of them recognize themselves as participants in social practices ruled by legal standards that are validated by public institutions.

The third section examines objections to the view defended. Specifically, I am responding to concerns about the binding force of claims made by de facto authorities, the extent to which accepting de facto authority implies approval of claimed legitimate authority, and the scope of de facto authority given that not all members of society are likely to accept the authority claimed.

Authority and Validity

The legal system of the state claims legitimate authority. More specifically, it claims legitimate *legal* authority. Law's dual claim to authority and validity is readily observed in the operations of legal officials. Officials tasked with legal decision-making in courts and other public authorities typically recognize the law as authoritative. They believe that the norms of the legal system ought to be complied with because they are the law. Judges, police officers, and desk-officers are acting on the premise that the law enjoys legitimate authority and that they are bound by the law. Yet, legal officials are acutely sensitive to the validity of legal claims made. Not just any claim about the law is accepted by them as a binding precept of the legal system.

Consider, for example, members of the public who call upon legal officials not to enforce a particular legal requirement. It may be, for instance, that protesters argue that the 'lock down' imposed by the government in response to the COVID 19 pandemic is morally wrongful and also inconsistent with fundamental constitutional rights. Legal officials are in that case confronted both with a moral challenge and with a claim about the legality of the policy. Of course, legal officials are unlikely to be swayed by that. For officials, legal norms are binding independently of their moral convictions in so far as these norms are valid elements of the legal system.[3] The only question that officials are worried about, is the extent to which legal claims can be affirmed as valid by appeal to relevant legal sources. Raz neatly summarizes this view as follows:

> [the members of judicial institutions] hold themselves bound to recognize and enforce certain reasons not because they would have approved of them had they been entrusted with the question in the deliberative stage but because they regard their validity as authoritatively settled by custom, legislation, or previous judicial decisions.
>
> *(Raz 1970: 213)*

The key point is that the law's claim to legitimate authority depends on the possibility of verifying the law by appeal to its sources. The sources of the law are all those facts, statutes, case law, methods of interpretation, and so forth, by virtue of which a norm is valid. In identifying what the law requires, officials look at what they perceive as authoritative sources of the law (Raz 2009a: 48). Legal claims are accepted as binding practical reasons only if they are validated by sources of law that are recognized as authoritative.

Indeed, Raz holds that the practical aim of law is incomprehensible unless the law is recognized as providing binding reasons for action. For law to be a 'practical authority' it must provide reasons for action; the law must be 'an expression of the judgment of some people or of some institutions on the merits of the actions it requires' (Raz 1994: 231). The task of legal officials is to identify the reasons for action that should be complied with because they are valid and authoritative. The sources of the law are both reasons that validate the law, and reasons that determine their authority. They are sources of the law in a dual sense.

How then do legal officials verify authoritative legal norms? The simple answer is that a norm is a valid precept of law only if authorized by a norm higher up in the hierarchy of legal norms. A local ordinance that is enacted by a local authority is valid only if that body is legally authorized to that effect by laws enacted by a body that is legally authorized to that effect, and so on. The chain of validation cannot be extended indefinitely, however. In the end, the question is: what renders the highest norms of the legal system valid?

Hart famously named the ultimate sources of legal validation the 'rules of recognition'; they represent the final standard by which officials determine the validity of the highest norms of the legal system (Hart 1962).[4] Since the rules of recognition are the final standards of validation in the legal system, they are neither declared nor enacted by legislative bodies (though they may overlap with rules that are). The rules of recognition literally cannot be legislated since acts of legislation are valid only on the basis of pre-existing standards of validation. Any attempt to regulate the rules of recognition are valid only in terms of already existing rules of recognition. Hence, the attempt to regulate the rules of recognition presupposes the existence of rules that already define the rules of recognition. Legal systems consequently do not allow for legal rules that confer the legal power to determine rules of recognition. The rules of recognition are, in this sense, both legal and non-legal features of legal systems: 'legal' because they generate duties among legal officials, 'non-legal' because they are not created by legally defined procedures (Kramer 2018: 107).

The fuzziness of the rules of recognition is unsurprising given that they are meant to identify the highest standard of validation for the normative system. In order for the rules of recognition to serve as the final benchmark of legal validity *for* the legal system, they cannot be norms *of* the legal system – or else *they*, too, stand in need of validation. The ambiguous nature of the rules of recognition is perhaps more adequately captured by the suggestion that they are legal norms that are neither valid nor invalid (Green 1996; Lamond 2014: 30; cf. Suber 1990).

Rules of recognition are not unique for legal systems. They are required in all normative systems. Consider the example of the 'meter standard' that validates all measures of distance in the meter system. Although the meter standard is the supreme norm of that system, the meter standard is not validated *by* that system. There is no rule in the meter system according to which the meter standard is the correct measure of the distance that we call 'one meter'. Similar to legal systems, the validity of the meter standard depends on rules of recognition that are neither valid nor invalid by the meter system. The question then is: how do the rules of recognition emerge?

Hart's answer is that the rules of recognition are constituted by 'social practices' among the subset of legal officials that are entrusted with judgments on the validity of the highest norms of legal systems. The notion of a 'social practice' is applicable to any social context where people do things together and share some basic understandings of what they are doing.[5] The participants of a social practice take the rules of that practice as action-guiding for them, though these rules are not necessarily created according to power-conferring norms. According to Hart, the rules of recognition are, instead, rules that emerge as the result of the activities by participants of that social practice.

Hart consequently held that all legal systems ultimately depend on social practices that sustain 'normative attitudes' that both guide conduct in these practices and provide critical standards by which others are evaluated (Hart 1962: 255). Following the standard reading of Hart, the validity of the highest legal norms – and by implication of the legal system as a whole – is contingent on normative attitudes among the participants of a social practice by special categories of legal officials (Kramer 2018).[6] As these practices serve normative purposes, it might be more illuminating to characterize them a 'normative web of practices' (Himma 2013a).

The normative attitude that emerges from participation in social practices are explained by Hart in terms of the 'internal point of view'. To adopt the internal point of view is to engage in social activities that depend on the existence of rules. When participants take the internal point of view towards rules, they accept them as authoritative for all participants including themselves. This is, arguably, a very common phenomenon, visible in the everyday dealings between the members of a family or in the interactions at the workplace. Unless participants adopt that point of view, they are unable to interact on the basis of shared understandings of norms. The internal point of view is necessary for participation guided by normative standards. This is not to say that the rules that guide conduct in social practices are available only for the participants who adopt the internal point of view. An external observer may be able to decipher the nature of the norms that regulate interactions in a particular social setting. Yet, an external observer does not perceive these norms as standards for conduct that should be complied with. A defining feature of the internal point of view is that the norms are accepted as binding.

The paradigmatic example of the internal point of view is how players relate to the rules of games. A game can be described as a social practice that is regulated by rules that are accepted as normative standards. The rules of the game are normative standards only for participants that adopt the internal point of view. Non-players may of course understand the rules of the game as well. But as they do not participate in the practice, they observe the rules only from an external point of view and therefore do no regard them as reason-giving.

In the context of law, the idea is that some legal officials engage in social practices that constitute the rules of recognition. They adopt normative attitudes because they adopt the internal point of view towards the practice such that its rules are recognized as standards of validity. The point is that the normative attitude adopted by legal officials in that context also provides the basis for their acceptance of these rules as authoritative. The rules of recognition would not guide judgments of validity unless they were not also accepted as authoritative. But the opposite is also true. Remove standards for the validity of law, and there is no 'law' to accept as authoritative. Hart's analysis shows why standards for the validity of law cannot be separated from belief in the authority of the law. In order for legal officials to accept law's claim to legitimate authority they must also be able to distinguish valid legal claims from those that are not valid. Officials who are guided by the internal point of view reproduce the highest standards of legal validity for the legal system, while also embracing its claimed authority.

However, it is one thing to explain how legal officials come to believe that legal claims are valid and authoritative. It is quite a different task to explain how legal claims come to be accepted as valid and authoritative by the *population at large*. Yet, that is something that must be explained for the legal system of the state to acquire de facto authority.

To that end, Hart has little help to offer. As noted by Gerald Postema (1998: 156), Hart's concept of the rule of recognition identifies the 'normative authority of the law ... in the practice of law-applying officials' and does in that measure leave the general population out of the picture. According to Hart (1962: 114), 'a great proportion of ordinary citizens, perhaps a majority – have no general conception of the legal structure or of its criteria of validity'. Ordinary citizens do not participate in the social practices that determine the validity of law and consequently do not necessarily adopt the internal point of view (Coleman 1999: 293; Perry 2006: 1180).

The consequent image is that of legal systems that are authoritative only for legal officials. While legal officials must be attuned to law's claim to legitimate authority in order for the legal system to exist, there is no corresponding requirement that ordinary members of society accept the legal system as authoritative. Postema (1998: 160) takes this as evidence for the conclusion that the Hartian framework is unable to explain how the law can be authoritative for the general population; 'authority does not and cannot extend to citizens'.

This observation is critical as it suggests that the legal system of the state may not achieve de facto authority for the general population. Elaborating on the implications of this view, Jeremy Waldron points out that Hart's view is consistent with the public relating to the legal system in much the same way as cats and dogs relate to their masters (Waldron 1999: 176). Though the dog may always be obedient, the master has no authority over the dog since dogs cannot recognize the master's claim to legitimate authority as the basis for compliance. In a similar vein, it appears that Hart's analysis leaves the legal system denuded of authority over the general population. Ordinary citizens may of course be very obedient. But the extent to which they are depends only on prudential reasons to that effect. However, that is a conclusion we cannot accept as it undermines the thesis that the all-subjected principle applies only to the subjects of legitimate claims to legal authority. The all-subjected principle is premised on the notion that legal systems are not merely systems of coercion or brute force and that the laws of the state are able to provide reasons for compliance that are widely recognized as such. Now, I believe we can avoid this pessimistic conclusion and that the Hartian framework can be used to explain how legal systems achieve de facto authority for people at large.

Two Failed Attempts

Before introducing the position that resolves the conundrum identified, two alternative attempts are examined. The first proposes that people at large recognize the authority of the law because they accept the 'more basic' rules of the legal system. The second is the proposal that law gains authority due to 'acquiescence' on the part of the general population. However, both attempts are bound to fail for reasons to be explained below.

In their influential analysis of social norms, Geoffrey Brennan, Lina Eriksson, Bob Goodin, and Nicholas Southwood, acknowledge that Hart's legal theory is unable to account for how the law can 'have some kind of *normativity* in the eyes of the ordinary members of the group in which they are norms'. In line with others before them, they point out that Hart's account only explains why the law is authoritative for legal officials. Generalized belief in the binding force of law is necessary, or else 'we cannot have a legal system in the full-blooded sense' (Brennan et al. 2013: 48).

The problem that Brennan and his colleagues seek to resolve is the same as we are interested in despite the fact that they do not refer to the 'de facto authority' of the law. They are trying to identify a basis for attributing beliefs in the authority of law beyond the inner circles of legal officials. Their solution is that citizens accept as normative the 'more basic' rules that underpin the legal system; people in general have normative attitudes towards the legal system's 'more basic and fundamental rules' (Brennan et al. 2013: 49). Citizens adopt normative attitudes towards the basic rules that grant authority to the state. Based on these attitudes, citizens are able to conclude that 'the state ... has a right to apply and enforce *whichever principles are law*' (ibid.).

Unfortunately, Brennan and colleagues do not explain where the 'more basic rules' of legal systems are to be found.[7] In the absence of such an explanation, it remains unclear that they have in fact solved the problem they set out to resolve. One possibility is that they mean to say that the authority of legal systems depends on general acceptance of some hypothetical basic rule. In that case, the solution proposed by them is reminiscent of Hans Kelsen's argument that legal systems ultimately depend on an abstract *Grundnorm*. Kelsen realized that a legal system must be validated by a norm that is not part of the legal system. A legal system cannot derive validity from the highest norms of that system (as also the 'highest' norms need to be validated) and we must therefore hypothesize the existence of a norm that is more fundamental than any norm within the legal system. The *Grundnorm* is not part of the legal system but a 'logico-transcendental condition' for the normativity of law (Kelsen, quoted in Delacroix 2004: 507).

However, what is the most original invention in the legal thinking of Kelsen is also what Hart identified as its greatest defect. In the Hartian analysis, no 'more basic' rule is to be found, except, of course, the rules of recognition. In fact, a major task of Hart's work is to dispel the notion that legal systems ultimately depend on 'fundamental rules' of the kind suggested by Kelsen. The rationale for his insistence is the insight that *actual* legal systems cannot be validated by *hypothetical* norms. And the fact is that Kelsen's *Grundnorm* is just a hypothetical norm. Legal systems cannot be validated by abstractions but only by empirically observable criteria. That is why Hart introduces the rules of recognition to replace Kelsen's *Grundnorm*. The rules of recognition are empirical phenomena as they are constituted by social practices; they provide a benchmark of legal validity that is embedded in social facts (Kramer 2018).

Hence, if Brennan and co-authors mean to say that we should follow in the tracks of Kelsen, their argument is inconsistent with the basic premises of the Hartian approach to which they are committed. In agreement with Hart, I conclude that we should reject the attempt to explain the authority of law by appeal to hypothetical norms of validation. The all-subjected principle depends on the fact that people are *actually* subject to the state's claim to legitimate authority. Democratic inclusion is a demand that arises when people are actually subject to claims to legitimate authority – no such demand can be inferred from hypothetical authority.

Now, let us finally consider a different attempt to explain the basis for law's de facto authority. Kenneth Himma argues that since the internal point of view is unavailable to citizens we should seek to identify 'some other attitude on the part of the subject that is sufficient to bind the subject to the rule'. The suggestion introduced is that citizens 'acquiesce' to the legal system (Himma 2013a: 153). Acquiescence is passive acceptance combined with a willingness to conform with the requirements of the law (Bix 2015: 138).

In Himma's account, citizens acquiesce to anything said or done by public officials as citizens are willing to do what the law expects from them. This is a troublesome view, however, as it obliterates the distinction between the authority and validity of the law. Himma presumes that any claim by legal officials to the effect that 'X is the law' is also a reason for the citizen to conclude that X is a valid precept of the law. But law's claim to legitimate authority applies only to valid legal claims. Reasons to comply with a legal requirement are in other words contingent on reasons to believe that X is valid. By contrast, Himma's account does not seem to allow for such considerations. From the claim that citizens 'acquiesce' to legal claims, it follows that citizens blindly conform to public officials and the authority claimed by them. No standard exists by which the general population can confirm the validity of the claims made by officials. The result is that acquiescence is required also in relation to corrupt or illicit claims by public officials.

In other contexts, the seriousness of this problem might be clearer. To say that the players of games are bound to follow the rules is to intend the *rules* of the game to be reason-giving. By contrast, Himma's account seems to imply that players are following the rules only because they acquiesce to what others tell them are the rules of the game. Players comply with *claims* about rules; they do not comply with the *rules*. In order to avoid this conclusion, and to be able to say that games are played by the rules, players need some standard to adjudicate between conflicting claims about the rules of the game. No such method of adjudication is available according to the view that citizens are expected to acquiesce to claims about rules.

The People and The Internal Point of View

Every now and then, individual members of society are making legal claims. As a member of a society that is regulated by the law, you make assertions about the legal rights of yourself or others, you make claims about the legality of the actions undertaken by authorities or corporations, and you frequently have to assess the legal claims made by others on you. These claims are often enough intended as normative; they seek to inform judgments about rightful and wrongful conduct. In making legal claims that are intended to be normative, we are participants of a social practice where legal norms are accepted as critical standards for behavior. Following Wendel (2006), we should think of these practices as society-wide practices of law-claiming where citizens take the internal point of view toward the law. Whenever citizens rely on the law as a normative standard of conduct, they adopt 'normative standards that define lawful action, including the rule of recognition' (Wendel 2006: 1486). According to Wendel, the ultimate criteria for the validity of legal systems – the rules of recognition – are internalized as normative standards among citizens at large.

However, for reasons already mentioned, this is implausible. Officials recognize the law as binding because of social practices that ultimately determine the sources of legal validity and these practices are necessarily highly specialized and restricted to minor circles of legal professionals. The rules of recognition are binding for them because they take the internal point of view with regard to these practices, and they take the internal point of view because they accept being a part of these practices. But it is unrealistic to expect ordinary members of society to be engaged in practices that determine the validity of the law and ultimately of the legal system itself. In other words, it is implausible that people at large participate in practices where the rules of recognition are relevant normative standards. The grounds for accepting law's claim to legitimate authority cannot be the same for public officials as for people at large.

The preliminary conclusion is that while ordinary people are engaged in social practices where 'law' is constitutive of the 'rules of the game', these practices must be fundamentally different from those of legal officials. The general public does not have access to the criteria for legal validation such that they can distinguish between valid and invalid claims of the law. The quest for an account that explains the authority and validity of law must continue.

In a powerful contribution, Zipursky (2006) professes to provide a solution to this problem. In his view, the internal point of view does not necessarily depend on participation in social practices constituted by the rules of recognition. Though Zipursky agrees that the internal point of view is key to how the law comes to have authority among people at large, he denies that the authority of law depends on participation in social practices. Instead, Zipursky argues that citizens are *taught* to adopt the internal point of view. Informed members of the public understand legal directives as requirements that ought to be followed; 'laws are conventionally treated by competent members of the legal community as specially positioned, general, standing injunctions to act a certain way' (Zipursky 2006: 1241). Not to understand that a legal directive is an 'injunction to act' is to misunderstand what law is. Zipursky believes the internal point of view is equal to the 'legally socialized point of view' of any 'citizen who is sufficiently trained and nurtured in our legal culture' (ibid.). The idea is that citizens are 'trained and nurtured' to recognize both the authority and validity of the law.

Now, people may certainly be socialized to believe in the authority of the law.[8] But belief in the authority of the law is not enough. In addition, people need the means to separate valid and invalid legal claims. Compliance with *legal* authority requires the capacity to distinguish between reasons for action that are legal and reasons for action that are not. Without a critical standard for the validation of legal claims, people are left with nothing but blind faith in public officials. This is essentially the conclusion of the theory of 'legal socialization'. Teaching citizens that law is authoritative is to ignore that the de facto authority of the state depends on widespread recognition of *legal* claims to legitimate authority.

We are now back to where we started; still searching for an account that can explain how the general population accept the claims of law as both authoritative and valid. Without a popular standard for legal validation, the legal system of the state does not achieve de facto authority with regard to the general population.

Maybe though, it is possible to formulate a standard for the validation of law that is akin to but not identical to the rules of recognition. As noted by Coleman (1999: 293), 'authority may require that there be a rule by which individuals can reliably identify which of a community's norms are its law. But *that* rule need not be a rule of recognition'. The sources whereby citizens validate legal claims are distinct from the complex rules of recognition that are used by legal officials. Of course, this means that the general population is not, strictly speaking, able to validate legal claims. Only public authorities and courts are competent to confirm the validity of legal claims. Publicly available standards of validation are, in that sense, more akin to 'cues' than criteria. These cues nevertheless allow ordinary members of society to distinguish between the laws of the state and other normative claims.

In fact, the ordinary member of society is frequently able to affirm legal claims as valid by appeal to the publicly available standards of constitutionality. Public knowledge to the effect that normative claims are made in accordance with the procedures required by the constitution is sufficient warrant for belief in their legal validity. The perception that the claims made by public authorities are constitutional is providing the general population with a degree of legal validation. The norms and procedures that govern the political system serve as publicly available and sufficiently reliable proxies for legal validation.[9]

The point is that every-day legal practices offer publicly available correlatives to the rules of recognition. Whereas legal officials depend on the rules of recognition as critical standards for legal validation, people at large depend on critical standards that are but cues for the validity of claims to legal authority. The implication is that the public's understanding of the law is unlikely to fully coincide with positive law as identified by legal institutions. The widely recognized 'folk law' is nevertheless sufficiently accurate with respect to law's more salient requirements (Crowe and Agnew 2020: 239).

Now, it is certainly conceivable that the general public is familiar with the constitutional norms that govern the political system and yet see no reason to recognize the law as either authoritative or valid. For proxies of legal validity to be normative standards, they must operate from the *internal point of view*. The perceived authority of the law consequently derives from the fact that the law is accepted as a normative standard among the participants of a social practice. Legal norms are accepted 'as if' they are reasons that should be complied with. This is how the legal system of the state comes to have 'a grip' over the members of society.[10]

This is significant because the de facto authority of the legal system depends on wide-spread recognition of legal norms as binding reasons for action. Legal norms are accepted as binding by ordinary people because they identify valid legal norms by sources that are recognized as authoritative due to their participation in social practices (Duff 1980: 66). Just as legal officials come to see the law as binding when they take the internal point of view towards the rule of recognition, people at large accept the law as binding because they take the internal point of view towards public proxies for the law. People at large adopt normative attitudes towards the sources of law that infuses them with authority. Thus, the law is accepted as providing reasons for compliance because citizens internalize the rules that guide everyday practices of law-claiming.

Challenges to De Facto Legal Authority

The dual challenge of generalizing the validity and the authority of the law to the general population can be solved. It is solved on the basis of empirical claims about the place of the law in everyday social practices that are premised on the 'internal point of view' toward reliable proxies of the law. The 'law' is validated by publicly available cues that are trusted sources of valid legal norms. To the extent that the general population view these sources from the internal point of view, they accept the law as normative standards for conduct.

There is no reason to think that such practices are always present or widespread among the population. In different places and times, due either to the brutality of the government or disruptions in the social and institutional infrastructure of society, the general population may be either unwilling or unable to participate in the social practice of law. The result is that the legal system fails to establish itself as a de facto authority. The legal system in such circumstances does not serve as a normative standard of conduct for the general public. However, in well-functioning societies the legal system functions as a normative yardstick of behavior among people in general.

There are certainly a number of concerns about this account, however. One worry is with the *authority* of the law that follows from the proposed account of everyday validation. Another worry is with the plausibility of assuming that people in general do accept the sources of the law as authoritative. Clearly, not every member in society will recognize law's claim to legitimate authority. Does it follow that only some members of society are subject to the law in the sense relevant for the all-subjected principle to apply? As I will argue, though the normativity of law is conditioned by widespread recognition of law's claim to legitimate authority, the applicability of law determines the scope of law's normative claims.

Are The Laws of The State Binding?

The legal system of the state enjoys de facto authority only if the general population accept the law as binding for them. Of course, there is no basis for the conclusion that people are morally bound to comply with the law just because they take it as binding for them: 'no general reason to comply' follows from 'mere acceptance' of legal rules (Schiner 1989: 15; Murphy 2018: 89). However, the argument here is not that the law is morally binding because it is accepted but that the law is perceived as morally binding because it is accepted. The general population act 'as if' the law is morally binding because they adopt the internal point of view towards publicly available standards of validity. The law is recognized as binding as a result of society-wide participation in social practices for which the law serves as a normative standard.

Again, social practices do not establish that the law gains moral authority for participants. Raz (1999: 57f.) made this specific point in response to Hart's attempt to explain how legal officials come to accept the law as binding because they participate in social practices constituted by the rules of recognition. Raz observed that social practices cannot generate morally binding reasons for action. This point is of course valid but irrelevant to the present account. Our aim is to show how the legal system can achieve de facto authority. As Raz has also made clear, the existence of moral reasons for compliance is not among the preconditions for the de facto authority of legal systems. In order for a system of law to possess de facto authority, it is sufficient that there is a widely recognized tendency among citizens to accept the law as binding for them. Obviously, no contradiction is involved in saying that the participants of social practices tend to accept the rules of that practice as morally binding although they are not in fact morally bound to comply with them.

There is nevertheless a problem with this explanation of de facto authority. Hart's understanding of the internal point of view is that it generates normative attitudes among the participants of social practices. These attitudes are normative in the sense that they confer authority to the rules of the practice while also providing reasons for action among participants.

The problem, though, is that de facto authority does not depend on attitudes but on *reasons* to believe in legitimate authority. Though a normative attitude is indicative of positive normative significance, it is not quite the same thing as *belief* in legitimate authority (Perry 2006: 1173). Hence, compliance with legal norms on the basis of normative attitudes fails to show that people believe in the legitimacy of legal authority. The implication is that normative systems that depend on normative attitudes do *not* satisfy the conditions for de facto authority. The attempt to explain how the law achieves de facto authority because citizens adopt the internal point of view towards legal practices may in the end prove to be futile.

Interestingly, it appears that Raz is prepared to accept this conclusion. Raz shares Hart's conviction that compliance with the law can be 'internal', 'fully committed', and 'normative' while not grounded in the belief that authority is legitimate (Perry 2006: 1204). Hence, following both Hart and Raz, people may come to accept that the law is binding 'for their own reasons' or 'for no reasons at all' (2009a: 155). People who accept the law as binding 'do mean to assert its binding force, though not necessarily its moral force' (Raz 2009a: 155). The point is that the de facto authority of law is normative only in the sense that it is accepted as normative. The subjects of de facto authority are subject to the claim that they should comply for moral reasons, and they are subjects of de facto authority only if sufficiently many of them accept that claim as binding. Yet, Raz insists that people need not accept the authority of law for moral reasons.

The startling conclusion is that a legal system can potentially induce general compliance that is 'normative' and 'fully committed' while still failing to meet the conditions for de facto authority – as this requires also generalized beliefs in the legitimacy of the law.

The same problem applies to normative systems that are not legal. The assertion that there is a social norm such that people ought to (or ought not to) act in particular ways is normatively salient only if recognized as binding by 'sufficiently many' (Koller 2014; Hage 2018) or by a 'significant proportion' of the members (Brennan et al. 2013: 230). Social norms are reasons for action only if people are in fact committed to act on the normative standard identified by the norm. But the commitment to comply with a norm is not necessarily a moral commitment. Individuals can believe that they ought to comply with a norm and yet hesitate as to whether that is what they morally ought to do. The point is that if the de facto authority of a normative system is premised on belief in the moral legitimacy of the authority it claims, it is not enough that members perceive themselves as bound to comply. It appears that normative systems are de facto authorities if, and only if, the authority claimed by them is believed legitimate such that members think compliance is morally required 'at least to some minimal extent' (Koller 2014: 172).

The way out of this conundrum is to re-interpret what it means for de facto authority to be widely accepted as legitimate. Clearly, the normative attitude towards law's legitimate authority is not the same thing as the *belief* in the legitimate authority of the law. Nevertheless, it is implausible for such a normative attitude to co-exist with belief in the *illegitimacy* of law. Hence, although the normative attitude that emerges from the internal point of view does not amount to belief in legitimate authority, it implies the rejection of belief in the *illegitimacy* of authority. Tony Honoré alludes to this understanding in the argument that accepting rules as binding does not presuppose the belief that the rule-maker wields legitimate authority. The acceptance of a rule as binding presupposes that the agent does not reject (in the absence of 'professed rejection') the legitimate authority claimed by the rule-maker (Honoré 1987). The de facto authority of the legal system can thus be sustained, albeit re-interpreted as premised on widespread belief that the authority claimed by the legal system is not illegitimate.

Approval and Acceptance of Authority

The practice account that we rely on does not depend on approval of laws that are accepted as binding. The participants of social practices recognize certain normative standards as valid. But the fact that they recognize some norms as authoritative does not entail approval of them. When you play chess, you need to recognize the rules of chess, or else fail to play chess at all. Yet, the fact that you recognize that the rules of chess are binding does not imply that you approve of them. Perhaps you are terribly annoyed by specific chess rules (for example, the rule that allows a pawn to strike *en passent*, or the rule that allows for a pawn to metamorphose into a queen when reaching the opposite edge of the board). But even if you disapprove of these rules, you will accept them as binding when you are playing chess to the extent that you participate in the social practice that is constitutive of that game. Chess players employ the rules of the game as a normative standard by which they judge the permissibility of moves in the game. The rules of the game are recognized as valid 'critical standards' with normative content.

The distinction between accepting a norm as binding and approval of the norm can be elucidated by the familiar distinction between the justification of a practice and the justification of actions within a practice (Rawls 1955). In order to justify an act within a practice you need not take a stand on the justification of the practice itself. Participants in social practices are in the business of justifying actions within it – they are playing the 'game'. They are not in the business of justifying the social practice itself – they are not evaluating the rules of the game.

An objection to this view is that norms are binding only if it is true either that participants approve of them or if it is true that participants approve of the authority that imposes them. Norms are reasons for action. And reasons for action – whether they are binding or not – apply to people only if they have reasons to accept them as such.

With respect to games, the analogy would be that rules are binding for players only if they approve of them. Rules are binding because the players have approved of the rules by freely choosing to play the game. The binding force of the rules is thus conditioned by prior approval. Rules are binding only if approved of. Generalized to the legal system of the state, the claim is that laws can be sources of normativity only for citizens 'who so choose' (Bix 2015: 315).

But the view that rules are binding reasons for action only if approved of is questionable. As pointed out by Kaplan (2017: 486), the claim that rules are binding only if approved of is a 'holdover' from moral theory. If approval is necessary for a rule to be binding, we should be able to separate between rules that are binding because they are practiced and rules that are binding because they are approved of. But the participants of social practices need not approve of the rules in order to accept them as binding. The chess player is expected to accept the rules of chess as binding, though no one expects her to 'approve' of these rules. From the perspective of the practice account, 'approval' is superfluous. Rules are binding because participants adopt the internal point of view towards the normative standards that regulate their behavior.

The Extent of Legal De Facto Authority

It is an ever-present possibility, and sometimes a tragic fact, that the conditions for the de facto authority of the legal system are not met. In cases where only public officials recognize the validity and authority of the legal system, the general population is not subject to the de facto authority of the law. Following Hart, though such a society would have a legal system, it would be 'deplorably sheep-like' (Hart 1962: 117). It would be sheep-like exactly because the general population does not recognize the authority of law and because the legal system thus fails to achieve de facto authority.

The fragility of the de facto authority of law has important implications for the account of democratic inclusion advanced here. If community-wide recognition is necessary for the de facto authority of the laws of the state, and if the all-subjected principle applies only to the subjects of de facto authority, the principle of democratic inclusion does not apply in societies where the legal system is not widely recognized as authoritative.

For these reasons, it is important to specify further the conditions for de facto authority. Of course, the conditions for de facto authority are not met in the event that *no* member of the general public recognizes the law as authoritative. Equally obvious is that the conditions for de facto authority are met when *all* members of the general public recognize the law as authoritative. But what if *some*, but not all members do? Should we then conclude that the laws of the state have achieved de facto authority only for some? That would leave us with a disconcerting conclusion; that the de facto authority of the legal system is limited to people that do accepts law's claim to legitimate authority – or that at least do not explicitly reject it. People that do reject the law's claim to legitimate authority would not be subject to the de facto authority of the law and hence not legal 'subjects' at all. Stefano Bertea takes this to be a serious flaw in the Hartian approach to legal obligation. If the normativity of law depends on people's subjective attitudes, the law is binding only for 'self-identified participants' (Bertea 2004: 404).

In response, we should make clear that the conditions of de facto legal authority are distinct from the conditions for *subjection* to de facto authority. De facto authority exists only if the law is widely recognized as binding. It does not follow that only people who recognize the law as binding are subject to law's claimed authority. Put differently, we should say that de facto authority is necessary but insufficient for subjection to the law. For a particular person to be a subject to the laws of the state, it must be true also that the person is the identifiable target of the claimed authority of the law. Hence, the necessary and together sufficient conditions for subjection to the laws of the state is that the legal system enjoys de facto authority and that it claims legitimate authority for that person.

Against this response to Bertea, it might be objected that it does not really help explain how the laws of the state can be *binding* also for people who are not self-identified participants of legal practices. It still seems that the law is not binding for people who reject the legitimacy of law's claimed authority. The objection is correct but is missing the point. The position defended here is not that subjection to the law is premised on accepting the law as binding. The fact that the law is sufficiently accepted as binding is a condition for the de facto authority of the state. It is not a condition for a person being a subject to the de facto authority of the state. A person can be a subject to the de facto authority even if that person does not recognize the law as binding.[11]

On the other hand, the fact that the legal system is generally accepted as binding is not without normative significance. This is most readily seen in the context of social norms. To illustrate this point, consider the following conversation about the existence and normativity of a particular social norm. As it happens, someone is asking you if it is the norm in your country that visitors take their shoes off before entering a home. If you believe that people rarely do take off their shoes in such circumstances, you might answer 'no, it is not the norm in the society where I live that visitors should take their shoes off'. The reply is based on the assumption that a normative standard that is not widely adhered to is not really a social norm at all. As is well known in the theory of social norms, a norm exists only if complied with. The claim that 'it is the norm that…' is correct only if it is true that a 'sufficiently large' number of people adhere to it (Bicchieri 2005: 11ff.). Thus, a social norm such that visitors should take their shoes off before entering a home exists only if 'sufficiently many' do in fact comply with that norm (Kaplan 2021: 7).

Now, imagine that in your country it *is* the norm that visitors should take their shoes off. The interlocutor then proceeds to ask if the social norm applies also to people who don't comply. The question is not about the existence of the norm but about the extent to which people recognize it as binding. It would be curious to answer that 'no, the norm is binding only for people who comply with it'. It would be curious since that answer would extinguish the normativity of the norm. Social norms would have no social function if they were binding only for people who already complied with them.

To make sense of the normativity of norms – whether social or legal – we should have to admit that norms claim also to be binding for people who do not accept them as such. Norms are 'socio-empirical' entities that exist only in so far that they have a 'grip' that generate reasons for action (Brennan *et al.* 2013: 48). Though norms exist only if they have a 'grip', it does not follow that only those gripped by norms are subject to claims for compliance with them. Norms generate expectations of compliance that are communicated through normative attitudes. The point then, is that while norms exist only if they are 'sufficiently' recognized and complied with, they present *claims* for compliance also for people who do not recognize them as binding.[12]

How claims for compliance extend to people who do not accept them as binding is perhaps best illustrated with respect to the rules of games. The rules of a game are binding if sufficiently many take the internal point of view towards them (Marmor 2009). Yet, it does not follow that rules are normative only for participants that actually do. As argued by Kaplan (2017: 486), the fact that the 'normativity of games and etiquette is attitude-dependent' does not preclude that normativity 'can apply to particular individuals irrespective of their attitudes'. If that was not the case, we would be compelled to say that the rules of a game are binding only for players that recognize them as binding and that the rules are not binding for players who do not. To take the internal point of view is to recognize yourself as a participant in the social practice of the game. As a participant of a game, the rules are viewed from the 'inside' such that you are 'disposed to guide and evaluate conduct' of self and others (Shapiro 2006: 1157). This is illustrated by individuals joining a game for the first time. As soon as they start playing the game, and before being fully aware of its rules, they are subject to the normative attitudes of other players. They are subject to claims for compliance even though they may not yet have internalized the norms that regulate the practice.

Returning to the legal system of the state, the conclusion is that it gains de facto authority only if recognized as valid and authoritative by 'sufficiently many'. This is not to imply that the de facto authority of the state claims to regulate only the conduct of the people that recognize it as such. The legal system of the state claims legitimate authority for society as a whole. Though the state's claim to legitimate authority does not reach out endlessly, it is not limited to persons who perceive themselves as bound to comply.

Notes

1 The normative significance of subjection to de facto authority also pertains to distributive justice, as argued by Sangiovanni (2007).
2 Raz's view is that every political authority makes a claim for legitimate authority and that this claim is possible only if the government enjoys de facto authority. However, authority that is not political need not possess de facto authority (Raz 2009a: 8). Hence, the fact that a government in exile (such as the Polish government in London during the Second World War) claims legitimate authority while lacking de facto authority shows that it is not a political authority. See also, Raz (2009b: 129).
3 According to Raz and others, the validity of legal norms depends exclusively on factual sources. This position is known as 'exclusive legal positivism' and contrasts with the view that the sources of legal validity can also include moral propositions (the 'incorporation thesis', traditionally attributed to Hart). The correct view on this issue does not affect the plausibility of the present argument, however, as it remains true that in either view the law is legally binding only if validated by the sources of the law (Eekelaar 2002: 503).
4 Following Hart, the rules of recognition are a special case of secondary norms that are indispensable for legal systems as they distribute legal powers, define standards for legal interpretation and, most importantly, identify the criteria by which a legal norm belongs to *this* legal system. According to Eleftheriadis (2010), the rules of recognition also confer 'disabilities in law-making' (Cf. Beckman 2020).
5 Cf. Noah Smith (2006) who argues that social practices require conceptual, epistemic and practical agreement, and commitment that is unlikely to obtain among legal officials.

6 These comments are not intended to serve as a justification of the social practice account. A regular objection against the claim that there can be rules that are constituted by social practices is that it fails to distinguish between social practices that give rise to normative attitudes and practices that do not – instead being mere behavioral regularities. For a response, see Lovett (2019).
7 Curiously, the notion of 'fundamental rules' is mentioned only twice (Brennan *et al.* 2013: 48) and discussed only briefly.
8 In fact, it is unclear that Zipursky (2006) accepts that legal authority exists at all. Though he speaks of 'legal duties' he argues that such duties 'push' the subject to pose 'the question' if he or she should 'breach one's legal duties' or not. But if that is what the law is doing, the law does not seem to provide exclusionary reasons for action in the first place.
9 A similar argument is made by Alexander and Schauer (2009).
10 According to Coleman (1999: 299) the argument that a social practice is perceived as normative by participants who adopt the internal point of view leaves unanswered whether the practice is so perceived because they do in fact participate in it, or because the participants adopt the internal point of view. If the former is the case, the internal point of view is, at best, a defining element of a social practice, but not one that contributes to the normativity of rules. If the latter is the case, the question is, instead, why people should recognize the rules as normative if the only reason for their normativity is that they are treated as such.
11 Indeed, it appears that Bertea is asking for an account that can explain how the law can be binding in the practical reasoning of every subject independently of the moral content of the law. But the search for such an account seems in vain.
12 Following Hage (2020) the normativity of norms refers to: (i) deontic normativity, or (ii) rule-based normativity, or (iii) the conjunction of deontic and rule-based normativity. Using this terminology, deontic normativity is part of the meaning of social norms, while actual social norms are either normative only in the rule-based sense (for those that are expected to comply), or normative in both the deontic and rule-based sense (for those that recognize them as binding).

5
THE SCOPE OF LEGAL AUTHORITY

The argument so far is that democratic inclusion in the context of the state is conditioned by subjection to the de facto authority of the legal system. For de facto authority to emerge, a substantial portion of society's members must accept its claim to legitimate authority. A legal system of the state that is thus embodied with de facto authority is subjecting the population to the law in the sense relevant for the all-subjected principle to apply. They are subject to the claimed authority of the law.

Though important elements of the all-subjected principle are now in place, there are still essential pieces missing. Similar to rival understandings of democratic inclusion, the all-subjected principle is intended to provide criteria by which members and non-members in the demos can be distinguished. The principle should offer criteria informing judgements about inclusion in the demos. Yet, in its current form, the all-subjected principle is nowhere near providing such criteria. The claim that the subjects of legal systems with de facto authority should presumptively be included in the demos is not yet specific enough.

In accordance with the authority thesis, I take it that the extent of democratic inclusion in the state should depend on the scope of subjection to the state's claimed authority. Membership in the demos is to be determined on the basis of the scope of the state's legal authority. The task then is to explain the scope of legal authority.

This chapter explores four distinct answers to this question. The first is that the scope of the state's claimed authority is conditioned by the territorial borders of the state. The basis for this view is that the state is a territorial organization that is able to exercise authority only within internationally recognized borders. The second alternative is the view that the laws of the state apply to any behavior described by legal norms. The authority of the law is not limited by territorial borders but extends to all conduct that fits the substance of the law. The third alternative is that the scope of legal authority is determined by the extent to which the state is able

DOI: 10.4324/9781003359807-5

to coercively enforce the law. A subject of legal authority is a person against whom the law can be enforced. The extent of coercive power determines the scope of legal authority.

These three views are nevertheless found inadequate. Instead, a fourth account of the scope of legal authority is defended. In this view, the extent of legal authority depends on the operations of legal institutions that confirm the validity of exclusive legal authority. The scope of legal authority is thus a function of the operations of legal institutions tasked with the determination of the law. I will refer to this as the 'legal determination' approach to the scope of the all-subjected principle.

The State-Based Argument

Given that legal systems and states are closely intertwined, the state seems the natural place to start for the purpose of exploring the scope of the all-subjected principle. The state is by definition a territorial organization as evinced by the fact that territory is a precondition for statehood according to international law. The 1933 Montevideo Convention on the Rights and Duties of States specifies the jurisdiction of the state as limited to 'national territory' (Art. 9; see also Shaw 1982).

Territoriality provides the bedrock for the view that the laws of the state apply only in the territory controlled by and recognized as belonging to the state. The question 'when are people subjected to the laws of the state?' is accordingly answered without much effort; only persons who are present in the territory of the state are subjected to the laws of the state. Let us call this the *state-based argument*. The gist of this view is that legal norms apply only in the territory of the state because states are territorially defined entities.

Yet, the state-based argument is inadequate for both empirical and conceptual reasons. First of all, the state-based argument is flying in the face of the empirical reality that states regularly engage in transborder activities. Every state is attempting to regulate and influence conduct beyond their own borders. Through economic policy, legal actions and even physical coercion, states are constantly attempting to extend their control to foreign shores. This tendency is accelerated by international commerce and trade, global climate change, migration flows and other transborder interactions that encourage the creation of transnational networks of governance and influence. Accordingly, the image of the world as separated into mutually exclusive areas of 'physical territorial possession and control' is commonly said to be in decline (Biersteker 2013). The assumption that state power is structured by territorial borders is a 'trap' analytically as well as descriptively, according to the influential argument by geographer John Agnew (Agnew 2015). The upshot is that the borders of the state are not impenetrable constraints on state action anymore.

This argument is open to debate, of course. Some would point out, for example, that state borders are currently regaining prominence due to growing nationalism, trade-conflicts, unilateralism, and anti-migrant sentiments (e.g., MacIsaac and Duclos 2020). However, the main issue with the state-based argument is not whether it captures the significance of state borders at any particular moment in history. The main issue with the state-based argument is conceptual. The state is an organization that claims legitimate authority over a distinct territory and that is equipped with the power to exercise effective control within it. Territorial control is a necessary attribute of the state and, yet territorial control is *not* necessary for legal authority. Legal authority is the ability to make people comply with norms and that ability can transcend territorial borders. Thus, legal authority does not encompass the defining attributes of the *state*. Although territorial control is a defining feature of what scholars of international relations call the 'Westphalian state', the state so defined is analytically distinct from that of legal authority (Philpott 2002).

The notion that we should separate the legal authority of the state from its territorial configuration pertains to the distinctions made in chapter three. As argued there, the state is a body vested both with normative and causal power. The state so conceived is an entity with a 'dual nature' (Lamond 2001; Lepsius 2020). The distinction between the state and the legal system allows for the possibility that legal authority extends beyond the realm controlled by the state. Potential examples include the fact that diplomatic emissaries remain protected by the laws of their own states even when they operate in the territories of other states; the claim by some legal systems to criminalize behavior abroad; the fact that laws of taxation apply to earnings from abroad and in some cases even to residents in other countries, and by the fact that corporations in other countries are increasingly targeted by the laws of the state. The laws of the state sometimes seem to apply 'extraterritorially', despite the fact that the international system of states does not allow states to use 'coercive power to enforce its rules outside its territory' (Ryngaert 2008: 24).

The preliminary conclusion then is that the state-based argument goes awry by ignoring the distinction between the state understood as an organization vested with causal power, and the normative authority claimed by it. Once the distinction is recognized, it should be clear that the scope of the state's claim to legitimate authority is not necessarily limited by the territorial borders of the state. The state is by definition a territorial organization and states frequently engage in actions with consequences for peoples and other entities abroad. But these are features of the state and not features of the legal authority claimed by it. According to the all-subjected principle, membership in the demos is premised on subjection to norms that claim to be binding. The extension of the demos is consequently a function of the scope of the state's claimed authority. And that claim is not necessarily limited by territorial borders.

In the following, the state-based argument is left to the side and our attention is shifted to three alternative theories of the scope of legal authority. The first holds that legal authority is limited only by the substance of legal norms. The law claims to regulate all conduct to which legal norms apply. This is what I shall term the substantive approach. The second view is that the scope of legal authority depends on the extent of coercive power. Legal authority prevails as far as the state is able to enforce the law by means of coercion. The third account, finally, explains the scope of legal authority by recourse to institutions with the capacity to authoritatively determine legal norms.

The Substantive Account

The first view is that the scope of law's claim to legitimate authority is determined by the content of legal norms. This corresponds to what Petter Asp (2017: 34) names the 'substantive' account of law. The basic idea is simple. Consider, for example, laws against murder according to which the intentional killing of a human being is a criminal offense. Following the substantive view, the law against murder applies to every action that corresponds to the conduct defined by that law.

The 'ambit' of the law against murder is, of course, considerable on this view. The conduct that laws against murder claim to regulate is found in all corners of the world: intentional killing is 'murder' and hence a criminal offense irrespective of where the relevant action is taking place. This conclusion is in line with Asp's (2017: 46) remark that legal norms against murder do have 'extraterritorial ambit' and the claim that there is 'nothing unreasonable' in the presumption that the law is binding beyond the territory of the state.

The substantive view outlined by Asp raises a number of questions, however. One is that it is awkward to submit that the law applies only to actions that fit the behavioral descriptions of the law. If the criminal law claims the authority to regulate only actions that are prohibited, the law against murder would claim the authority to regulate only the intentional killing of others. Consequently, the law against murder would not apply to non-murderers since they do not engage in the activities that are regulated by the law against murder. But if the law claims to provide reasons for action, the criminal law is intended to provide reasons *not* to engage in the actions prohibited by the law. The authority claimed by the law is a claim that the subject should not perform the action prohibited by the law. If so, the law is not addressed only to persons who actually undertake the action that is prohibited. The law claims to be reason-giving for 'everyone'. The law creates legal obligations that are 'universally borne', as argued by Edmundson (2004: 216). In the case of laws against murder, the point is that this law purports to establish practical reasons not to murder that apply to murderers and non-murderers alike. Of course, since only murderers violate the norm, only murderers should be held accountable before the law. But that is not because only murderers are subjected to the law. Murderers who violate the law are held accountable because they have violated a norm that already applied to them.

On the basis of these considerations, the substantive view needs to be reconsidered. Instead of saying that the law claims to regulate only the conduct that is described by legal norms, we should say that the law claims to regulate the conduct of any subject with the capacity to act on the reasons provided by the law. The authority of the law extends to everyone for whom the law can be reason-giving.

This revised version of the substantive view still implies that the ambit of the law is very wide and that territorial borders are of no or little importance in deciding the scope of legal authority. Indeed, it appears that the scope of legal authority is even wider in this view. The consequent 'juridical' interpretation of the law implies that 'everyone everywhere in the world is strictly subject to those laws' (Goodin 2016: 381).

Before proceeding to examine this view, we should pause to note one important reason in its favor. The substantive account is particularly well-placed to recognize the idea that criminal law protects the interests of victims. This is the main rationale for criminal law. Since victims of criminal behavior can be found anywhere, it makes a lot of sense to insist that the law against murder applies to everyone, everywhere. After all, all human beings have a strong interest in protection against murder and it would be repugnant to presume that only *some* people's interests in protection are relevant to the justification of the law against murder. The substantive view takes the interests of all victims equally seriously and that is why it applies irrespective of the location of the crime (Ryngaert 2008: 44; Asp 2017: 38).

Despite these benefits, the substantive view is arguably problematic. According to Abizadeh, the view that a legal norm applies to everyone, everywhere is 'absurd' and should be rejected. To see the absurdity, Abizadeh asks us to consider what it would mean to *fulfil* the requirements of a duty-imposing law. A legal requirement is fulfilled when people act in accordance with it. The fulfilment of the law against murder requires, for example, not engaging in acts of murdering. The implication is, of course, that every person in the world who presently does not engage in murder is fulfilling the legal requirement against murder. The reason why that conclusion is absurd, according to Abizadeh, is realized by the possibility of rewarding compliance. The plausibility of rewarding legal compliance is a method for testing 'intuitions about the legal requirement's scope' (Abizadeh 2021: 608). Following this test, the substantive view implies that rewards for compliance should be extended to everyone in the world. That is patently absurd according to Abizadeh (2021: 608) and thus sufficient to conclude that the substantive view should be rejected.

It is not clear that this objection is particularly powerful, however. Legal systems scarcely ever offer rewards for compliance. And if they did, we might simply deny the alleged absurdity of extending rewards to everyone in the world.

The real problem with the substantive view is different and due to the fact that it pays no regard to the claimed authority of the law. The point is that the authority claimed by the legal system is inconsistent with the substantive account. To see this, we must recall that claims to authority are claims about reasons for action. The subject of the law is presumed to have a reason for action that is binding such that it represents an 'exclusionary reason' not to act contrary to the law. Accordingly, the statement that the law claims legitimate authority to regulate everyone's conduct (that is, anyone with the capacity to act on the reasons provided by the law) implies that the law claims to provide exclusionary reasons for everyone. But that is arguably incoherent; the legal system *cannot* provide exclusionary reasons for everyone.

To understand why, consider, again, the criminalization of murder. Laws against murder are found in virtually every legal system in the world. They are present in the legal code of all 204 member states of the United Nations (Mikhail 2009). Now, if every legal system in the world claims to regulate all conduct, it follows that everyone, everywhere is subject to the authority claimed by every legal system. Every person is accordingly presumed to be subject to the claimed authority of 204 legal systems – each insisting on exclusionary reasons not to act contrary to the law against murder.

In the case that the laws against murder found in all legal systems are identical, it is *possible* for every person on earth to comply with all of them. However, we should more often expect that distinct legal systems provide for conflicting legal requirements. Whereas murder is criminalized in every jurisdiction, other actions are criminal offenses in some places but not in others. This is true of abortion, for example. On the assumption that legal systems claim to provide binding practical reasons for everyone, the implication is that everyone is subject both to duties not to engage in abortion, and to claims that abortion is permissible. Hence, the notion that legal systems apply to everyone, everywhere implies that people are subject to claims of compliance with irreconcilable reasons for action.

Of course, conflicting legal requirements provided by different legal systems do not necessarily obtain in all circumstances. But the problem is more fundamental and remains even if legal requirements do *not* conflict. To see this, recall that binding reasons for action are *exclusionary* reasons. The law purports to give us reasons for action that 'exclude' acting on other reasons. Hence, the suggestion that people are subjected to the authority claimed by all legal systems implies that people are subjected to exclusionary reasons by all legal systems. But that is incoherent. If legal system X provides A with exclusionary reasons not to p, legal system Y cannot simultaneously provide A with exclusionary reasons not to p. Exclusionary reasons are reasons *not to act* on the basis of any other reason. They are reasons for action that are intended to exclude 'all reasons from outside the [legal] system' (Raz 1999: 145). This is significant as it means that a person can only be bound to comply with the authority claimed by one unique legal system. The claim to legitimate authority by the legal system intends to deny all competing claims to authority. These observations are devastating for the substantive account. The claim that legal norms apply to all conduct regulated by the norm is inconsistent with the exclusive nature of law's claimed authority.

The Coercion Account

In the domestic setting, the state has at its disposal a wealth of powers for the enforcement of the law. The state enforces the law by the threat of imposing sanctions that depend on its capacity to use violence and physical force to secure conformity. Individuals and other entities governed by the state are in other words 'subject to coercion' (Blake 2001).[1] Indeed, it is commonly believed that the coercive powers of the state renders coercion a defining element of subjection to the laws of the state.

The notion that law and coercion are intimately related has a long pedigree. Following the famous words of Thomas Hobbes (1651) in *Leviathan*: 'covenants, being but words and breath, have no force to oblige, contain, constrain, or protect any man, but what it has from the public sword' (Venezia 2014). For Hobbes, agreements are 'but words' and ultimately ineffective in the absence of the coercive power manifested in 'the sword'. Indeed, coercive power is not employed merely for practical reasons – to induce conformity with the law – but is for Hobbes a necessary precondition for the existence of legal obligations. There is no obligation to comply with the law unless the claim for compliance is backed up by a credible threat of coercive enforcement. The duty to obey the law is accordingly to be found only among subjects 'exposed to the possibility of sanction for noncompliance' (Edmundson 2004: 216).

The *scope* of subjection to the laws of the state is in this view markedly different from that of the substantive account. Whereas the latter view implies that anyone with the capacity to undertake the action regulated by the law is under a legal obligation to comply, Hobbes's view is that the scope of the law is limited by the ambit of the state's power to coercively enforce the law.[2] The coercion approach thus offers an antidote to the expansive scope of the substantive account.

Despite Hobbes's insistence that legal obligations are conditioned by the capacity to enforce them, his view is not that the legal system and consequent legal obligations are *just* a euphemism for the organized capacity to enforce the will of the sovereign. In Hobbes's mind, the subjects of the state are obligated to comply with the 'sovereign' as a result of the social compact (Goldsmith 1996: 276; Dyzenhaus 2011: 414). In this respect, Hobbes's account differs markedly from that of John Austin. Both underline the importance of coercive sanctions in the process of making subjects conform to the commands of the sovereign. But in contrast to Hobbes, Austin thinks that the laws of the state can be fully explained in terms of sovereign commands sustained by coercive sanctions. Whereas Hobbes acknowledges that the subject is obligated to obey the sovereign because of the rationality of the social contract, Austin offers no basis for the existence of either actual or claimed duties to comply with the laws of the state. For Austin, the state is not a body that claims the authority to rule, but a body with the ability to coercively enforce its will. The subject of the laws of the state is but the recipient of the sovereign's 'command' to do as told or else suffer the pain of coercive sanction (Yankah 2008: 1202).[3] The legal system does not claim the legitimate authority to regulate conduct – the law does not pretend to create rules that the subject *should* comply with. Austin's account is consequently inconsistent with the thesis that subjection to claimed authority is a necessary precondition for democratic inclusion.

Let us therefore leave Austin behind and return to the Hobbesian view that subjection to the law is not merely predicated on coercion. The more influential and in many ways also more sophisticated version of this idea is formulated by Hans Kelsen. In opposition to Austin, Kelsen denies that the claims of law are ultimately traceable to the coercively enforced commands by 'the Sovereign'. The law is instead conceived of as a hierarchical system of legal norms, communicating 'oughts', that ultimately depends on a hypothesized *Grundnorm*. Legal norms are imperatives directed to the officials tasked with the application of the law; 'legal norms ordering coercive acts are addressed to legal organs and not, or at least not immediately, to the persons whose behavior is the condition for these coercive acts' (Kelsen 1991: 54). The purpose of the legal system is to regulate the coercive powers of the state. The law is that invention, or 'technology', by which the coercive powers exercised by the agents of the state are controlled and directed (Raz 1970: 121; Stevenson 2003).

The implication is that the individual citizen is encountering the law only indirectly, as a result of the 'coercive acts' by public officials that are in turn legally regulated.[4] Since the law is regulated coercion, Kelsen comes close to *defining* the law in terms of coercion: 'no norm is a legal norm unless it represents a condition for a coercive sanction' (Edmundson 2012: 452). By contrast, for both Austin and Hobbes, coercion does not define the *content* of law though it is necessary as a *means* for enforcing it (Bobbio 1965: 321). Following Kelsen, people at large are subject to the law only because they are subject to the legally regulated coercive acts of public officials. Hence, the capacity of the state to impose coercion defines the outer limits of subjection to the law.

Kelsen's account of what it means to be subject to the laws of the state has been enormously influential. Yet, it completely ignores the authority that the legal system is arguably claiming for itself. In the view defended by Raz and others, that inspires the present account of the all-subjected principle, the state and the legal system claims the moral right to be obeyed. The subject *should* comply with the law because the legal system of the state allegedly wields legitimate authority. The law is making a claim for compliance that is premised on its capacity to provide practical reasons that are binding.

By contrast, Kelsen and many of his contemporaries were convinced that human behavior is governed by volition, not by practical reason. The very idea of 'practical reason' is considered as 'logically untenable' by Kelsen. Accordingly, he rejected the notion that legal systems claim the authority to regulate behavior by binding practical reasons because he did not see reasons as action-guiding in the first place. Clearly, the law cannot be modelled as an attempt to establish *reasons* for action if true that 'will' rather than practical reason is governing the behavior of the subject (Alexy 1992: 231; Green 2016).[5]

There is nevertheless one insight in the work of Kelsen that is helpful. For Kelsen, legal systems must be *effective* if they are to regulate human conduct. Given that the capacity to enforce the law by means of coercion is how the law becomes effective, it follows that coercion is a precondition for the existence of the legal system. Law is a coercive order, and that is essential to distinguishes law from other normative systems (Golding 1961: 376; Oberdiek 1976).

Indeed, Kelsen is not alone in thinking that effectiveness is a necessary precondition for the existence of legal systems. Hart, too, maintained that the capacity to impose sanctions on the offender is necessary for obligations under the law. The 'continued normal operation of the system of sanctions' is presupposed by the claim that a person is bound by the law (Hart 1962: 84–85). Kelsen's account of the existence-conditions of the legal system may in that regard be more attractive than his account of what the legal system *is*.

Kelsen's insight that coercive institutions are required for the existence of legal systems may in the end prove consistent with an authority-based understanding of the subjects of law. In order for the legal system to claim the authority to regulate conduct by binding practical reasons, it must satisfy the conditions for its existence. Following Kelsen, laws that 'lose their effectiveness or the possibility of effectiveness' are not laws at all (Kelsen 1991: 140). The institutional capacity to enforce the law is a precondition for the existence of a legal system that claims authority because only effective legal systems do exist and the capacity to enforce the law is what makes them effective.

This point might be illustrated by the occurrence of 'dead-letter' laws. An ordinance or statute is a 'dead-letter' if not formally repealed, and yet ignored by law-applying institutions. It seems plausible to submit that no-one is subject to claims for compliance with dead-letter laws. A 'dead' law should not be complied with and the reason why, Kelsen would add, is that such laws are not enforced; laws exist only if 'observed and applied by and large' (Kelsen 1991: 139).

However, we should not confuse the claim that coercion is necessary for the existence of legal *systems* with the claim that coercion is necessary for the existence of legal *norms*. The assertion that law must be observed and applied 'by and large' in order to exist does not entail that only legal norms that are in fact applied by means of coercion do exist. In other words, from the claim that a legal system is 'dead' unless it is effective in enforcing the law, it does not follow that coercion is a prerequisite for the existence of a legal norm.

Hence, the thesis that coercion is required for effective legal systems does not help explain why dead-letter laws are not laws. Of course, that would be easy to explain, if we accept that the law is by definition coercive. But that argument is a conceptual claim, not a claim about what is required for the law to be effective.[6]

I submit that the thesis that coercion is necessary for the effectiveness – and existence – of legal systems is ultimately of little use in identifying the scope of the law. Though it establishes that people are subject to the law only if they are subject to legal systems that are coercive, it does not imply that they are subject to the law only if subject to coercion. The thesis considered thus says nothing about the *scope* of the law and who is subject to the law. For example, the thesis that legal systems are necessarily coercive appears fully consistent with the substantive view of the law discussed previously. On the substantive view, a person is subject to the law only if the content of legal norms applies to the person. As noted, that view arguably has the implication that everyone, everywhere is subject to legal norms and this implication is not undermined by the additional claim that legal norms must be part of legal systems that are coercive in order for them to exist.[7]

The Legal Determination Account

The extent of subjection to the legal system of the state is still unresolved. For reasons spelled out above, the scope of the state's claim to legitimate authority cannot be accounted for either in terms of the substance of legal norms or in terms coercion. In this section, I argue that a better approach is to look at the operations of legal institutions tasked with the application of the law. The extent to which people are subject to the state is determined by the capacity of legal institutions to validate the exclusive claim to legitimate authority professed by the legal system of the state.

The starting point is that legal systems are not just normative systems but also institutionalized systems. They are institutionalized in the sense that they depend on some mechanism for 'ensuring conformity' and 'dealing with deviations' from the claims made by the law (Raz 1999: 52).[8] The law is a system of norms that pretends to regulate conduct. But it is able to do so only if it includes institutions that translate sometimes abstract and vague legal norms to individuated legal claims. A legal system requires institutions tasked with the 'authoritative determination of normative situations in accordance with pre-existing norms' (Raz 2009a: 108). In fact, Raz is more specific and claims that legal systems depend on the fact that 'the law is identified through the eyes of the courts' (Raz 1979: 71). This is a slight exaggeration, however. Though courts are empowered to 'authoritatively determine' legal claims, they are not the only public bodies so empowered. A wealth of other public authorities is similarly involved in the making of judgments about the specific legal rights and obligations that apply to the subject. The point then is that subjects of the law are necessarily subject to institutions with the capacity to determine the legal requirements that apply to them.

What is the basis for the view that subjection to the laws of the state is premised on the operations of legal institutions? One answer is that the authority claimed by legal systems represents a claim for compliance only if this authority is explicitly claimed by someone. Authority must be practiced in order to impose its normative claim for compliance. The claims made by legal institutions on the subject population is therefore necessary for the state's legal authority to generate legally binding claims.

The legal determination approach repudiates the notion that legal norms are themselves sources of legal authority. A legal norm forms the basis for a claim for compliance only if it is practiced and determined as a valid member of the legal system by legal institutions. This is effectively to recognize that the legal norms are not self-authorizing; they depend on the existence of an institutional order for them to be authoritative. The claim to legitimate authority that is associated with legal norms is conditioned by legal institutions; 'a law is part of a [legal] system only if it is acted on by the law-applying organs', as insisted by Raz (2009a: 87ff, 105ff).

This point is well illustrated by the above example of dead-letter laws. Legal norms that are 'dead' are present in the sources of law but are not practiced by legal institutions. They are effectively 'dead' exactly because they are not determined as valid norms by legal institutions. Though dead letter laws remain part of the normative system, they do not belong to the *institutionalized* normative system. The legal determination approach is thus able to explain how dead letter laws may at once be 'laws' while not grounds for claims to legal authority.

Indeed, the current approach also helps distinguish between dead and living *legal systems*. There is a wealth of legal systems that have long since gone extinct. However, 'dead' legal system are still normative systems since they include primary and secondary norms. A student of the history of law might be able to re-create the normative system that constituted the legal system of the Roman Empire or of the Sumerian kingdom, for instance.

Yet, no-one is a subject to claims of compliance with dead legal systems. These legal systems are no longer sources of authority. But why exactly is that? The answer is obvious following the legal determination approach: there are no legal institutions tasked with determining the norms of dead legal systems. Though they are still normative systems, they are not institutionalized normative systems and therefore not sources of claims to legitimate authority.

The thesis that law's claim to legitimate authority depends on the operations of legal institutions has implications for the scope of subjection to the laws of the state. It indicates that the presence of institutions is critical for the scope of the state's authority. But in explaining how far the state's claimed authority travels in space, it is necessary also to attend to the fact that legal systems insist on *exclusive* authority.

The legal system of the state insists on exclusive authority to regulate the conduct of its subjects. The norms determined as valid by legal institutions aim to 'exclude the application of reasons, standards, and norms which do not belong to the system or are not recognized by it' (Raz 1999: 150; Raz 2009a: 145). The legal system is exclusive within its domain and the scope of that domain is a consequence of the extent to which legal institutions are successful in imposing exclusive legal authority.

The exclusivity of claimed authority is mirrored by the fact that the legal system of the state claims *comprehensive* authority. It is comprehensive in the sense that it claims the right to regulate all entities and behavior within its realm (Raz 2009a; Green 2016: 167; Besson 2019: 121). In order to be comprehensive, the authority must also be exclusive. The demand for exclusive authority is effectively the demand that all other normative systems in its domain accept the supremacy of the authority of the state.

The exclusive and comprehensive nature of the claim to legitimate authority is also reflected in the authority thesis. The claim to legitimate authority implies that the subject is required not to act on other reasons than those supplied by the law. As we recall, the subject of the law is bound to comply and the statement that legal norms are binding is equal to the presence of exclusionary reasons to act as required. Just as exclusionary reasons are meant to 'exclude' other reasons for action and thus 'trump' rival legal claims, the legal system is exclusive in the sense that it insists on 'excluding' rival sources of authority in its domain.

The implication of the exclusive and comprehensive nature of the authority claim by the state is that other normative systems that seek to regulate conduct are successful only if permitted by the legal system of the state. A subject of the state's authority can of course be a subject of also of the authority claimed by other associations. But these associations are authoritative only to the extent that they do not rival, undermine, or challenge the authority claimed by the state. In fact, the subject of the state's authority can also be bound to comply with the legal norms of foreign legal systems. Again, however, these foreign legal norms are valid sources of claims for compliance only if validated by the legal system of the state. Not all legal norms recognized as valid *by* the legal system need be norms *of* that system.

For example, a couple married according to the laws of country A is usually also treated as a married couple by the laws of country B. This is consistent with Raz's observation that legal systems are 'open' as they can accept the validity of norms created by other legal orders (Raz 1999: 152). Legal norms that originate from the legal system of another state, or from international law or even from sub-national legal systems can be tolerated and applied by the legal system of the state. It seems a mistake then to argue, as advocates of legal pluralism often do, that the exclusive authority claimed by the legal system of the state necessarily implies the rejection of the idea that 'nation-states should ever take into account international, transnational, or non-state norms' (Berman 2007: 1165).

The recognition afforded to norms from other normative systems is necessary conditional, however. The conditional incorporation of foreign legal norms is illustrated by the recent trend among Western nations for revising the laws of marriage. Marriage is a legal institution, and it is happily a common practice among legal systems to recognize the legality of marriages registered abroad. Yet, some marriages concluded abroad are increasingly seen as inconsistent with the commitments of western liberal democracies. Thus, the lawmakers of the Netherlands introduced the Forced Marriage Prevention Act in 2015 in order to limit the recognition afforded to marriages concluded abroad to those between adult persons. Foreign marriages that involve minors are no longer recognized as legally valid in the Netherlands (Wijffelman 2017). Consistent with the exclusive and comprehensive authority claimed by the Dutch legal system, this invalidated legal claims that originated from legal systems abroad that were previously recognized as valid.

The notion that the legal system necessarily claims exclusive and comprehensive authority may not *entail* that it is unable to sustain its claimed authority beyond the territory of the state. On the other hand, it is uncertain that it can do that according to the legal determination approach. This view holds that legal systems are able to establish valid claims for compliance only to the extent that legal institutions are able to determine *exclusive* claims for compliance. Legal institutions are not just shaping the content of the norms with which the subject ought to comply but also set limits to the extent to which claims for compliance can be sustained. The fact that the scope of the state's legal authority is dependent on the operations of legal institutions and their ability to establish exclusive authority is a reason to believe that territorial control is pertinent after all.

In this chapter, I have tried to explain what decides the scope of the law's claim to legitimate authority. In contrast to approaches that emphasize either the substance of legal norms or the coercive powers of state institutions, the account advanced here calls attention to the operations of legal institutions. This is, I believe, a natural implication of the overarching thesis of this book, which is that the all-subjected principle is concerned with claims to legitimate authority. The legal system of the state claims legitimate authority and exclusive rights to compliance of the subject. Yet, other legal systems will often seek to regulate the same persons and entities. In the competition over supremacy, legal institutions are needed and indeed sufficient to determine exclusively valid claims to legal authority.

Notes

1 I am, in the following, ignoring the distinctions between coercion, force, prevention, and sanctions. *Coercion* is pressure exerted against the will of the subject and leaves the subject with a choice. *Force* is exerted when the subject is unable to resist pressure. Handcuffs are not coercive but instruments of force (Morris 2012). Furthermore, some insist that *preventive* actions are neither coercive nor exercises of force. By stealing your car, I am not subjecting you to either coercion or force, although I do prevent you from using the car (Miller 2010: 114). Finally, not all coercive actions of the state are sanctions against norm-violations. Expropriation of property is typically coercive but not a sanction (Oberdiek 1976).
2 Notions of coercive *enforcement* are distinct from accounts of coercive *consequences*. In some radical views, the 'coercive effects' of the state extend far beyond the territory of the state as when, for example, they coercively restrict the autonomous actions of people in foreign territories (Valentini 2014).
3 Austin's 'sanction theory of duty' can be understood to mean either that sanctions are commanded, that sanctions are probable in case of non-compliance, or that non-compliance is the reason for sanctions (Hacker 1973).
4 Kelsen understands coercion as roughly equivalent to compulsion. This usage sets him apart from recent Anglophone theorists, who distinguish between coercion and compulsion (Edmundson 2012: 452).
5 However, Vinx (2007) argues that Kelsen believed that 'subjects of the law have a legal duty not to perform actions that are conditions for the application of a sanction' (42). Vinx's point is that Kelsen's view is consistent with general beliefs in the normative legitimacy of the legal system and that subjects who accepts the legitimacy of the law may think that they have moral duties to comply with the law. Yet, this does not establish that Kelsen believed that the legal system claims legitimate authority.
6 MacCormick (1997) makes the related point that it is a mistake to include coercion in the definition of law as it would turn into 'an analytical truth what is in fact an achievement of statecraft'.
7 Indeed, there is reason to think Kelsen saw this. In the *General Theory of Norms* he argues that 'Effectiveness is a condition for validity to the extent that a single norm and a whole normative order lose their validity—cease to be valid—if they lose their effectiveness *or the possibility of effectiveness.*' (1991: 139 emphasis added). The claim here is that 'possibility of effectiveness' is sufficient for legal validity, which requires merely that it is not impossible to comply with the norm. The point is that legal norms remain effective and valid in so far as compliance is possible, whether or not they are actually enforced. See also Vinx (2007: 38, n. 37).
8 The institutionalization of law is explained by Neil MacCormick (1997: 1058) in terms of the capacity to 'settle and finalizing disputes' about norms.

6
AUTHORITY AND EXTRATERRITORIAL JURISDICTION

Does the authority claimed by the state extend beyond its own border? One reason to think not is that territorial jurisdiction remains an important feature of the international state system. If the *jurisdiction* of the state is limited by its territorial borders, it seems a natural conclusion that the legal authority claimed by the state is also limited by territorial borders. Yet, jurisdiction is a multi-faceted concept, and it is not clear that all jurisdictional claims by the state are constrained by its borders. More importantly for our purposes is that the authority claimed by the state does not fully align with its jurisdiction. The argument pursued here is that a claim to jurisdiction by the state sometimes fail to establish a valid claim to authority. The scope of the authority claimed by the state is not determined by the extent of jurisdiction but by the ability of legal institutions to establish the exclusive validity of the law. This is the argument made in the first part of this chapter.

The second part surveys four contested cases of extraterritorial jurisdiction: the legal duties of diplomats in foreign countries; the prosecution of non-nationals by recourse to 'universal jurisdiction'; the attempt by the state to regulate and sanction corporations in foreign countries and, finally, the practice of international taxation whereby the state seeks to tax nationals abroad. In each case, I argue that the legal determination approach proves instructive in explaining the scope of the state's claim to legitimate authority. The conclusion is that the state is unable to subject anyone to its claimed authority outside of its own territory.

Jurisdiction and Authority

The concept of 'jurisdiction' denotes the legal right (power) to take legal action. Accordingly, the claim that a decision-making body has jurisdiction conveys 'lawful power to make and enforce rules' (Oxman 2007; Besson 2019: 100f.). *Territorial* jurisdiction is the legal right to take action within the bounds of a given territory.

DOI: 10.4324/9781003359807-6

The principle of territorial jurisdiction, when applied to the state, is the legal power of the state to act in the territory of the state.

The notion that the jurisdiction of the state is circumvented by territorial borders is relatively recent. The ascendance of place-based legal regimes followed in the wake of the wars in early modern Europe and the emergence of *the state* as the chief unit of political organization. The standard view is that the norm of territorial integrity and respect for sovereign statehood were crystalized by the Treaty of Westphalia in 1648 that concluded the Thirty Years' War.[1] The treaty established – or at least reinforced – the idea of equality between states, understood as independent and territorial sites of authority. The doctrine of territorial jurisdiction is in other words intimately bound up with the birth of the territorial state.[2]

However, it is controversial that 'territorial jurisdiction' adequately reflects interstate relationships today. A prominent argument is that the convenient mapping of legal systems into territories controlled by states is a relic of the past. The geographer Peter J. Taylor (1994) influentially argued that the state is a 'leaking container' that no longer has exclusive control over people and things in its territory. The presumption that the state enjoys undisrupted jurisdiction and control over its own territory is destabilized by the cumulative effects of economic globalization and the fact that powerful states and international organizations increasingly interfere with the activities of weaker states and their populations (Sassen 2013). The conclusion according to Kal Raustiala (2005) is that 'geographic borders in fact coincide quite imperfectly with the reach of national laws'. Instead of assuming that law is bounded by territory, Raustiala proposes that we should accept the 'rebuttable presumption' that the legal claims made by the state extend neatly into foreign territories. Territorial jurisdiction is a mere hypothesis that is often false. Since state law does not always map onto the territory of the state, prevailing legal practices are more adequately captured by the notion of 'legal spatiality' than of territorial jurisdiction.

The tenet that the jurisdiction of the state is fully determined by international borders is evidently mistaken. Yet, it is also a mistake to presume that 'territorial jurisdiction' carries the implication that *all* legal claims made by the state are limited by the territorial borders of the state. States are legally empowered to act in many ways and there are consequently many distinct forms of jurisdictional claims to be made. The point is that a proper evaluation of the thesis that territorial jurisdiction is in demise must differentiate between them. The literature usually distinguishes between the state's jurisdiction to *prescribe* law, *enforce* the law and to *adjudicate* the law (Ryngaert 2008).

Jurisdiction to enforce the law is indeed strongly territorial; no one state is legally entitled to enforce the law in the territory of another state. In *that* sense, jurisdiction is limited by the borders that separate the territory of one state from another. This is why, for example, forced abductions ('snatch-and-catch operations') in foreign territories are illegal by the standards of international law. Operations by one state in the territory of another state are permissible only with the consent of the state controlling the territory (Kamminga 2012).

Jurisdiction in either enacting norms or adjudicating conflicts between them is not conditioned by the territory of the state, however. Indeed, the claim that territory does not restrict exercises of jurisdiction in either sense is confirmed by the Permanent Court of International Justice in the paradigmatic *Lotus* case from 1927. The court concluded that 'all that can be required of a State is that it should not overstep the limits which international law places upon its jurisdiction' (S.S. Lotus [Fr. v. Turk.], 1927 P.C.I.J. [ser. A] No. 10 [47]). The jurisdiction of the state is limited by the borders of national territory only to the extent explicitly ordained by international law. For instance, without norms to the contrary, states possess prescriptive jurisdiction with regard to conduct abroad and adjudicative jurisdiction to prosecute individuals for their actions in foreign territories.

On the other hand, since international law recognizes that every state is equally entitled to exercise jurisdiction on their own territory, all states have the authority to prevent or invalidate the legal claims made by other states in their territories. The consequence is that while extraterritorial legislation is not prohibited, states do not have the unconditional legal power to regulate conduct abroad. In sum, the doctrine of territorial jurisdiction is consistent with the power to regulate conduct and adjudicate legal conflicts that occur in foreign territories, while each state retains the legal power to block legal claims by foreign entities on its territory (Lowe and Staker 2003: 319; Florey 2019).

The question of interest to us is not, however, the type and scope of jurisdictional claims of the state. The fact is that jurisdictional claims are not equivalent to claims of legal authority. Jurisdiction and legal authority are distinct concepts. This is shown by a brief look at the conditions for the validation of jurisdictional claims and claims of authority. A sufficient condition for a valid claim to jurisdiction is that it coheres with, and is authorized by, the relevant normative sources of the legal system. By contrast, a valid claim to legal authority depends both on validity in the former sense and on the extent of de facto authority. Jurisdictional claims are not necessarily limited to objects and persons over which the state enjoys de facto authority. But claims to authority are limited to objects and persons over which the state does enjoy de facto authority. The implication is that a person may be 'subject' to the state's jurisdictional claim and yet not a subject to the state's claimed authority. Lawful exercises of power do not incontrovertibly translate into effective exercises of authority. Hence, it remains an open question if the legal authority claimed by the state extends to all entities over which it claims to exercise jurisdiction (Hovell 2018: 429).[3]

The rift between jurisdiction and legal authority is accounted for by the legal determination approach according to which claims to legal authority must be validated by legal institutions. A person is subject to claims to legitimate authority only to the extent that legal institutions are able to recognize such claims as valid exercises of authority. Jurisdiction is the legal right to take action. But the fact that a legal body is legally empowered to regulate the conduct of a person is not sufficient to establish that this person is subject to legal authority. The practical implications of this distinction are shown in the following discussion.

The Limits of Territorial Authority

It is a frequent proposition that 'national law applies to all within the state' (Dorsett and McVeigh 2012: 39). The familiar image is that people and things in the territory of the state are subject to the state's claimed authority. But, as noted by Kal Raustiala, the law does not literally apply to *everyone* in the territory of the state. A flagrant exception to the norm that everyone in the state is subject to its laws is the legal immunity enjoyed by diplomats and ambassadorial residences. They are not ruled by the laws of the nation where they reside but by the laws of the nation for which they are emissaries (Raustiala 2005: 2510). If the laws of the state are unable to penetrate the doorsteps of diplomatic missions, the statement that the law applies to 'all within the state' cannot be correct. Although foreign embassies are located on state territory, the state does not possess the authority to regulate them. Here, then, emerges what appears to be a blatant incursion into the territorial jurisdiction of the state that seems to disrupt the state's claim to legitimate authority over its own territory.

On the other hand, the issue is ultimately *why* states are unable to enforce their laws in foreign legations located on their territories. In fact, the legal basis of this presumed limitation of the legal authority of the state is the Vienna Convention on Diplomatic Relations (1961). The convention is acceded to by most contemporary states. The parties to the convention have consequently agreed to the legal immunity of diplomatic agents that therefore remain under the jurisdiction of the sending state.[4]

Hence, the legal immunity of diplomats derives from treaties of international law that are conditioned by the consent of the state. Because the legal immunity of diplomats derives from international law, the limited authority of the host state in relation to diplomats is not due to a decision by the sending state. No state possesses the legal power to unilaterally confer immunity on officials abroad.

From the perspective of the host state, it is also clear that its authority is not limited by the fact that it cannot exercise jurisdiction over foreign embassies and diplomats on its territory. By acceding to a treaty that grants immunity to diplomats, the state has waived its legal right to regulate their conduct by its own legal system. The state has, in effect, voluntarily decided to abstain from exercising jurisdiction over entities that it does have the authority to regulate. We must therefore conclude that the case of embassies and diplomats is not evidence to conclude that states are unable to claim legitimate authority over all entities and conduct in their territories.

Extraterritorial Jurisdiction

A more challenging objection to territorial jurisdiction is found in the notion of extraterritorial jurisdiction. Extraterritorial jurisdiction refers to legal actions by the state beyond the territory of the state; it either includes all such actions or only actions that are not authorized by international agreement. The jurisdiction over diplomats and embassies in foreign territories is a case of extraterritorial action in the first sense, as it is a prerogative exercised in accordance with existing treaties.

Extraterritorial jurisdiction in the first, treaty-based, sense had a different and more radical meaning in the past. An early example is the agreement between Suleiman the Great and the king of France in 1536, ensuring that the Franks in the Ottoman Empire would remain under French jurisdiction (Cobbing 2018). Later on, Great Britain, France, the United States, and many other Western nations, established extraterritorial jurisdiction in weaker states and Empires abroad, particularly in the Ottoman Empire, China, and Japan (Kayaoğlu 2013).

These early examples of extraterritoriality are similar to the privileges afforded to ambassadorial representatives today; they are treaty-based and grant legal immunity to foreign nationals in the territory of the state. Yet, the scope of the colonial practice of extraterritorial jurisdiction was significantly wider as it conferred legal immunity on all nationals of the sending state. For example, all British nationals present in China were presumed to remain under the jurisdiction of His Britannic Majesty's Supreme Court for China in Shanghai. Likewise, all British nationals in the Ottoman Empire were under the exclusive purview of the British Supreme Court in Istanbul, which was subsequently complemented by His British Majesty's Supreme Court for the Dominions of the Sublime Ottoman Porte in Alexandria (Slys 2014). The scope of extraterritorial jurisdiction in the colonial era was consequently of a different order of magnitude in comparison with contemporary practices that extend immunities only to limited categories of persons. Indeed, past practices also conferred the legal power to create courts and other public agencies abroad (including police and postal services). The result was that the territorial integrity of the Ottoman Empire, China, and other states were effectively compromised.

However, the most contentious feature of extraterritoriality in the past was that it was non-reciprocal. The treaties that granted Western powers jurisdiction overseas did not create corresponding immunities for nationals of non-Western states in *their* territories (Slys 2014). The agreements were 'unequal treaties' and gradually became more unpopular following growing national consciousness and relative shifts in the balance of power.[5] The present world does not tolerate foreign states to operate courts on the territory of other independent and sovereign states.[6]

Yet, extraterritorial jurisdiction in the second, non-treaty based, sense remains a feature of global politics. Four principles of extraterritorial law are commonly identified. The principle of *active personality* is that the state can hold nationals legally accountable for an offence committed abroad. The more radical principle of *passive personality* is that the state is in certain circumstances entitled to prosecute foreign nationals for offences undertaken in other countries. According to the *protective principle*, the state is entitled to take legal action against anyone, or anything, posing a threat to the sovereignty or independence of the state. The principle of *universal jurisdiction*, finally, refers to claims by the state to criminalize particularly egregious offences regardless of the perpetrator's nationality and the location of the crime (Ryngaert 2008: 85; Kamminga 2012; Florey 2019: 8).

These distinct types of extraterritorial jurisdiction are not equally tolerated by the international community. The principles of passive personality and universal jurisdiction are generally understood to be more controversial than either the active personality principle or the protective principle (Ireland-Piper 2017). In Ryngaert's (2008: 92) estimate, universal jurisdiction represents the 'most aggressive' form of extraterritorial jurisdiction.

Now, of foremost interest in this context is to what extent the state is able to claim legitimate authority beyond its own territory at all. Does the state possess the capacity to claim legitimate authority over persons and entities in foreign territories? That is, is anyone or anything not present in the territory of the state ever subject to the state in the sense relevant for the all-subjected principle?

Does Universal Law Claim Universal Authority?

The potential radical implications of extraterritorial jurisdiction are best illustrated by the principle of universal jurisdiction. States that claim universal jurisdiction assume the right to prosecute and punish crime exclusively by reference to the nature of the crime. No connection between the state and the perpetrator is required according to universal jurisdiction.

The origins of universal jurisdiction are standardly attributed to attempts by states to outlaw and prevent acts of piracy on the high seas (Bassiouni 2010: 43). In fact, all currently existing states reportedly claim universal jurisdiction with regard to piracy. Many states additionally claim universal jurisdiction with respect to slavery, crimes against humanity, acts of terrorism, genocide, war crimes and torture.

The fact that claims to universal jurisdiction are frequent in the contemporary world might be taken as evidence for the conclusion that the authority of the state does in fact extend beyond the territory of the state. In fact, Bob Goodin argues that universal jurisdiction is testimony to the radical implications of the all-subjected principle of democratic inclusion. Legal systems that pursue universal jurisdiction claim to regulate conduct that falls under the relevant sections of criminal law wherever the offence is committed. Claims to universal jurisdiction impose legal duties on 'everyone, everywhere' that would seem to trigger claims for democratic inclusion applicable to everyone, everywhere according to the all-subjected principle. In Goodin's estimate, the all-subjected principle implies that states that recognize universal jurisdiction 'must give a vote in the making of such laws to all foreigners abroad who would be subject to them' (Goodin 2016: 385).

Clearly, Goodin's argument is premised on the substantive approach to the scope of subjection to the law. That is not the view taken here, and we shall return to this shortly. The first thing to notice, however, is that it is not factually correct to say that claims to universal jurisdiction are legal claims that apply to the conduct of everyone, everywhere. Claims to universal jurisdiction are often conditional claims. That is, as a matter of legal practice we are not entitled to conclude that the law applies to everyone just because the state insists on universal jurisdiction.

For instance, there is a generally acknowledged difference between universal jurisdiction with respect to acts of piracy, on the one hand, and acts of genocide, on the other. Acts of piracy are subject to universal jurisdiction only if they take place in international waters. The state is not entitled to universal jurisdiction over acts of piracy in waters that are not international, for example, lakes or shorelines. No such limitation applies to the universal jurisdiction claimed with respect to genocide (Hovell 2018). It is a mistake, therefore, to assume that claims to universal jurisdiction are necessarily universal in scope.

A further indication of the spatial limits of universal jurisdiction is that criminal law sometimes includes specific conditions for the applicability of the law. The provisions of Swedish criminal law that regulate sexual relations between adults and minors is a case in point. According to Swedish law, sexual relations with a child are a criminal offence for anyone irrespective of the location of the crime. The authorities are therefore empowered to prosecute relevant offences committed abroad. From this fact it may seem to follow that the legal system of Sweden claims to apply 'everywhere'. On the other hand, the criminal code also includes the proviso that an offence is to be prosecuted only if the suspect is 'present within the realm' (Asp 2017: 35). The universal application of the law accordingly does not entail that the law will be enforced everywhere. The legal system of Sweden claims the authority to enforce the law only against a perpetrator who is present in the territory of the state.

In response to these observations, Goodin might reply that the extent of prosecution is not relevant in judging the extent of subjection to the law. On the substantive approach (or the 'juridical' reading, as Goodin calls it), a person is subject to the law even if neither apprehended nor prosecuted (Goodin 2016: 371). The fact that a person is 'not much affected by the law' is no reason to deny that the person is 'still subject to it' (Goodin 2016: 375).

Goodin is certainly correct in pointing out that subjection to the law is not conditioned by actual prosecution. The fact that no legal action is taken against a person does not imply that she is not subject to claims for compliance with the law. Indeed, public authorities may fail to initiate prosecution for a variety of reasons that are unrelated to the extent of authority claimed by the law, including lack of evidence, inadequate resources, or just sheer incompetence. An offender who evades the law has still violated the law and is still a potential subject of legal authority.

However, conceding this point does not commit us to accept the premise of Goodin's argument, which is that the extent of subjection to the law can be fully accounted for by the substance of legal norms. Following the legal determination approach, people are instead considered as subject to the legal authority claimed by the state only if legal institutions have the capacity to determine the law in relation to them. Hence, if legal institutions decline to enforce a legal provision on the grounds that the laws of the state do not apply to that person, the conclusion is that the person is not subject to the state's claim to legitimate authority in that regard. In other words, *some* decisions not to prosecute *are* grounds to conclude that the law does not apply to the person. For example, legal institutions may decline to prosecute by appeal to a valid international treaty stipulating that prosecution should be reserved for offences that are criminalized in the country where the offence took place. In that case, a decision not to prosecute *is* evidence to conclude that the suspect is not subject to claims of compliance with the authority of that legal system.

A second critical observation is that Goodin pays no attention to the validation of legal claims. For Goodin, legal claims are 'juridical facts' that can be determined by reading the relevant sections of the law-book. What is required by the law is fully accounted for by the substance of legal norms. By contrast, the legal determination approach holds that people are subject to a law's claim to legitimate authority only if also subject to institutions that determine the law. In order to conclude that a person is legally required to comply with a provision of universal jurisdiction, some procedure is required by which the validity of the legal requirement can be determined. The point is that a person is subject to universal jurisdiction only if legal institutions are able to confirm that these claims apply to that person. In the domestic setting, this is not usually an issue. A well-functioning state typically includes legal institutions with the capacity to verify the authority claimed by the state in the territory. The question, then, is do legal institutions have the capacity to determine the validity of laws of universal jurisdiction beyond the territory of the state?

A case that illustrates how the operations of legal institutions determine the validity of the state's claimed authority is the high-profile case of Augusto Pinochet. In 1998, a Spanish prosecutor took the initiative to press charges against Pinochet for his actions while in office as the dictator of Chile. The legal system of Spain at the time accepted universal jurisdiction with respect to crimes against humanity and thus permitted the prosecution of non-nationals in foreign jurisdictions.[7] As the prosecutor learned about Pinochet's presence in London, Spanish authorities issued an international arrest warrant to which British authorities responded promptly by issuing a preliminary warrant for Pinochet's arrest.

Up to this point, it may seem as if the legal system of Spain successfully claimed legitimate authority with respect to Pinochet. After all, Pinochet's arrest in London was a direct consequence of the actions taken by Spanish authorities. Yet, the validity of the arrest warrant was not for Spanish authorities to decide. It was a matter to be decided by legal institutions in the United Kingdom (Orentlicher 2004). It was up to the judicial system of the United Kingdom to determine whether the charges pressed by the Spanish prosecutor were admissible and if the request for the extradition of Pinochet to Spain was legally valid in the United Kingdom. While Pinochet was held in custody, British authorities engaged in a series of legal decisions, some reversing prior judgments. These decisions involved the highest judicial institutions of the country (the House of Lords) and were finally resolved by the intervention of the British government that decided to release Pinochet on reasons of health.

The point is that the legal basis for the prosecution of Pinochet was eventually decided by the legal institutions of the United Kingdom, despite the universal jurisdiction claimed by Spain over Pinochet. Although Spain claimed jurisdiction over Pinochet, it appeared that Pinochet was only subject to the authority claimed by the state where he resided at the moment. The British legal system responded to the requests made by the Spanish legal system but reserved the right to determine the fate of Pinochet. This illustrates the position defended here, according to which the scope of subjection to the law does not depend on the content of legal norms but on the operations of legal institutions. It appears mistaken, then, to argue that it is 'a juridical fact' that claims of universal jurisdiction apply to individuals in foreign territories (cf. Goodin 2016: 375).

The Effects Doctrine

Commercial law represents a lively scene of extraterritorial law due to the tendency of the United States to regulate foreign corporations and their activities. The legal basis for the actions taken by US authorities is found in the so-called 'effects doctrine' that evolved in the case-law of American courts. The doctrine holds that the US can regulate 'conduct occurring outside its territory that has an effect within its territory that creates a genuine connection between the conduct and the prescribing state' (Florey 2019).[8] The underlying principle is that the state – or the United States in any case – is entitled to protect is own commercial interests from the activities of foreign entities abroad.[9] Unsurprisingly, that claim has ignited a continuous stream of controversy in international politics and law (Putnam 2016).

Domestic commercial interests are considered to be at risk if, for instance, foreign corporations adopt bogus business practices that give them an edge in competition over contracts. Accordingly, the US has introduced legislation that grants the US Department of Justice and the Securities and Exchange Commission (SEC) 'considerable authority' to initiate prosecution against foreign corporations whenever bribery is suspected (Kaczmarek and Newman 2011). Through the effects doctrine, the United States seeks to regulate bribery and cartels, but also trade with nations that are subject to economic sanctions.[10]

The effects doctrine allows the state to take legal action against foreign entities in foreign territories. The question is whether such actions represent extraterritorial claims to legitimate authority? As argued above, the scope of such claims is determined by the operations of legal institutions. Only legal norms that are validated by legal institutions generate claims of compliance with legal authority. The effects doctrine grounds extraterritorial claims of legitimate authority over foreign corporations provided that legal institutions confirm the exclusivity and validity of the claim that such corporations are subject to legally binding norms.

An important observation, to which we shall shortly return, is that corporations may have incentives to conform with the authority claimed by the state even if not subject to it. A corporation that expects to suffer from non-conformity with legal claims has strong *prudential* reasons to accommodate them, even if the corporation does not strictly speaking have a legal obligation to obey. The point is that the corporation may choose conformity to legal claims even though these are *not* valid claims for compliance.

Yet, Austen Parrish (2008) has argued that the effects doctrine does subject foreign entities to the laws of the state. For that reason, he also believes that the effects doctrine is violating fundamental democratic principles. By extending legal claims beyond its borders, the state regulates persons and entities that are unable to vote and participate in the law-making process. When the US imposes fines or other sanctions on foreign corporations and their management it 'forces foreigners to bear the costs of domestic regulations, even though they are nearly powerless to change these regulations' (Parrish 2008: 1483). But if democracy is to mean anything, Parrish (2008: 1486) asserts rhetorically, it should at least mean that 'those whose conduct is to be controlled by a particular law must have some voice'.

Parrish insists that a democratic voice should be granted anyone (or anything) bearing 'the costs' of the law and 'whose conduct is controlled' by the law. However, it is not clear if Parish means to say that costs suffered as a result of legal actions are sufficient for a democratic voice, or if he means to say that a democratic voice is required only if the subject is also controlled by the law. As it turns out, it is implausible to submit that an entity that suffers costs as a consequence of legal actions should therefore be entitled to democratic voice.

Consider the following example: one state introduces legislation that increases the costs of productive activities for domestic corporations by raising legal standards of labor safety. As a result, the cost of consuming the products of these corporations increases. Now, in export-driven and internationalized economies some of the consumers are likely to be present in foreign countries. Hence, legislation that improves safety for workers and thereby raises the cost of consumption of the relevant products domestically is destined to also increase the costs of consumption for foreign individuals and corporations. Should we therefore conclude that consumers in foreign countries are entitled to a democratic voice because they suffer costs as a consequence of the actions undertaken by the state? That seems doubtful, to say the least. Indeed, the current conception of the all-subjected principle explains why. The fact that you must pay more for a product as a result of decisions taken by the state is no reason to conclude that you are subject to the claimed authority of that state. No reason for compliance with the state is generated by the fact that some options are rendered more costly by the state.

This observation is not sufficient to rebut the argument made by Parrish, however. In a more plausible interpretation of his argument, the claim defended is that democratic voice should extend to all legally required to pay. Penalties are legally required costs and are in that respect distinct from costs that are *caused by* but not *required by* the law. Penalties rather than costs are, presumably, the relevant concept.

In fact, significant penalties have been imposed on foreign corporations by appeal to the effects doctrine on many occasions. In 2015, US courts ordered the French bank BNP Paribas to pay 10 billion USD in penalties for violation of US sanctions against Sudan, Iran, and Cuba. Earlier, a total of nine foreign banks had been penalized by the United States on similar charges (Amariles and Winkler 2018). In all these cases, the banks relented and paid the amount ordered by US authorities.

However, the fact that the banks conformed to the claims made by US authorities is not evidence to conclude that the banks were subject to the authority claimed by the United States. Just like other multinational corporations, banks have strong business interests in maintaining relations to the US market. A corporation that declines to cooperate with US authorities risks forfeiting valuable economic opportunities, such as the right to list stocks on US markets, or being licensed for business in the US. In addition, the authorities of the US could freeze assets registered in the US in retaliation for non-cooperative behavior (Amariles and Winkler 2018: 510). Multinational corporations consequently face strong incentives to do as told by the US.

The point is that a foreign state can incentivize conformity with the law even if the person or entity is not subject to the legal authority it claims. This is of course not sufficient to reject the hypothesis that foreign corporations are subject to the legal authority claimed by the United States. However, it is sufficient to reject the hypothesis that corporations that conform to legal claims made by the United States are therefore subject to its claimed legal authority.

For legal claims to be exemplars of legal authority, they must be both valid and exclusive. The legal claim that BNP Paribas is guilty of violating the laws of the US was determined by US legal institutions and in other words valid by the standards of the US legal system. But the fact that a decision is *valid* is not enough to conclude that the decision renders a person or entity subject to the legal authority claimed. For that to be the case, it must also be true that the decision is able to establish *exclusive* authority with respect to the conduct that it seeks to regulate. Legal claims are exclusive only with respect to persons and entities that are not regulated by other legal systems.

Now, legal actions taken under the effect's doctrine do not appear to be exclusive in that sense. This is indicated by the reactions of other states to the attempt by the US to impose its laws on corporations elsewhere in the world. Intending to block US assertions of extraterritoriality, the EU and its members introduced measures that made it unlawful for corporations in Europe to cooperate with US authorities. The EU made compliance with US sanctions illegal and allowed corporations targeted by US extraterritoriality to recover legal damages and costs suffered (Layton and Parry 2004; Putnam 2016).

The European response to the measures taken by the US also affected legal institutions. In 1996 the European Union prohibited courts and authorities from recognizing and applying judgments that would give legal effect to US extraterritorial claims (Yaser Ziaee 2016). Similar actions were taken by Canada and other nations in order to block, limit, or mitigate the effects of US legal actions against corporations in their territories.

The capacity to introduce blocking legislation shows that legal systems are exclusive and have the power to deny legal claims by foreign states in their territories. In fact, it shows that the legal effects of foreign legal systems are conditioned by authorization by the domestic legal system – even when blocking measures are *not* introduced. In the case that European states had not introduced blocking measures, US legal claims would have been legally effective in Europe. But their legal effectiveness would still be conditioned by the European legal system tolerating them. As noted by Raz (1999: 151) 'actions are regulated by a norm even if it is merely permitted by it'. Thus, foreign legal claims are effective only if they are permitted by the domestic legal system. The fact that legal claims are effective only if permitted shows that extraterritorial legal claims are not valid unless recognized by the legal system in force in the relevant territory.

Taxing People Abroad

Taxation is a legal power exercised by the state for the purpose of collecting revenue from individuals, business, and other entities. The effects of taxation are sometimes hard felt by the individual and it is not surprising that taxation bears an important historical connection to demands for political participation. 'No taxation without representation', is a familiar slogan from the American colonies under British rule. It also informs the hypothesis that expansions of the tax-base by the state is one important driver of democratization (Ross 2004).

The all-subjected principle provides a rationale for the connection between taxation and democratic participation. Because legal claims to tax are claims for compliance with legal authority, the people subject to taxation law should be included in the demos. The point though is that tax-payers should be included in the demos because they are subject to the authority asserted by the state, not because the taxpayer has contributed to the public purse.

Yet, some states do seek to impose taxes on people and entities beyond their territory. If we ignore taxes levied on corporations and focus exclusively on taxes on individuals who are not residents in the territory of the state, the question is can the state claim the legitimate authority to tax foreign residents? The case to consider is the principle of international taxation according to which citizens are required to pay income tax even if not a resident of the state.

The principle of international taxation is rare though notoriously recognized by both the United States and Eritrea. Following the US tax code, income tax applies to 'every citizen of the United States, whether residing at home or abroad' (Schneider 2012). US citizens are subject to pay US income tax regardless of residential status. Eritrea employs a specifically designed 'diaspora tax' that levies two percent of the income. The diaspora tax is particularly controversial due to the fact that many Eritreans emigrated for either humanitarian or political reasons. Thus, the government effectively imposes taxes on persons who were forced to emigrate (Hirt and Mohammad 2018).

Consider, first, the extent to which US tax agencies are able to enforce rules of international taxation against their citizens abroad. Of course, there are formidable challenges in collecting the information necessary to determine the amount of taxes that should be paid. Because it is an income tax, the authorities need access to all sources of income in a given year in order to calculate the amount to be paid. This might not be excessively difficult in relation to US citizens residing abroad who are also employed by US registered corporations. As long as the employer is active in the United States, the employer is subject to the claimed authority of the US government to provide the necessary documentation. The situation is different with regard to US citizens employed by corporations that are not registered in the United States. On their own, US authorities are hard pressed to collect the information needed from these citizens and must instead rely on incomplete and unreliable data submitted voluntarily (Schneider 2012: 55f.).

The Eritrean government appears slightly better positioned to garner the information needed to determine the diaspora tax. One reason is the assistance provided by embassies and consulates abroad. The agencies of the Eritrean foreign office are, in effect, acting as tax authorities that decide the tax obligations of citizens abroad. However, the decisive reason for the relative effectiveness of the Eritrean diaspora tax is the pressure exerted by the government of Eritrea on foreign nationals. The government has made full compliance with the diaspora tax a condition for various legal services, such as renewal of passports, assistance in administrating property or inheritance, and even for permission to re-enter Eritrea (Hirt and Mohammad 2018).

In terms of the capacity to enforce laws of international taxation, a preliminary conclusion is that US authorities are less successful than the government of Eritrea. Yet, securing conformity with the law is not the same as securing compliance with the law. Compliance is premised on claims of legitimate authority, not on the power to incentivize conformity. It thus remains an open question if the Eritrean government is able to claim legitimate authority with respect to fellow countrymen abroad.

The authority claimed by Eritrean officials in foreign territories is frequently resisted by other states. In 2014 the Canadian government ordered the consulate of Eritrea in Toronto to 'cease and desist' all activities related to the collection of taxes in Canada. Similar measures were taken by other states. The Swedish parliament adopted a resolution stating that the diaspora tax is illegal. Authorities in Sweden subsequently encouraged Eritrean residents to report any attempt by the Eritrean government to solicit taxes in the country (United Nations 2014: 38). Eritrean citizens in Sweden were effectively legally required *not* to pay the taxes demanded by the government of Eritrea.

The conclusion is that the state of Eritrea could not claim the legitimate authority to collect taxes abroad. Residents in other countries were not subject to the diaspora tax because they were subject to the exclusive claim of authority by the state in which they resided. Though states may be successful in incentivizing conformity with the law abroad, they are unable to claim legitimate authority in the territories controlled by foreign legal systems.

Not all taxes levied on foreign residents are based on laws of international taxation. Much more common is the practice of taxing foreign residents on property that is registered in the territory of the state. Property taxes are levied on the property, irrespective of the 'domicile' of the owner. Thus, a US citizen with property in New Zealand is legally required to pay property taxes in New Zealand and vice versa. Similar to the case of international taxation, property taxation law appears to extend its claimed authority beyond national borders. And just as in the cases of international taxation, legal institutions may face considerable difficulties in enforcing taxes on foreign property-owners (Cassidy 2017).

The obvious difference between extraterritorial income taxation and extraterritorial property taxation is that only in the latter case does the asset taxed necessarily remain in the territory controlled by the state. The person legally required to pay the tax may be abroad, but the asset taxed is not. For that reason, incentives to conform with taxation law are stronger for non-residents in the case of the property taxation.

In any case, the conditions for subjection to the law's claim to legitimate authority are not fulfilled simply because a person has the incentive to act in accordance with the law. A person is subject to legal claims to pay property taxes only if subject to the authority claimed by the state. And, just as in the case of international taxation, the scope of claims to authority depends on the ability of legal institutions to validate the exclusivity of that claim. Now, tax collectors and other authorities involved in the enforcement of the property tax cannot operate in foreign territories and foreign authorities are under no obligation to assist in the enforcement of foreign tax-claims.[11] Hence, just as in the case of international taxation, people are subject to property taxation only within the realm under the control by the legal system. The law according to which property in New Zealand is subject to taxation is exclusive only in the territory of New Zealand. Hence, the law of the property tax in New Zealand does not apply to a person who is present in a foreign jurisdiction. Although non-resident property owners have incentives to conform with the law, they are not subject to the laws of the state.

Notes

1 The significance of the Treaty of Westphalia to the formation of the state system is of course debated (e.g., Krasner 1995 and Piirimäe 2010). A number of alternative hypotheses on the origins of the modern state exist, including: the view that it emerged as a result of the wars fought in the 13th century between Spain, France and Britain; the view that it developed following the demise of the Italian city states as a consequence of the invasion by France in 1494; and the claim that the state appeared as the result of the Treaty of Worms in 1122 between the Catholic church and European monarchies (see Sofier 2009 for an overview). The literature on the origins of the state and the emergence of territorial borders is voluminous and I do not pretend to be able to do it justice here. See also Sassen (2006), Caporaso (2000) and Murphy (1996) for instructive accounts of the debate.
2 As noted by Ford (1999) and (Dorsett 2006), the notion of territorial jurisdiction is conditioned by technological inventions in cartography. Territorial control requires the capacity to organize space on the basis of abstract 'maps'.
3 Cf. Grant (2017: 513) who argues that jurisdiction depends on legitimate legal authority (not claims to legitimate legal authority) which seems mistaken given that the de facto authority of the state and other entities is not necessarily legitimate.
4 There are some exceptions to the legal immunities enjoyed by diplomatic agents according to the Vienna Convention, for example, with regard to commercial activities unrelated to the official functions of diplomats (Hestermeyer 2009).
5 The so called 'capitulations' in the Ottoman Empire by Western nations came to an end during or directly after the First World War. Germany renounced its legal privileges in exchange for military cooperation, as did Austria, while the new Soviet government unilaterally terminated the privileges of Russia in 1921. The remaining capitulations ended with the Treaty of Lausanne in 1923 (Slys 2014).
6 The era of unequal treaties is said to have ended with the closing of the US extraterritorial court in Morocco in 1956 (Raustiala 2005: 2510). Great Britain nevertheless kept extraterritorial courts running in the Persian Gulf until 1971. Today, lesser forms of 'extraterritorial-type judicial arrangements' remain in some islands (Puerto Rico, Guam, and the Northern Mariana Islands by the US: in French Polynesia, Wallis, and Futuna by the French; in Netherlands Antilles by the Dutch and in Bermuda, the Cayman Islands, and the Falkland Islands by Great Britain). See Putnam (2016: 19).

7 The Supreme Court of Spain has since ruled that a nationality tie is necessary for universal jurisdiction by the laws of Spain (Roht-Arriaza 2004).
8 The doctrine originates with the 1945 judgement *United States v. Aluminium Co. of America* (the 'Alcoa' case). See Sandage (1985) for an overview.
9 The effects doctrine is arguably a unique feature of the legal system of the United States. Lowe and Staker (2003: 322).
10 The effects doctrine applies also to environmental interests, allowing the state to regulate activities abroad that have effects on domestic environmental interests. See Cooreman (2016).
11 This fact is acknowledged in international law through the so-called 'revenue rule' according to which tax-claims by a foreign state are not enforced by other states. Of course, we could imagine bi-lateral tax agreements that would allow for the enforcement of tax-claims by foreign states. Yet, even in that event, tax-claims would be valid extraterritorially only if accepted by the domestic legal system and consequently do not represent evidence for the validity of extraterritorial claims to legitimate authority. See generally Schneider (2012).

7
AUTHORITY AND STATE BORDERS

The notion that state borders should be assigned importance for rights to democratic participation is controversial. One reason is that state territories and the borders that separate them are often contested and sometimes sources of political, even violent, conflict. David Miller (2014) labels territories with contested borders 'debatable lands'. Land is 'debated' if there is a territorial border subject to conflicting claims by at least two states. Miller's prime example is that of the Kashmir, a region claimed by both India and Pakistan and currently divided between them. Another example is Crimea which is subject to territorial conflict between Ukraine and Russia. It is not hard to imagine additional examples.

In fact, the expression 'debatable land' is misleading as border disputes are not necessarily about 'land' at all. The territory of the state does not just comprise the surface land mass but also seas, airspace and outer space, the seabed, and the subterranean (Buchanan 2003: 232; Jessop 2015: 31). For instance, the 'Cod Wars' between Iceland and the United Kingdom in the 1970s were not about land but about economic zones in international waters. Similarly, the conflict between China and its neighbors in the South China Sea is not primarily about 'land' but about controlling the seas, trade routes, and natural resources. In any case, since people predominantly reside on land, only conflicts about land are relevant in exploring the relationship between territorial borders and the demos.

There is a popular argument to the effect that border disputes pose a difficult challenge to the all-subjected principle. The argument is, in brief, that conflicts about territorial borders cannot be resolved democratically by principles of inclusion that are premised on existing territorial borders for the purpose of delimiting the demos. Specifically, if border conflicts are to be resolved by democratic procedures, it appears that the all-subjected principle is instructing us to rely on the very object of dispute in order to identify who should participate in the decision. According to critics, this renders the all-subjected principle incoherent, or overly ambiguous, at best.

This objection is strengthened by the perception that disputed borders are illegitimate. Many now existing borders were determined in the past by powerful actors without consulting the resident population. These borders are morally problematic and should not now be used to identify the demos in decisions that seek to make borders legitimate.

However, the observation that state borders are disputed is no reason to conclude that they are illegitimate. The fact that land is 'debated' in Miller's sense implies an ongoing political conflict about territorial borders. But borders are not rendered illegitimate just because they are subject to conflict. The question, then, is not whether the demos should be identified by reference to existing territorial borders in cases where state borders are illegitimate. The question is rather whether the demos should be identified on the basis of territorial borders in cases where democratic procedures are mobilized to resolve territorial disputes. That is the question addressed in the final section of this chapter. Can the demos be identified by the all-subjected principle in what I call 'border decisions' – decisions seeking to resolve disputes on state borders?

The argument ultimately defended is that the debate about border decisions is largely based on the mistaken assumption that state borders *can* be decided by states. In reality, however, no state has the legal power to decide state borders as they are determined by international law. The point is that if states are unable to regulate state borders, they are also unable to make democratic decisions that regulate state borders. Hence, the argument that the all-subjected principle fails to identify the demos in border decisions is based on a false premise.

Before getting there, however, we are to examine two other arguments about the relationship between state borders and the demos. The first is the claim that border controls can trigger demands for democratic inclusion. The claim is that border controls frequently subject potential immigrants to coercion. In response, I caution against conflating territorial *borders* with border *regimes*. The all-subjected principle takes territorial borders as relevant for the scope of the demos but has nothing or little to say about border regimes.

The second argument examined is that the all-subjected principle is implicitly nationalist as it attaches normative importance to the congruence between territory and democratic participation. In response, I draw a distinction between the claim that territorial borders *define* the scope of the demos and the claim that state borders are *consequential* for the scope of the demos. The theory of democratic inclusion advanced here does not define the demos in terms of the territory of the state though it implies that territorial borders have consequences for the scope of the demos given certain assumptions about the state and the authority it claims.

Borders and Border Regimes

According to the 'democratic borders argument', the territorial borders of the state are pertinent to the scope of democratic participation. The rules that determine who is entitled to cross the borders are increasingly important as many states seek to limit access to their territories for migrants and refugees. These rules are laws that provide instructions for public authorities; rules that regulate and that authorize coercive measures against potential as well as actual immigrants. The rules that regulate cross-border movements are consequently bound to have repercussions far beyond the borders of the state, even though they are primarily practiced only *at* the border.[1] Laws that authorize public officials to communicate that unauthorized migration will be punished are effectively communicating coercive threats to potential immigrants. Because they are subject to coercive threats, the options available to potential immigrants and refugees are circumscribed. Given that autonomy depends on the availability of valuable and unobstructed options, it thus follows that coercive laws that restrict migration encroach on the autonomy of people abroad (Abizadeh 2008; Parvu 2015).

Whereas the democratic border argument is concerned with the rules that regulate migration, it is worth keeping in mind that these 'border regimes' also regulate cross-borders flows of capital and goods. The border regime of the state is consequently affecting economic opportunities and well-being just as much as it constrains freedom of movement and prospects for refuge.

To evaluate this argument, we need to begin by reflecting on what state borders are. A popular view in the discipline of 'critical border studies' is that state borders are 'socio-spatial practices' that are sustained by multiple social, political, and economic processes (Parker et al. 2009). Yet, this perspective muddles the distinction between the territorial border and the policies that regulate access to the territory of the state. That there is a distinction to make is indicated by their separate origins. As already remarked, state borders are as old as the state system and reaches back to the times of early modernity in European politics. By contrast, border *regimes* that regulate cross-border transfers of capital and goods are incomparably older. Customs duties and tariffs on merchandise have been known since the beginning of human civilization. On the other hand, the systematic regulation of the cross-border movements of *people* is a more recent phenomenon. Earnest attempts to legally regulate migration have only been made since the late 19th century (Torpey 2009).

More importantly, there is reason to acknowledge that legal regimes for the regulation of cross-border movements – the border regime – are not determined by the status of the territorial borders of the state. The border regime is a matter of public policy. Like other policies of the government, the border regime is adjusted according to the perceived needs and interests of the state. A border regime that is at one point lax and liberal can quickly turn to strict, and back again. Lax policies impose few barriers on cross-border trade and migration; strict policies include visa restrictions, closed border checkpoints, heavy tariffs, and regulative barriers on trade (Biersteker 2013). Furthermore, the border regime comprises several 'functional areas' that can be regulated separately. The regime may be tough on migration while at the same time 'liberal' with respect to the cross-border flows of capital and goods (Little 2015).

By contrast, the status of territorial borders is not a matter of public policy; 'states cannot choose to have a border' (Parker and Adler-Nissen 2012). The nature of the border is not for the state to decide by means of public policy. The territorial border is a defining attribute of the state as construed by the international state system and is not a product of unilateral choices made by states.

Now, the claim that the border regime is separate from the borders of the state does not necessarily disprove the argument that coercive border regimes are relevant to democratic inclusion. All it shows is that the democratic border argument is not concerned with territorial borders but with the policy that regulates cross-border movement. The argument correctly understood is that border policy that enforce limitations on border-crossing renders prospective immigrants and refugees subject to the coercive powers of the state. This is arguably deeply problematic, given the democratic principle that all subject to state coercion should be able to participate in the democratic process.

The premises of the democratic border argument are controversial, however. The first premise is that border regimes are coercive. But in the case that coercion necessarily involves pressure to undertake a particular action against one's will, laws that prevent a person from entering the territory of the state are not coercive. The subject who is denied entry is still free to choose from many available options. The threat communicated by the border regime to prospective immigrants is in that case *preventive* rather than coercive (Blake 2008; Miller 2010; cf. Abizadeh 2010).[2] The second premise is that prospective immigrants are subject to coercion *by* the border regime. But it is not clear they are subject *only* to the border regime. The coercion that is exercised by border authorities is ultimately authorized by the constitutional framework. A subject of the border regime is effectively subject to the legal system of the state. There are no subjects of border regimes, only subjects of the state (Beckman 2013).

In this context, however, the relevant premise of the democratic border argument is a different one. Following the current version of the all-subjected principle, the coercive nature of public power is unimportant. The relevant feature of the state is instead the authority it claims. The question then is whether the border regime claims the authority to regulate the conduct of prospective immigrants who are not yet present in the territory of the state. The democratic borders argument represents a challenge to the current interpretation of the all-subjected principle only if it shows that the claimed authority of the border regime reaches out to prospective immigrants.

The response to this challenge is nevertheless clear from previous chapters. The state's claim to legitimate authority is limited by the legal authority of other states. Authority is a claim to establish *exclusive* reasons for compliance. The exclusive authority claimed by the legal system nullifies the claims made by foreign states in the domain that is subject to sovereign control. The function of territorial borders in the current state-system is to identify the endpoints of de facto authority. The borders between states both constrain and make possible a world divided into states that claim exclusive legal authority.

Though indisputable that border regimes affect migrants and refugees in morally salient respects, border regimes do not claim the authority to regulate conduct beyond the territory of the state. The extent of subjection to the laws of the state is not affected by the extent of control exercised by the state at the border. Following the current version of the all-subjected principle, prospective immigrants are not subjects in the sense relevant from the point of view of democratic inclusion.

Territorial Borders and Nationalism

A frequent complaint against the all-subjected principle is that it takes existing territorial borders for granted. This is arguably problematic for the reason that nationalist ideas are accepted as the primary building blocks for democratic theory. By drawing the boundaries of democratic peoples along territorial borders, the message of the all-subjected principle coincides with the nationalist standpoint that political rights are privileges of peoples delimited by 'the boundaries of states or nations' (Ochoa Espejo 2014; Whitt 2014). The all-subjected principle is allegedly 'nationalist' as it condones the existing territorial division of the world (Eckersley 2020: 220).

The validity of this critique evidently depends on what is meant by 'nationalism'. I will return to this shortly. First, however, I want to address the relationship between territorial borders and democratic inclusion that is implied by the all-subjected principle. The claim defended in previous chapters is that territorial borders should determine the scope of the demos. The question though is what it means for the borders of the state to 'determine' the demos.[3]

In one reading, territorial borders determine the demos if the borders of the state decide the *extension* of the demos. Extension is the range of objects to which a concept applies at a particular moment. For example, the extension of 'the European Union' equals all current member-states of the EU. Note that this is an empirical fact that follows only given a particular definition of the EU. Claims about extension are, in other words, not definitions. The extension of 'the European Union' varies from time to time, even if the definition is the same. Accordingly, the assertion that the extension of the demos coincides with the population that resides in the territory of the state is not a claim about the definition of the demos. Rather, it is an empirical claim that presupposes a particular definition of the demos.

In the second reading, the claim that the demos is determined by the territorial borders of the state *is* a conceptual claim. If territory is a defining attribute of the demos, 'the demos' is by definition the population in a given territory. The claim that territory determines the demos is on this version a claim about the *intension* of 'the demos', not about its extension.

The distinction between intension and extension illuminates the relationship between territorial borders and the demos. On the principle that the demos should presumptively include all and only all subject to the state's claim to legitimate authority, the demos is defined in terms of authority. The intension of the demos makes reference to authority, while the extension of the demos is in this view decided by territorial borders. The point is that territorial borders are not part of the definition of the demos. Membership in the demos is not conceptually linked to territory. This is realized by the fact that the all-subjected principle also works to identify the demos in non-territorial associations.

Consider, for example, the members of the demos in the International Chess Federation (FIFE) that organizes more than 200 chess associations active around the world. Given that all and only all the members of FIFE are subjected to the authority claimed by FIFE, the demos of that organization should presumptively include all and only all the members of FIFE following the all-subjected principle. The point is that since the FIFE is not a territorial organization, the *extension* of the demos is not determined by territorial borders. Moreover, the *intension* of the demos in the case of FIFE is the same as the demos in the case of the state; it includes all and only all subjects to de facto authority.

In sum, territorial borders are only contingently relevant in deciding the extension of the demos. Territory is relevant in deciding the demos of the state because the de facto authority of the state is limited by territory. The state is a territorial organization that authoritatively regulates conduct only in the territory it controls. This is, of course, only a contingent factual claim that may at some point prove false. In the case that the authority of the state would extend beyond its borders, the all-subjected principle implies that the demos of the state should also extend beyond its borders.

The difference between the intension of the demos and the extension of the demos is relevant also for rival principles of democratic inclusion. Consider, for example, the principle that only the relevantly affected should be included in the demos. Territorial borders are clearly not part of the intension of the demos in that view. Nevertheless, it is an open question whether territorial borders determine the extension of the demos according to the all-affected principle. In the event that all and only all present in the territory of the state are relevantly affected by the decisions of the state, the extension of the demos following the all-affected principle would be limited by the borders of the state. The point is that the relationship between the territory of the state and demos membership is the same for the all-subjected principle as for the all-affected principle. Neither one of them defines the demos in terms of territory, though both may determine the extension of the demos by reference to territory.

Now, let us return to the charge that the all-subjected principle implicitly condones a nationalist understanding of 'the people'. In order to reply to this concern, we need to know what the demos would be according to the theory of nationalism. But nationalism is not a theory of democracy and consequently does not propose a theory of demos membership at all. Nationalism is foremost a theory of national self-determination that applies to peoples with shared ethnicity, language or other traits that are assumed to define nationality. Nationalism endorses the precept that groups that share a national identity should be afforded collective rights to territory. Ideally, national identity should be congruent with territorially defined political units (Buchanan 2003: 231; Moore 2015: 113).

Now, let us imagine a democratic version of nationalism according to which membership in the demos is conditioned by shared national identity. Democratic nationalism, so conceived, is the theory that the state should be ruled by a demos that includes only the group that shares the same national identity. In the case that the state is populated by a group with a common national identity, the nationalist demos of the state would include all residents on the territory of the state. But that situation is quite unlikely. More probable is that the territory of the state is not exclusively populated by people with a shared a national identity. It is also likely that some people who are not resident in the territory of the state share the relevant identity. In either case, the nationalist demos is neither limited by territorial borders or inclusive of all residents in the territory. Instead, the demos should exclude residents who are not members of the 'nation' and include non-residents who are.[4]

The logic of democratic nationalism is demonstrated by the law on citizenship introduced in the newly created Croatian state in 1991. The new law on citizenship effectively denied citizenship to ethnic minorities in Croatia while simultaneously offering citizenship to Croatians abroad (Pogonyi 2014: 132). Since the equally new election law reserved voting rights only to citizens, the demos that emerged conformed neatly to the nationalist conception – the demos included all members of the relevant ethnic group irrespective of the extent to which they were subject to the authority of the state. As illustrated by the case of Croatia, the nationalist demos is not necessarily congruent with the territorial borders of the state.

By contrast, the demos as defined by the all-subjected principle presumptively includes all present in the territory of the state. Shared national identity is irrelevant to demos membership, in this view. The claim made by critics that the all-subjected principle is nationalist seems categorically mistaken. According to the all-subjected principle, the demos is not linked to national identity but to the claimed authority of the state.

None of this is to deny that nationalism might coincide with the prescriptions of the all-subjected principle. The demos is the same on both principles if the population that occupies a territory subject to control by the state is homogenous in terms of national identity (and if no member of the 'nation' resides outside of that territory). The nationalist principle then implies that the demos should include everyone within the borders of the state because of their shared national identity. The all-subjected principle similarly prescribes that the demos should include everyone within the borders of the state, albeit for different reasons. Though the intension of the all-subjected principle and the nationalist conception are distinct, they can be extensionally equivalent.

The Demos in Border Decisions

In an influential article, Gustaf Arrhenius (2018) has argued that 'the territorial state principle cannot give any guidance in cases where borders of territorial states are in question.' To believe otherwise is to 'falsely assume' that borders can be taken 'as something already fixed and undisputed'. By the 'territorial state principle', Arrhenius does not mean to refer to the all-subjected principle. Yet, the prescriptions of the all-subjected principle do seem to be identical in the context of the current state system. The criticism delivered against the territorial principle is *mutatis mutandis*, valid also for the all-subjected principle.

One curious facet of Arrhenius's criticism is the claim that the territorial principle cannot 'guide' judgments about the proper boundaries of the demos in border decisions. But why can it not? Presumably, the objection is rather that the principle is guiding such judgments on the false assumption that territorial borders are 'already fixed and undisputed'. The charge then is that the territorial principle, and by implication the all-subjected principle, should be rejected because these principles entail a commitment to false premises when applied to border decisions.

Arrhenius follows Whelan (1983) in referring to Northern Ireland as a case that illustrates the defects of the all-subjected principle in relation to border decisions. Part of the long conflict between unionists and nationalists in Ireland is rooted in conflicting perceptions of the legitimacy of the border that separates Northern Ireland from the Republic of Ireland. Given the intensity of the conflict, it would be of great value to resolve it peacefully by a democratic process. But what would the demos of that decision be? The answer offered by the all-subjected principle is that the demos should be delimited by the territorial borders now in force. That is allegedly asking for the impossible as the border between Northern Ireland and the Republic of Ireland is the very object of dispute and not something that can be accepted as a premise for the decision. The conclusion according to Whelan (1983: 24) is that 'democratic theory offers no guidelines on this question'. In fact, the precept that border decisions challenge the cogency of the all-subjected principle has become widely accepted: 'when the boundaries are themselves the issue to be decided, there is no uncontestably 'democratic' way of deciding *who* makes the decision' (Briffault 1992: 802, emphasis added).

Let us begin, however, by paying attention to one critical premise of the above reasoning; the claim that border conflicts *can* be resolved by democratic procedures. The validity of that premise is essential for the argument to bite. It is no good objecting that the all-subjected principle is unable to define the boundaries of the demos in decisions that *cannot* be resolved by democratic procedures. In fact, below I argue that border decisions cannot be resolved by democratic decisions taken by the members of the states involved and that the critique is therefore premised on assumptions that are false.

I will nevertheless provisionally accept that conflicts about state borders *can* be decided by states and their members. Is the critique effective if we presume that this premise is valid? To find out, we must examine the extent to which the all-subjected principle can identify the demos in decisions about borders. The challenge is to identify the demos without 'falsely assuming' that the border is 'fixed and undisputed'. At first glance, a variety of alternatives do in fact appear available.

One possibility is that the demos should include only the people in the territory where people are dissatisfied with the border. I will refer to this view as the 'unilateral demos' solution. This view tends to be the default position in political life as illustrated by increasingly frequent 'independence referendums' that include Quebec (1980), Montenegro (2006), Scotland (2014), the United Kingdom (2016), South Sudan (2011), and the many referendums in New Caledonia (2018, 2020, and 2021).⁵ In all these cases, the decision on the future political status of the territory and its borders included only the residents in the territory that was the object of dispute.⁶

The unilateral demos solution has been attempted also in Northern Ireland. In 1973 a referendum was organized on the future of its border with the Republic of Ireland. The Northern Ireland border poll of that year was a referendum that produced an overwhelming majority in support of remaining part of the United Kingdom. It should be added that the procedural legitimacy of the referendum is contentious due to the boycott initiated by the nationalists and the consequent low turnout rate (Canovan 2005: 111; Tierney 2012: 72).

However, it is unclear that a referendum organized within a single region or state is sufficient to determine the border between adjacent political units. The status of the border between two political units is arguably not for the people in one of them to decide unilaterally. Whereas a democratic decision within a political unit can resolve conflicts in that unit, a democratic decision within a political unit cannot resolve conflicts between the members of *different* political units.

In fact, the all-subjected principle corroborates this concern by offering at least one reason against unilateral referendums on border decisions. A decision that revises the territorial border is a legal decision that depends on the claimed authority of the legal system. The claimed authority of the legal system conditions the validity of border decisions just as it conditions all other decisions by the state. But the notion that the legal system of the state can authorize a decision that regulates the border of the state is incoherent. The reason is that territorial borders are *shared*: A's territorial border with B is also B's territorial border with A. Hence, the notion that A is legally empowered to decide its territorial border with B is inconsistent with B being legally empowered to decide its territorial border with A. It consequently makes little sense to say that the legal status of territorial borders should be decided by a single state and its legal system.

To illustrate this point, consider the 1919 referendum on the Åland Islands on the question of seceding from Finland and becoming a part of Sweden.⁷ The referendum was unilateral in the dual sense that it included only the resident population of Åland and was organized in defiance of the Finnish government. The outcome was overwhelmingly in support of seceding from Finland and to become part of Sweden.

The question, however, is could the resident population of Åland revise the border between Finland and Sweden? Even on the questionable assumption that national borders are regulated by the authority of national legal systems, it appears that the shared border between Sweden and Finland can only be revised with authorization from both legal systems. Unilateral referendums on the territorial borders that separate independent states are therefore fundamentally ineffective. The problem is not that they fail to identify the demos. The problem is rather that they are unable to determine the issue at stake.

More in line with the all-subjected principle is the idea that border decisions should be made *jointly* by the residents of territories with shared borders. Though neither residents of A nor B can unilaterally determine the legal status of their shared border, A and B *can* determine the legal status of their shared border. If the border is regulated by the legal system of both A and B, the members of these units are both subjected to decisions to revise the border. Hence, members of A and B should together form the demos for the decision that determines the status of their shared border.

Now, a joint decision by the members of two territorial units can in principle be organized in two separate ways. Either the joint decision is effectuated through a *single* decision including the members of A and B. Or the joint decision is effectuated by *separate* decisions. Both alternatives do seem consistent with the all-subjected principle.

Of course, the notion of a joint decision on territorial borders is likely to be politically controversial. Consider for example the independence referendums that were organized in the process of de-colonialization following the Second World War. Numerous referendums on independence from the colonial empire were organized in Asia and Africa, including for example one in Cambodia in 1945 and another in Malta in 1962.[8] Now, it is surely difficult to imagine that the peoples of either Cambodia or Malta would have also accepted the inclusion in the demos of French and British citizens residents in the metropolitan country. On the one hand, political controversy is not necessarily a reason to conclude that a proposal lacks normative justification. On the other hand, the very rationale for a joint referendum is missing in the case where successful secession would not result in a shared border. In fact, neither Malta nor Cambodia would share a border with their past colonial metropoles following their independence. The general point is that the fact that A wants to secede from B does not imply that A will eventually share a border with B. The joint model for the democratic resolution of border conflicts appears more plausible in cases where the border under dispute is to be shared in the future.

Let us therefore return to the running example of Northern Ireland. A joint single decision to resolve the border conflict in that context would necessitate a referendum including the members of both territories. However, as Northern Ireland is a part of the United Kingdom, the implication is that all citizens of the Republic and the UK should participate in a single democratic decision about the border. Though that proposal appears consistent with the all-subjected principle, it runs into another problem. As a matter of fact, elections are legally effective only if authorized by the legal system. Hence, a referendum in the UK can only be authorized by the laws of the British legal system and a referendum in the Republic can only be authorized by the legal system of the Republic. But a joint referendum does not seem reconcilable with the exclusive authority claimed by the two legal systems involved. Thus, there can be no joint single referendum between independent states.

The notion of a joint single decision is accordingly workable only in intrastate border disputes. Yet, intrastate borders are rarely resolved by joint single decisions and for good reasons (Reinikainen 2022: 60f.). The usual procedure followed in the case of a geographically concentrated part of the population that seeks independence is to include only the members of the potentially seceding unit in the demos. Including both the members of the secessionist unit and the members of the larger unit in the demos can be expected to disadvantage secessionist movements. Consider for example the 2006 referendum in Montenegro on independence from Serbia or the 1995 referendum in Quebec on independence from Canada. In the event that these referendums would have included all the members of Serbia and Canada respectively, it is unlikely that they would have had any chance of success.

A rare case of a joint single decision on territorial borders is the 1991 referendum in the Soviet Union. The question put forward to the voters was whether the Union should be reformed and allow for the enhanced independence of its constituent republics. In practice, few if any of the Soviet republics (except Russia) were interested in enhanced independence as they sought complete sovereign statehood. As a result, they either declined to participate or organized separate referendums on sovereign independence that made the original referendum irrelevant (Tierney 2012: 68).

This brings us to the second option: joint dual decisions, as the democratic way for the resolution of border conflicts. This alternative is rare but not unheard of. Separate referendums were organized in Schleswig and Denmark in 1920 for the purpose of determining the shared territorial border. The residents in Schleswig took to the polls to decide whether they wanted to be part of either Germany or Denmark. Later the same year Denmark held a referendum on the constitutional changes necessary to integrate what they termed 'Southern Jutland' with the Kingdom. In effect, the peoples on both sides participated in deciding their shared border.

A similar procedure can be imagined in the border dispute between the Republic of Ireland and Northern Ireland. The governments in both units could agree to resolve the issue by separate referendums. Indeed, the model was employed following the 1998 Belfast agreement (the Good Friday agreement). Separate referendums were held on May 22 that year to ratify the agreement. The demos in each referendum conformed, more or less, with the principle that all and only all subject to the legal system in the relevant territory should be allowed to participate.[9]

As is clear from these examples, and contrary to the claims made by the critics of the all-subjected principle, a territorially defined demos *can* make a democratic decision on borders without 'falsely assuming' that the border is 'something already fixed'. There is no contradiction involved in deciding territorial borders by democratic decisions while at the same time relying on territorial borders in identifying the demos.

A final challenge is the argument by José Martí (2021) that the all-subjected principle is *indeterminate* in border decisions. Marti invokes the conflict between Spain and Catalonia to illustrate this point. As became clear in the dramatic events that unfolded in 2016, when the regional government unilaterally organized a referendum on independence, the conflict ultimately concerned the territorial integrity of the state of Spain.

Following the all-subjected principle, it would seem that all Spanish citizens should have had the opportunity to participate in the referendum. After all, the dispute concerned the integrity of the state of Spain. All subject to the claimed authority of the Spanish state would be subject to a decision that either granted independence to Catalonia or not. However, the point stressed by Martí (2021) is that the creation of a new Catalonian state would also have legal consequences for other European countries. It would change the composition of the EU and the European political system. There is consequently a case to be made for the claim that all members of the European Union would be subject to the decision. For Marti, this observation is sufficient to conclude that the all-subjected principle is 'ambiguous' and therefore unsuitable as a principle for democratic inclusion (Martí 2021).

Though Marti is right to stress that the all-subjected principle is 'ambiguous' in the case of border decisions, he is mistaken in assuming that the principle is to blame. The reason is, instead, that the legal status of territorial borders cannot be determined by decisions taken by individual states; the legal status of international borders depends on the authority of international law.[10] If the legal status of international borders depends on international law, national legal systems are not empowered to establish international borders. Consequently, the problem is not that border decisions reveal any inherent weakness of the all-subjected principle, but that states do not have the authority to determine international borders. There can be no democratic procedure at the level of the state that decides the territorial borders between states.[11]

This conclusion applies to independence referendums generally, whether they are unilateral, jointly singular, or jointly separate decisions. A referendum on the territorial border between two or more states is not authorized to determine the status of state borders. Possibly the clearest example of the failure of a democratic process to effectuate a border decision is the referendum called in Crimea in 2014 on its secession from Ukraine and incorporation into the Russian Federation. Though the referendum produced overwhelming support in favor of the secession of Crimea from Ukraine, the international community did not recognize the validity of either the referendum or its results.[12] As a result, the referendum failed to decide the border between Russia and Ukraine.

The conclusion is also illustrated by the (illegal) referendum in the Åland islands in 1919. The referendum failed to achieve the secession of Åland from Finland, not just because the government in Helsinki opposed the solution, but because the political system in Åland lacked the authority to determine its own borders. Indeed, according to the Treaty of Versailles the future of the Åland islands was for the League of Nations to decide, not for the peoples of Åland, nor for the peoples of neighboring states to decide (Åkermark 2009). The referendum allowed the people to *speak*, it did not allow the people to *decide*. It served the purpose of communicating a political opinion in the hope that the bodies with the authority to decide would take it into account.

At other times, what at first glance appears to be a referendum on state borders turns out to be something else. The 1980 referendum in Quebec was not arranged for the purpose of deciding the territorial border between Quebec and Canada. The question resolved by the referendum was whether the provincial government should be granted the political mandate to negotiate for sovereign independence or not.

None of this is to deny that independence referendums sometimes do have tangible legal consequences. Norway's referendum in 1905 on the dissolution of the union with Sweden gave legal effect to the divorce as it confirmed the condition for independence decided by the Swedish government. But the legal fact established by the referendum was, in the end, of political significance only. The sovereign status of Norway in international law had to await recognition by the international community. In a similar vein, the referendums in both New Caledonia and South Sudan were decisive on the basis of antecedent agreements by the relevant governments. The same applies to the Scottish independence referendum in 2014 as the vote was recognized as binding through prior agreement between the regional government and the UK government.[13] The referendum in Schleswig-Holstein in 1920 is a special case as the prior legal agreement had been decided by the international community. The vote of the people was decisive due to the stipulations of the Treaty of Versailles signed by the Western Allies and Germany in 1919 (Laponce 2004).[14]

Independence referendums only have legal significance on the basis of prior agreements and do not establish the legal status of international borders. At best, they contribute to the political legitimacy of the winning alternative. In conflicts about territorial independence, a referendum at times serves as a 'trump card' that effectively eliminates other alternatives from the political agenda. (Tierney 2012: 62). It is, therefore, a mistake to assert that border decisions represent a challenge to the all-subjected principle or to any other principle of democratic inclusion. The mistake is due to the false assumption that states *can* make border decisions. The legal status of territorial borders between states is determined by international law and not by domestic legal decisions, whether effectuated by democratic procedures or not.

Notes

1. The coercion imposed by border regimes does not only take place at the border. It extends beyond it when the state engages in extraterritorial enforcement of migration law, through carrier restrictions imposed on airlines, boardings of vessels carrying migrants in international waters, and asylum centers in foreign countries. See Moreono-Lax (2017) for a particularly helpful overview. The extraterritorial enforcement of migration law does represent a challenge to the territorial scope of the all-subjected principle that I intend to address in future work.
2. Incidentally, Abizadeh (2021: 609) now denies that the laws of the state apply beyond the territory of the state for reasons that are criticized in chapter five above.
3. For a helpful discussion on intension and extension in linguistic theory, see Alston (2012).
4. A rare defence of this view is found in Östbring (2019).
5. See Qvortrup (2014) for a detailed overview of independence referendums in the world since 1860.
6. In the case of New Caledonia, not all residents in the territory were entitled to participate as the right to vote was limited to residents with more than ten years of domicile on the islands. The special rule was defended by highlighting the importance of securing sufficient influence for the indigenous population and was accepted by the European Court of Human Rights in *Py v. France* (2005).

7 The referendum in Åland was technically illegal as it was not authorized by the government in Helsinki. The same applies to a few other independence referendums, including the 2016 referendum in Catalonia and the 1991 referendums in Krajina and Kosovo. For discussion of de facto referendums of independence, see López and Sanjaume-Calvet (2020).
8 The referendum as a method for independence was most extensively used in the decolonization process when France introduced a new constitution in 1958. All members of the French Union (all colonial dependencies) were called to confirm the constitution in eighteen separate referendums. In practice, these referendums turned into opportunities for independence as the rejection of the new constitution would have precluded membership in the French Union. Perhaps surprisingly, only the voters of Guinea voted against the constitution and thus opted for independence.
9 The all-subjected principle does seem to justify the inclusion also of the residents in the UK as they are equally subjected to the agreement. Yet, the British government was, arguably, permitted to delegate the power to determine a decision binding for the UK to the population in Northern Ireland alone based on the historical fact that Northern Ireland is a less integrated part of the UK than either Wales or Scotland. On this point, see Rose (1982: 129).
10 Borders between sovereign states are legal when they are recognized by the international community based on criteria of effective government control over population and territory. It remains debatable whether recognition of state borders is a requirement for the existence of state borders, or if recognition of state borders is required when and because states satisfy the criteria for recognition (Fabry 2010).
11 A similar argument about the difficulties facing the all-subjected principle can be made concerning decisions about administrative borders *within* the state. Local and regional borders are not regulated by either local or regional authorities. Ultimately, the authority to decide sub-national territorial borders belongs to the supreme legal body of that system, though the lawmaker, the courts, or the constitution are of course free to delegate that power to subordinate bodies. See Briffault (1992) for an illuminating analysis.
12 See the opinion expressed in the report by the Venice Commission (European Commission for Democracy through Law) Opinion 762, 2014, and the resolution adopted by the UN General Assembly A/RES/68/262.
13 It is of course a possibility that democratic decisions can be made on the norms of international law – including the norms that regulate state borders (Agné 2006; Jurkevics 2019). That would require a global state, however.
14 As recounted by Laponce (2004) the referendum in Schleswig Holstein is a particularly interesting case of demos composition as it involved two separate referendums, one in Schleswig, the other in Holstein. Moreover, in order to fine-tune the borders to the preferences of the voters, the referendum in Holstein was organized in smaller districts effectively allowing each separate district to decide for itself.

8
DOES IT MATTER THAT STATE BORDERS ARE ARBITRARY?

As elegantly summarized by Carmen Pavel, the territorial borders between states are the result of 'the shifting winds of historical accident, the arbitrary whim of powerful nations, and wars of conquest and colonialism' (Pavel 2018). Indeed, little knowledge from the history books is needed to corroborate this view. The straight-lined borders that now divide the African continent were largely drawn on maps by leaders in the capitals of colonial powers. Though the less sharp-lined borders between European nations are in some cases also the result of map-drawing exercises in the capitals of alien powers, many of them are products of failed and sometimes successful attempts at territorial aggrandizement by the rulers themselves.[1] Whatever the political origins of state borders are, the conclusion is that they are the enduring and ultimately arbitrary marks of past exercises of 'naked power' (Bartelson 2004: 55; also, Näsström 2007 and Kaltwasser 2014).[2]

The statement that state borders are 'arbitrary' is regularly considered a powerful objection to the notion that democratic rights should be determined by territorial borders. According to Antoinette Scherz, the all-subjected principle is problematic as it entails that the boundaries of the demos should depend on territorial borders that are 'normatively arbitrary and often in question as they are defined through war and power struggles in the course of history' (Scherz 2013). The arbitrariness of state borders is regarded as a challenge to the all-subjected principle.

But what, more precisely, is wrong with a demos that is delimited by arbitrary borders? One way to understand the intuition driving the perception that democratic peoples should not depend on state borders is that arbitrary exercises of public power are *pro tanto* wrongful. The rules that decide membership in the demos are exercises of public power. Hence, if membership in the demos is decided by territorial borders that are ultimately arbitrary, the implication is that the demos

DOI: 10.4324/9781003359807-8

is determined by arbitrary exercises of public power. If arbitrary exercises of public power are wrongful, demos membership should not depend on arbitrary state borders.

Now, the force of this argument is sensitive to the meaning of 'arbitrary'. In fact, this term is notoriously ambiguous; making the analogy to arbitrary exercises of public power somewhat vulnerable (Wright 2010; cf. Lovett 2012). Only if the term is defined more carefully can we hope to grasp the power of the above objection. In the following, three versions of the argument are distinguished.

One sense in which state borders may be arbitrary is that they are 'contingent'. A state of affairs that is 'contingent' could have been different. It seems obvious that current geographical borders could have been different. Contemporary state borders were not destined to be drawn where they currently are; existing state borders are just one possibility among many other possible worlds. The borders of the state are thus arbitrary because they are contingent.

Another sense in which state borders may be considered arbitrary is that they are *morally* arbitrary. What is morally arbitrary, should not be considered relevant to moral conclusions. The tenet that state borders are morally arbitrary consequently entails that we should not attach moral significance to the territorial borders of the state. Clearly, this is a very distinct understanding of 'arbitrary' compared to that of contingency. Claims to the effect that some feature of the world is morality arbitrary does not entail that it is contingent. Equally, it is not clear that all contingencies are necessarily morally arbitrary.

The third understanding of 'arbitrariness' in the context of state borders is that they conflict with justified normative principles. 'Arbitrary' in this sense implies 'unjustified'. The claim that state borders are arbitrary accordingly means that they should either be revised or abolished.

Once again it is important to observe that the third sense of arbitrariness is analytically distinct both from the claim that state borders are contingent and from the claim that state borders are morally arbitrary. It is perfectly conceivable that some state of affairs is contingent while not being unjustified, and vice versa. Also, the claim that some fact is morally arbitrary does not entail that it is unjustified. The fact that the weather is awful today may be morally arbitrary in the sense that it does not affect our moral rights and obligations. Obviously however, the fact that the weather carries no moral implications does not entail that the weather is 'unjustified'.

Though there are certainly additional usages of 'arbitrary', the three notions briefly introduced here are sufficient for present purposes. The overall question is whether the all-subjected principle can withstand the challenge that state borders are arbitrary in any of these senses. The argument defended is that the arbitrariness of state borders neither contradicts nor undermines the all-subjected principle. The argument is developed in the following five sections. The first two focus on the argument that state borders are arbitrary in the sense of being contingent. The third section moves on to consider the claim that state borders are morally arbitrary. The fourth and fifth sections, finally, engage with various versions of the claim that state borders are arbitrary in the sense of being morally unjustified.

Contingent Borders

In what sense are state borders 'contingent' and how does it undermine the claim that the demos should be limited by state borders? Arguably the most well-known account of contingency is that introduced by Stephen Jay Gould in the context of the evolution of animal species. Gould claimed that the species that are present on earth today would be radically different if the process of evolution were to be replayed (Gould 1994). Evolutionary processes are not replicable because they are extremely sensitive to small changes in initial conditions. Even from roughly similar starting points, the outcome is bound to be radically different (Turner and Havstad 2019). The consequent account of contingency is historical. Whether the subject matter is the evolution of the species, or the history of state formation, the claim that long chains of causally interconnected events are contingent means to imply that minor divergences accumulate over time and produce surprising and unpredictable results (Ben-Menahem 1997).

A different notion of 'contingency' is present in the following argument by political theorist Adrian Little. According to Little, state borders are 'highly contingent entities undergoing processes of transformation' that are for this reason deprived of 'normative certainty'. Contingency is said to undermine the moral and political status of territorial borders (Little 2015: 444). Now, this statement is not just a claim about historical explanation. Rather, it echoes a particular theory about the nature of the world where 'contingency' is associated with a commitment to an 'anti-foundationalist metaphysics of knowledge'. The implicit theory that informs attributions of contingency to features of the world is 'anti-necessitarian' in the sense that it rejects determinism and causal explanation (Joas 2004). The assertion that territorial states are 'contingent' is meant to convey the claim that territorial states are arbitrary entities due to the indeterminate nature of the world.[3] The claim is not that outcomes are sensitive to initial conditions, but that they are not determined at all.

There are, consequently, two conceptions of contingency at play: the historical and what can be termed the 'metaphysical' idea.[4] Though both are adverse to the ideal of predictability in the social and natural sciences, only the latter eschews the notion of causal explanation altogether.

It is not always apparent if the claim that borders are 'contingent' is meant to convey a metaphysical claim or if the claim is just that they are hard to predict. Consider, for example, Bernard Yack's argument that 'contingencies of history' are contrary to the 'rhetoric of popular sovereignty'. Yack's point is that contingent state borders abjure the precept that all public power belongs to the 'the people'. In so far as state borders are contingent, the ideal of popular sovereign control is futile. Only if the people take back control of territorial borders can the people escape domination by the contingencies of history (Yack 2001: 528f.). It is not clear, though, whether this argument is premised on contingency in the historical or metaphysical sense.

Maybe the distinction is not very important for our purposes, however. Few believe that state borders can be predicted. In a more mundane sense, the notion that state borders are contingent can be translated into the claim that they 'could have been different' (Schedler 2007).

So, what about the thesis that contingency undermines the normative status of state borders? One reading of this claim is that the perception that borders are mere historical constructs is fuelling political conflict. The idea is that territorial borders are contested *because* they are formed out of 'contingent societal processes' (Paasi 2009: 216). The contingent nature of state borders encourages the desire to either remake or abolish them by depriving the state of a secure normative foundation.

But the tenet that state borders are disputed is scarcely relevant to the normative status of territorial borders. The fact that elements of the state are contested does not imply that they lack normative justification. Furthermore, the validity of the claim that state borders are contingent is not dependent on the claim that they are subject to political conflict. If borders are contingent, they are contingent even if not disputed.

The decisive question is if there is a valid argument against the all-subjected principle that is premised on the claim that state borders are contingent? Does the fact that state borders 'could have been different' constitute a reason to reject the claim that the scope of the demos should depend on the territorial borders of the state?

Now, contingency is a reason to reject the all-subjected principle *if* that principle depends on the assumption that state borders could *not* be different. Yet, the principle does not depend on that assumption. The all-subjected principle holds that membership in the demos is decided by the extent of subjection to the claimed authority of the state. The scope of the state's claim to authority depends on facts of the world, irrespective of how they are explained and, indeed, irrespective of the extent to which the state and its territorial borders can be explained at all. The tenet that subjects of de facto authority should be included in the demos is not conditioned by any specific explanation of territorial borders. Hence, no contradiction is involved in asserting both that states, their borders, and the peoples delimited by them, 'could have been different' *and* that the subjects of the claimed authority of the state should presumptively be included in the demos.

Contingent Peoples

Critics of the all-subjected principle might conclude that the above analysis is missing the point intended by the argument from contingency. A restatement of the argument is that contingency is shaping the people, not just territorial borders. The suggestion that state borders 'could have been different' constitutes an objection against the all-subjected principle because it implies that the *peoples* delimited by territorial borders are also contingent. In the case that borders are just accidents of history, so are the collectives we call 'peoples'. The gist of that argument is well summarized by Rainer Bauböck:

In other words, there is no point arguing for the right of individuals to be included in a particular demos if the legitimacy of that demos itself is either blindly accepted as a contingent result of historical processes or fundamentally rejected based on inclusion claims that are per se incompatible with drawing legitimate political boundaries.

(Bauböck 2018a)

According to the view described by Bauböck, the contingency of state borders impresses on the demos as it renders the demos a product of arbitrary 'historical processes'. The point can be illustrated by the simple observation that the composition of the electorate would be different if the borders of the state were different. Consider a person who is now subjected to the state of Sweden (Paul) and another person who is now subjected to the state of Norway (Anne). The all-subjected principle requires that Paul should be able to vote in Sweden and that Anne should be allowed to vote in Norway. Yet, this pattern of voting rights is evidently contingent. It is contingent because the borders that decide the outer limits of the state's claim to legitimate authority – and thus where Anne and Paul should be able to vote – could have been different. The very fact that Paul is a subject of the Swedish state, and that Anne is a subject of the Norwegian state is a contingent result of historical events. Hence, the presumption that Paul should be entitled to vote in Sweden and that Anne should be entitled to vote in Norway are contingent accidents of history.

While it appears inevitable that the demos is contingent in that sense, this observation does not inevitably amount to an objection against the all-subjected principle. Why is there 'no point' in arguing for a right to democratic inclusion if the demos is 'a contingent result of historical processes'?

To fully appreciate the argument, it is necessary to uncover its basic normative premises. The first is that peoples are not 'legitimate' if shaped by arbitrary historical forces. Ochoa Espejo makes this point clear in the argument that democratic legitimacy is jeopardized by 'relying on a people that is solely defined by chance' (Ochoa Espejo 2011: 178). The additional steps of the argument can be summarized as follows:

1. The all-subjected principle takes pre-existing territorial borders as a given.
2. Peoples who are constituted by pre-existing territorial borders are contingent.
3. Hence, the demos as identified by the all-subjected principle is not legitimate.

Arguably, the conclusion that the all-subjected principle does not provide for the 'legitimacy of the people' is a valid inference from the premises. State borders are contingent and a demos as identified by the all-subjected principle is therefore contingent. Given that peoples that are contingent are not legitimate, it follows that the demos as identified by the all-subjected principle is not legitimate

We should bear in mind, however, that the all-subjected principle is not designed to secure that peoples are legitimate bodyies in the sense assumed as necessary by the argument. The all-subjected principle is an account of democratic inclusion, not an account of the legitimacy of the people. The relevant question then is not if the argument is valid but if the premises are plausible and worth taking seriously. Only if the premises are salient to the democratic ideal does the argument spell trouble for the all-subjected principle.

The essential premise of the argument is that a democratic people need to be legitimate and are legitimate only if they escape contingency. That claim is worth taking seriously only if escaping contingency is possible. If lack of legitimacy is wrong, and if something is wrong only if avoidable, it follows that it is wrong for a people not to be legitimate only if it is possible for the people to be legitimate. So how could the people be legitimate and avoid the debilitating consequences of contingency?

The solution, according to critics, is found in the redeeming power of self-constitution. The idea is that the deficit in legitimacy is remedied only by 'popular access to the constitution of the people' (Näsström 2007: 646). A people with access to a process of 'self-constitution' avoid contingency as they avoid being determined by external forces (Lindahl 2007). The question now is whether the ideal of the self-constituting people is viable.

Consider, once again, Paul in Sweden and Anne in Norway. Evidently, not just the location of the state border determines where they should be entitled to vote. If Paul had been born in Oslo instead of in Stockholm, Paul would have been entitled to vote in a different political unit. In other words, not just borders but also places of birth are contingent determinants of the demos. However, the fact that birthplace is contingent indicates that 'contingency' is at work at several levels. The point is that if Paul had been born in Oslo, Paul would not have been the same 'Paul' as if he had been born in Stockholm. A person is an individual with a particular identity and that identity is largely determined by the person's social and biological circumstances.[5] The person is therefore 'contingent' in the sense that any person 'could have been different'. Birthplace is among the circumstances that shape the identity of the person and that determine the identity of the members of the demos. That observation may seem trivial and irrelevant. But though it *is* trivial it is *not* irrelevant to the argument under consideration. The fact that the identity of the person is contingent does have implications for the possibility of a non-contingent demos.

At this point, we might want to consider that the demos is a collective entity, not an individual person. The collective identity of the demos is arguably unaffected by the contingency of its individual members (Page 1999: 63). Yet, even if this point is accepted, the main point remains effective. The proposed remedy of contingency is that the demos is self-constituted. A 'self-constituting' demos makes its collective identity a function of its individual members. But, if the identities of individual members are contingent, the decisions taken by individual members must also be contingent. While the process of self-constitution seeks to eliminate the contingency of the demos, it inadvertently intensifies the consequences of the contingency of its individual members. The result is that the collective unit of the demos is contingent *because* it is self-constituted. Hence, the argument designed to eliminate contingency from the demos by a process of self-constitution turns out to be self-defeating.

Self-constitution is no remedy for contingency, and it is hard to imagine what could be. The members of the demos are unavoidably contingent as the identity of each person who is a member of the demos is shaped by factors beyond individual and collective control. The self-constituting demos is no panacea for the contingency of the people in a democracy. The ideal of a non-contingent demos is beyond reach. Ultimately, there is no reason to worry about the fact that the demos, as identified by the all-subjected principle, is contingent.[6]

Moral Arbitrariness

Although every person is born in a territory controlled by a state, no-one deserves to be born in any particular territory. From the widely accepted principle that no-one is to be blamed or praised for features that one does not deserve, it follows that no person is to be either praised or blamed for one's place of birth. In that respect territorial borders are morally arbitrary.

At the same time, birthplace is highly consequential for future well-being, whether measured in terms of life-expectancy, happiness, or quality of life. Simon Caney alludes to this reasoning in making the argument that it is 'highly perverse' that being born on one side of the border rather than another 'should affect what people are entitled to' (Caney 2008: 505). Borders are 'morally arbitrary' in the sense that they undeservedly determine a person's present and future well-being.

This is particularly clear in the case of citizenship. Though few legal systems recognize the principle of *jus solis*, according to which the birthplace determines citizenship, there is a strong correlation between being born in the territory of the state and the right to citizenship of that state. As already observed, citizenship status is at present a necessary precondition for the right to political participation in virtually every democratic state. It consequently follows that one particular fact (birthplace), that is morally arbitrary, is deciding where people are entitled to exercise the rights to political participation or, indeed, if they enjoy any such rights at all. As influentially argued by Aylet Shachar, the existing territorial order effectively translates a 'morally arbitrary circumstance, that none of us can control (birth)' into 'solid democratic grounds for exclusion' (Shachar 2009: 135).

The upshot of Shachar's argument is that citizenship and political rights in territorially defined communities is morally suspect due to the morally arbitrariness of places of birth and the borders that separate them. Yet, the arbitrary nature of birthplace should not be conflated with the potential arbitrary nature of state borders. The notion that citizenship status is arbitrary due to the fact that state borders are morally arbitrary is distinct from the notion that citizenship status is arbitrary due to the fact that birthplace is morally arbitrary. This we can recognize from the fact that birthplace would remain morally arbitrary even if state borders were *not* morally arbitrary. There are, in other words, two versions of the thesis that citizenship and associated political rights are morally arbitrary: the first relies on the alleged moral arbitrariness of birthplace; the second relies on the alleged moral arbitrariness of state borders.

Now, how do any of these versions of the argument from moral arbitrariness represent an objection to the all-subjected principle? As we already know, the all-subjected principle implies that the extension of the demos depends on the territorial borders of the state. But if state borders are morally arbitrary, it seems that the all-subjected principle is bound to reproduce morally arbitrary patterns of democratic inclusion. The analogous objection to the all-subjected principle can be made on the basis of the claim that birthplace is morally arbitrary. Since a person's place of birth is morally arbitrary, the all-subjected principle is bound to reproduce morally arbitrary patterns of democratic inclusion.

At this point we should pause to consider the normative implications of the claim that an event or state of affairs is 'morally arbitrary'. There are at least two distinct ways to understand it. The first is that what is morally arbitrary should not ground attributions of moral blame (or praise). The second is that what is morally arbitrary should not ground any moral conclusion at all. In what follows, I examine each in turn.

On the first account, the claim that state borders and birthplace are morally arbitrary implies that they are not grounds for either blame or praise. It is quite obvious, however, that considerations that are not grounds for blame or praise can still be pertinent to moral conclusions. The proposition that an attribute is undeserved does not entail that it is irrelevant to any moral claims that apply to a person. Clearly, birthplace and state borders are undeserved features of the world. It does not follow from this observation that either birthplace or state borders are morally irrelevant, however.

To illustrate this point in a different context, consider the case of a physical or mental disability acquired by birth. It is uncontroversial that a disability acquired by birth is morally arbitrary in the sense that it is undeserved. Individuals born with disabilities do not deserve them and should not be blamed for their condition. But the fact that their condition is morally arbitrary does not preclude counting the disability as morally relevant for them (Miller 2009: 296).

The analogous point applies to state borders as well as to birthplace. Arguably, both are morally arbitrary in the sense that people do not deserve either that the border is drawn in one particular geographical location or that they are born in a particular place. Yet, since state borders and birthplace are of immense importance to future well-being, it may still be true that they are normatively salient to judgments about the rights and duties of the person (Blake 2005: 227).

Now, consider the second understanding of moral arbitrariness; the idea that what is morally arbitrary is not grounds for moral claims. The idea is that no significance should be attached to attributes that are morally arbitrary; they should be excluded from the moral equation. The first thing to notice about this view is that it does not depend on the assumption that the morally arbitrary attribute is underserved. Consider the color of a person's eyes, for example. It is plausible to assume that eye color is morally arbitrary in the sense of not being relevant to judgments about a person's political rights and duties. That is true even if the color of a person's eyes is *not* morally arbitrary in the sense of being undeserved. Perhaps you changed the color of your eyes by cosmetic surgery or perhaps you changed it by wearing colored lenses. In that event, you *can* be credited or blamed for the color of your eyes. But even if individuals 'deserve' their eye color, that feature of the individuals remains irrelevant to judgments about their political rights and duties. Thus, the claim that some attribute is morally irrelevant in the sense that it should not be allowed to determine moral judgments does not depend on the attribute being either deserved or undeserved.

It is doubtful, however, if any feature is morally arbitrary in the strong sense that it *never* grounds moral claims. After all, even eye color may be morally relevant in some situations. For example, consider a statement made in a court of law where eye color is referred to by a witness called to confirm the identity of the person prosecuted for a crime. In that context, eye color is arguably morally relevant to the extent that it proves pertinent to the judgment of the court. Hence, even though eye color is often morally irrelevant, it does not follow that it must always be.

The more plausible view is that the moral arbitrariness of a particular attribute implies that it is morally irrelevant to *some* normative claims (Armstrong 2010: 325). The contention that X is morally arbitrary implies that X must not be taken into consideration ('is impermissible') in reasoning about what is morally required or valuable in *some* but not all circumstances (Nine 2008: 262). The moral arbitrariness of an attribute is in that view always 'local'. The claim that an attribute is morally arbitrary intends to screen the attribute out from some, but not necessarily all, moral judgments.

This modified account of moral arbitrariness helps make sense of the claim that a disability acquired by birth is morally arbitrary. The fact that individuals' disabilities are morally arbitrary, because they could have done nothing to avoid them, rules out as impermissible some normative claims grounded in the fact of their disabilities. This is of course fully consistent with the claim that their disabilities are morally relevant to other claims. The claim that an attribute is morally arbitrary should be understood as providing a reason for ignoring that attribute in the justification of *some* normative claims. That is fully consistent with accepting the attribute as providing a reason that is relevant to the justification of *other* normative claims.

The claim that state borders are morally arbitrary in this second sense should accordingly be understood to mean that state borders are irrelevant for some but not necessarily all normative claims. Consequently, reasons to submit that either state borders or birthplace are morally arbitrary is not reason to conclude that either state borders or birthplace could not justify democratic rights. It remains an open question, then, whether it would be morally wrong to delimit democratic rights only to people born in particular places or to the residents of particular state territories.

Historical Injustice

The claim that state borders are morally arbitrary can be predicated on the fact that they were formed through a historically wrongful process. The territories now controlled by states around the world, are outcomes of past aggressions and wars;

they are products of 'a history of accident, force, and fraud' (Yack 2001: 523). The point is that territorial borders depend on morally wrongful actions in the past. The borders of the state are sites of historical injustice.

This claim allegedly has implications for the shape of the demos. If the borders of the state are sites of historical injustice, we should hesitate to conclude that they should decide the boundaries of the demos. The people entitled to participate and vote in democratic states should not be delimited by features of the present world that are plainly unjust.

The scope of this argument may have to be moderated, however. Though history teaches us that the formation of the present state-system is often the result of war, conquest, and colonialization, it does not necessarily follow that all territorial borders are tainted by historical wrongs. In some cases, the territorial border may be the result of reasonable and legitimate processes of reciprocal adjustment to geography, kinship, and economic interests. This might for example be true for the territorial borders of some island states. In the case that the borders of the island state coincide with its geographical shape and emerged by a spontaneous process of social interaction with other territories, there is at least pro tanto reason to believe that no injustice was involved in its creation.[7]

In sum, the argument that territorial borders are illegitimate because they are based on historical injustices does not automatically apply to all states and should therefore not lead us to conclude that state borders must never influence the boundaries of the demos.

Furthermore, we shall distinguish between two versions of the argument that historical injustice renders the borders of the state illegitimate. In the *first* version, state borders are illegitimate if they are the product of morally wrongful events or actions. Hence, the fact that territorial borders are the result of historical injustice is *sufficient* to conclude that they are illegitimate. Not so in the *second* version of the argument. In that view, state borders are illegitimate only if it is true *both* that they are products of moral wrongs in the past *and* that states or peoples today have duties to remedy these wrongs. The question then is whether historical injustice is sufficient reason to conclude that territorial borders are illegitimate. Consider the following way to structure the argument that the boundaries of the demos should not depend on the territory of the state.

i. The boundaries of the demos must depend on legitimate territorial claims.
ii. Territorial claims are illegitimate if historically unjust.
iii. State borders are territorial claims subject to historical injustice and are therefore illegitimate.
iv. Hence, the boundaries of the demos should not depend on state borders

I take it that the argument is valid in the sense that the conclusion follows from the premises. This is of course neither to accept that the conclusion applies to all states, nor even that the premises are valid. Indeed, there is reason to question the second premise, according to which the territorial claims of the state are necessarily illegitimate if historically unjust.

One reason to question this premise is that historical wrongs are not always sufficient to undermine normative entitlements in other contexts. Consider John who purchases an artefact in a public auction that he later learns was stolen a long time ago from an indigenous community. Though John believes he is entitled to the artefact, as he bought the object in good faith, it is perfectly possible that his claim to legitimate ownership is not valid after all. John's claim to ownership is potentially trumped by the legitimate claims of either the descendants of the original owners, the present-day indigenous community, or by public institutions tasked with the preservation of the common heritage. Yet, it seems plausible that John's claim to ownership in the artefact remains valid in so far as no countervailing and legitimate claim exist. The point is that legitimate ownership is not undermined *merely* by the fact that the artefact was originally stolen. Hence, historical injustice is not sufficient to establish that claims made today are invalid.

If this objection is sound, it follows that the territorial claims made by states today are not necessarily nullified by historical injustice. The observation that a territorial border was created by morally wrongful actions in the past is not sufficient to justify the claim that the state does not have legitimate territorial rights. There is consequently no reason to believe that the boundaries of the demos must not depend on state borders just because they are historically unjust.

However, historical injustice remains pertinent if there are moral duties to remedy past wrongs. In other words, wrongs committed in the past undermine territorial claims only if they are grounds for moral duties. The objection against the all-subjected principle is consequently that it is impermissible to delimit the demos by territorial borders that for reasons of historical injustice are sources of moral duties. As this objection depends on the existence of moral duties that are based on wrongs committed in the past, the first question is to establish that such duties do in fact exist.

That they do is not self-evident. International law typically rejects as invalid territorial claims that are based on historical grievances. Following the principle of *uti possidetis* ('as you possess') there is a presumption in favor of the legitimacy of existing borders of internationally recognized states. The principle favors the status quo and makes it difficult to gain credence for political efforts to revise state borders based on historical injustice or deprivation (Shaw 1996; cf. Elden 2006). The principle that we should remedy historical injustices caused in the formation of state borders is therefore controversial.

On the other hand, the fact that principles of international law tend to ignore historical grievances is no reason to conclude that they should be ignored. There might be reason to believe that just acquisition and moral rights to occupancy should play a larger role in our thinking of state borders and rights to territory than is currently the case (Moore 2015). Historical injustice may be reason to conclude that the principles of international law are sometimes morally deficient, and that states and peoples do have moral duties to revise existing territorial borders.

Specifically, unjust territorial conquests in the past can be grounds for 'rectificatory' duties towards victims.[8] Duties to rectify past wrongs in the creation of territorial borders are typically duties of restitution such that the status quo ex ante is restored. Rectificatory duties accordingly imply duties to revise territorial borders, possibly including the duty to create new independent states or self-governing territories.

Rectificatory duties are not necessarily duties of restitution, however. Compensation is an alternative for the rectification of the victim. In cases of theft, compensation is required when returning the stolen goods is either not feasible or desirable. While duties of compensation are often plausible, it is controversial that they are ever appropriate in discharging duties of rectification for historical injustice in the acquisition of territories. Some insist that historical dispossession of territory cannot be compensated for and that only territorial revisions can properly undo the initial wrongs suffered (Meisels 2005: chap. 4).

When do historical wrongs justify duties of rectification? Historical wrongs are duties of rectification towards victims. Individuals are victims of historical wrongs if, and only, if they are currently worse off because of the wrong (Sher 1981: 13). Duties of rectification consequently apply only in relation to victims who are worse off now because of historical wrongs than they would otherwise have been.

The proviso that duties are owed only to victims who are 'worse off' implies that not all historical injustices are grounds for duties of rectification. It is, for instance, plausible to think that no now existing person is worse off because of wrongs committed a thousand years ago or more. One reason is that, over long periods of time, initial losses inflicted by acts of dispossession tend to be compensated for by the 'progressive diminution in the transferability of entitlements' (Sher 1981: 13). Another reason is that, over the long haul, it may be that the victims of historical wrongs do not have any living descendants who could be worse off. Consider for example the hypothesis that the Neanderthal species became extinct partly because of deliberate acts of violence by members of the homo sapiens species (Lahr *et al.* 2016). Or consider the wrongs undertaken by the Normans during the invasion and colonization of the British Isles that followed the battle of Hastings.[9] Duties of rectification in either case are probably out of the question either due to the non-existence of recipients of duties of rectification (the Neanderthals) or due to the fact that initial losses in well-being have been superseded by later developments (the population on the British Isles).

The extent to which the passing of time diminishes the relative importance of the losses suffered in the past is of course controversial, particularly in relation to acts of territorial dispossession that took place in more recent times. Meisels (2005), for one, insists that the passing of time does not fully eradicate, though it may weaken, legitimate interests in regaining lost territories. This point reminds us of the fact that claims to historical reparation raise concerns of justice also in relation to the current inhabitants of unjustly occupied territories. As they can be presumed morally innocent of the wrongs committed in the past, justice also requires attention to their interests. That is why, according to Waldron (2002), claims to redress historical injustice are unlikely to require full rectification even to victims today who are worse off as a result.

We are now in a better position to summarize the argument under consideration. Again, the claim is that the boundaries of the demos must not depend on territorial borders that are illegitimate as a result of historical injustice. However, territorial borders are illegitimate in this sense only if historical injustices also provide grounds for duties of rectification to others who are now worse off because of them. Moreover, potential duties of rectificatory justice to victims are arguably weakened by the passing of time as well as by the legitimate interests of non-victims. Hence, historical injustice may not be sufficient to conclude that the territorial borders of the state should be revised when all things are considered.

Let us nevertheless assume, for the sake of the argument, that historical injustice is sufficient to establish that the borders of the state are illegitimate and that they should therefore be revised. Is the all-subjected principle then undermined? Following that principle, the subjects of the de facto authority of the state are presumptively entitled to inclusion in the demos. Since the de facto authority of the state is typically limited by territorial borders, the all-subjected principle typically entails that only people in the territory of the state should be included in the demos – state borders delimit the extension of the demos. The *objection* now is that the demos must not be limited by territorial borders that are illegitimate for reasons of historical injustice. State borders that for historical reasons give rise to rectificatory duties to victims should not be instrumental in defining the boundaries of democratic peoples.

One way to understand this argument is that the claim to democratic inclusion by the people delimited by the territorial borders of state is *in conflict* with moral duties to the victims who suffer from the creation of these borders. The idea is that we are unable to discharge duties towards victims and also include in the demos the people subject to the state in its territory.

But it is unclear that this amounts to moral conflict. Consider, first, the duty to revise state borders. Perhaps there is a moral duty to revise the border such that one region of state A should be shifted to state B. Is discharging that duty inconsistent with the claim that everyone subjected to state A should be included in the demos of state A? It is hard to see why. Either the region has not yet been shifted to state B, in which case the all-subjected principle holds that the residents of that region should for now be included in the demos of state A. Or, the region has just been shifted to state B, in which case the all-subjected principle holds that the residents of that region should be admitted to the demos of state B. In neither case does the all-subjected principle conflict with duties to revise the border. The claim that state borders should be revised does not contravene the claim that people presently subjected to the authority of the state are entitled to democratic participation.

In a different reading of the argument, the problem is not concerned with moral conflict but with the normative status of state borders. The idea is that illegitimate state borders are not *legitimate sources of normative entitlements*. This version represents a valid objection against the claim that people are entitled to democratic inclusion *because* of legitimate territorial claims. Illegitimate territorial claims should not ground democratic inclusion if it is accepted that only legitimate claims can ground entitlements. For example, the merits of A's claim to exercise sole authority in a house is undermined if it turns out that A acquired the house unjustly and therefore should not be considered the rightful owner of the house.

Though this version of the argument is more successful, it is unclear that it is relevant. In fact, state borders are *not* grounds for democratic inclusion according to the argument that state borders determine the extension of the demos. The claim by the all-subjected principle is not that people are morally entitled to demos membership because they are morally entitled to existing territorial borders. The only normative entitlement implied by the all-subjected principle is that the subjects of claims to legitimate authority should be included in the process of decision-making. It just so happens that the border of the state marks the end point of the de facto authority of the state. Consequently, state borders are not sources of normative entitlements, although they delimit their scope by defining the edges of the state's claim to legitimate authority.

Thus, I conclude that the territorial implications of the all-subjected principle are not undermined by the observation that state borders are often the result of unjust wars and processes of colonization in the past.[10] Though historical injustice may give grounds for duties to victims that entail territorial revisions, duties to rectify past wrongs do not undermine the precept that subjects of the de facto authority of the state should be included in the demos.

Global Injustice

State borders can be morally wrongful even if not tainted by historical injustice. One reason to believe that state borders are wrongful is that they have distributive effects that contribute to unjust economic disparities between people around the globe (e.g., Mollendorf 2009). These problematic consequences are arguably exacerbated by the fact that territorial borders condition existing systems for global trade and cooperation that serve to perpetuate exploitative relationships with harmful consequences (Beitz 1999). A further point is that territorial borders sustain norms of sovereignty and non-intervention that indirectly legitimize states that violate the human rights of their own populations (Pogge 2002). State borders might accordingly be considered wrongful due to their instrumental role in maintaining inequality, exploitative relationships, harm, and rights-violations on a global scale. The consequent 'global justice argument' holds that state borders are unjust and that they should be abolished. Morally speaking, state borders cannot be justified.

We should note that the global justice argument – or any of its variants – is not conclusive with regard to the moral status of state borders. Clearly, if it is true that state borders are instrumental to global injustice, it does follow that state borders are pro tanto unjust. But as observed by others, pro tanto reasons to think that state borders are unjust do not exclude other pro tanto reasons to think that state borders are required by justice (Caney 2005: 158; Nine 2008).

Let us nevertheless assume, for the sake of argument, that no countervailing reason in favor of state borders exists. Hence, we accept, *arguendo*, that state borders are unjust, all things considered, because they contribute to inequality of wealth and income, exploitation, harm, and rights-violations. Does it follow that state borders should be abolished? In fact, it is not clear that this conclusion follows.

To see why a conclusive argument that state borders are unjust is not necessarily underwriting the conclusion that state borders should be abolished, we shall begin by observing that public policy is the main driver of global injustice. Global injustice is an intended or unintended consequence of the fact that governments consistently pursue policies that primarily aim to benefit their own populations. Policy is hence the root cause of global injustice, not territorial borders. This insight is helpful in estimating the force of the global justice argument.

By contrast, according to some, the borders of the state aggravate global injustice because they 'structure where individuals of the world can travel, settle and work' (van Parijs 2007). However, this view is not correct if the cause of global injustice is traceable to the border regime and not to territorial borders. In that event, territorial borders have none of the consequences attributed to them by van Parijs as barriers to travel, settlement, and work are caused by government decisions.

Against the notion that global injustice is caused by policy rather than by border, it can be objected that the social and political roots of human well-being are much more complex. To illustrate this point, consider the powerful example offered by Mollendorf (2009) where he compares the life prospects of a child born to a banker in Switzerland and the life prospects of child born to a poor farmer in Mozambique. As the world is at present, it is likely that the expected well-being of these children will follow very different trajectories. However, this is not simply explained by the fact that the banker is wealthy and the farmer is poor. The main reason to expect that the child in Mozambique will be worse off in the future is that the quality of public institutions in that country is much lower. The point, then, is that territorial borders allow some to enjoy the benefits of high-quality public institutions while others are condemned to suffer the consequences of low-quality public institutions.

Although Mollendorf's example is important, it is questionable whether it supports the conclusion that state borders should be abolished for reasons of global justice. The reason why this conclusion does not necessarily follow is that wealthy and well-functioning state *could* pursue policies of global redistribution that would mitigate global inequality. The fact that the Swiss government does not pursue such policies at this moment does not cause poverty in Mocambique but explains it.[11] By a different mix of economic and other policy decisions, the rich countries of the world could alleviate global poverty. The point is that global injustice can be reduced even within the current framework of territorially delimited states. Although global poverty is maintained by the state system, it is not necessarily true that state borders must be abolished in order to address it.

On the other hand, the prospect of global justice appears slim in a world populated by sovereign states that continue to prioritize the interests of domestic populations. Even if global justice is strictly speaking *possible* in a territorially divided world, global justice is unlikely to materialize anytime soon in the current state system. The point is that the abolishment of state borders does not have to be *necessary* in order to be a justified precept of global justice. It is arguably enough that the abolishment of state borders is *effective* for the realization of global justice.

The final test for the all-subjected principle then is if it is negated by the claim that state borders should be abolished. Is the claim that the boundaries of the demos should be limited by existing territorial borders undermined by the proposition that state borders should be abolished for reasons of global justice?

The force of this argument depends on what it means for the all-subjected principle to be 'undermined' by a normative proposition. One possibility is that the principle is undermined if it conflicts with the prescriptions required by principles of global justice. Another possibility is that the principle is undermined if it depends on facts that are impermissible according to principles of global justice. Let us examine each version in turn.

The first version is that there is a normative conflict between global justice and the principle of democratic inclusion. A normative conflict is a situation where two normative statements that are pro tanto valid cannot both be performed (e.g., Horty 2003). For two principles to conflict, it must be true that both apply to a particular situation and that both provide conflicting recommendations for action. The relevant normative statement following the global justice argument is that state borders should be abolished. That statement evidently conflicts with the statement that state borders should not be abolished. In a particular situation, it is impossible to comply both with the statement that borders should be abolished and with the statement that they should not. Hence, the global justice argument is in conflict with the principle of democratic inclusion *if* the latter implies a commitment to the statement that state borders should not be abolished.

Yet, it is a mistake to presume that the all-subjected principle is committed to the preservation of existing territorial borders. The claim of that principle is that the demos should be limited by territorial borders – not that the borders of the state must remain as they are. There is no contradiction involved in affirming both the statement that all residents in the territory of the state should be included in the demos and the statement that state borders should be abolished. The only claim to which the all-subjected principle is committed is, thus, that all residents in the territory of the state should be included in the demos *as long* as they are subject to the de facto authority of the state. If state borders are abolished, the boundaries of the demos should be revised so that it aligns with the newly erected normative system that claims legitimate authority.

The second version of the argument is that principles of global justice undermine territorial borders as a source of normative entitlement. If the state system is an unjust public institution, territorial borders should not ground normative entitlements to democratic inclusion. The notion that unjust public institutions cannot be invoked as the basis for entitlements is a familiar one. For example, slave owners cannot justify ownership of slaves by appeal to an existing regime of property rights that permits it. Analogously, states cannot claim moral rights to existing territorial borders if the system of existing territorial borders is unjust.

At this point, we need to recall the considerations invoked earlier in responding to the argument from historical injustice. The all-subjected principle is not premised on a *moral right* to inclusion among the subjects of claims to legitimate authority. The principle provides an account of democratic inclusion such that procedures for democratic decisions should include the subjects in order to be democratic. The moral basis for the all-subjected principle is consequently conditional on prior moral reasons that justify democratic procedures. Of course, it is conceivable that democracy is justified on the basis of the territorial rights of the resident population. In that case, it appears that democracy and the right to participation in public decisions depend on considerations that are unjust according to the global justice argument. There are, nevertheless, many other potential justifications of democratic rights and it is therefore unlikely that principles of global justice undermine the normative entitlements necessary to justify democratic procedures.

Notes

1 For an overview of the artificial origins of state borders and an attempt to empirical measure their colonial origins, see Alesina, Easterly, and Matuszeski (2011).
2 See also Yack (2001), Ochoa Espejo (2011: 41) and Little (2015).
3 Causal indeterminism can be either epistemic or ontological. Epistemic causal indeterminism holds that indeterminism is just the way the world appears, given lack of knowledge of all the determinants of social and natural phenomena. Ontological causal indeterminism holds that the nature of the world *is* indeterminate, not just a consequence of limited knowledge (Hoefer 2016). Curiously, anti-foundationalists are more prone to defend the ontological version of causal indeterminism and are consequently more prone to endorse a particular metaphysics.
4 A third conception of contingency figures in the discipline of logic and applies to propositions that are neither necessarily true nor false. This version of contingency is propositional, neither an attribute of historical processes or of the ontological status of the world, and consequently has no implications for the status of territorial borders (van Inwagen and Sullivan 2018).
5 There is extant literature on the so-called 'non-identity problem' that undergirds this claim. For a discussion of the non-identity problem in relation to genetic and psychological accounts of personal identity, see Finneron-Burns (2016).
6 A related version of this argument is that because the demos is contingent, no principle of democratic inclusion is morally justified. For a critical assessment of this view, see Maltais, Rosenberg and Beckman (2019: 457).
7 Two potential explanations of legitimate origins are when state borders are created as the result of just wars (wars of liberation and wars of self-defence), and when state borders are created as the result of voluntary agreements that are ratified by democratic procedures. On the latter, see Qvortrup (2014) and Tierney (2012).
8 By duties of rectification, I refer to duties owed by wrongdoer towards victims. Duties of rectification either include duties of restitution, bringing the victim back to the situation prior to the wrong, or duties of either compensation or public recognition when reparation is unfeasible (Ivison 2009). The alternative to duties of rectification is perpetrator-centered responses, including either punishing the perpetrator or duties to 'disgorge'

benefits derived from past wrongs. (Goodin 2013: 480). Yet, I take it that historical injustice in the creation of territorial borders are primarily duties to victims. As noted by Simmons (1995), the terminology of rectification, compensation and reparation is often confusing.
9 Stilz (2018: 377) offers additional examples of ancient wrongs in the acquisition of territory that she argues carries little weight in contemporary settings.
10 Nili (2017: 123) makes a similar point in relation to the boundary problem in democratic theory more generally.
11 For the distinction between explanations and causes, see Davidson (1967).

9
END DISCUSSION
The Limits of Democratic Inclusion

The guiding idea of the all-subjected principle is that democratic inclusion is premised on subjection to a body that claims legitimate authority. Democratic participation is the right to partake in decisions of bodies that claim the moral right to regulate behavior. In a democracy, the people are the co-authors of the rules that constrain them, whether they are made by legal systems, or other normative systems.

Throughout the book, I have explicated this reading of the all-subjected principle with particular emphasis on its implications for democratic inclusion in the state. In this final chapter I focus on the limitations of this account by bringing to attention settings where it does *not* apply and situations where a demand for democratic inclusion accordingly cannot be made. These limitations follow from the fact that democratic inclusion applies only to the subjects of normative systems with de facto authority. Democracy is possible only on the premise that a rule-governed system – that claims the authority to regulate conduct – is already in force. The implication is that demands for democratic inclusion cannot be made in the absence of a normative system with de facto authority.

The first limitation of this account is manifested in situations where people are subject to rules that are binding, albeit not enacted by a body with authority. The typical case is that of social norms. Social norms are behavioral rules that are binding in the sense of providing exclusionary reasons for action. But social norms are neither enacted nor dependent on normative systems that claim the authority to regulate action. People may consequently be 'subject' to reasons that are normative in the sense of regulating conduct even in the absence of authority. Should we therefore conclude that the all-subjected principle applies to people who are subject to social norms? In that case, it seems as if subjection to claimed legitimate authority is not a necessary precondition for democratic inclusion.

DOI: 10.4324/9781003359807-9

The second situation to which the all-subjected principle does not apply is where people are subject to decisions that claim to be authoritative but not binding. A body that claims authority with respect to truth – epistemic authority – is the paradigmatic example. Epistemic authority determines belief, not action. The question, then, is does the all-subjected principle apply to the subjects of epistemic authority such that they are presumptively entitled to participate in their decisions? Further, below I show why this is not the case and why precepts of democratic participation pertain exclusively to decisions that purport to regulate behavior.

The third limitation on the all-subjected principle is more controversial and is concerned with decisions that are 'private'. A frequent contention is that claims for democratic participation are viable only in relation to *public* decision. There is no right to participate in the *private* decisions of others. But if the public/private distinction is contested, this precept is of limited use. As it turns out, however, a solution is offered by the present conception of the all-subjected principle. Decisions are private if they do not claim the authority to regulate the conduct of others. Private decisions are in other words not binding for others. Since the all-subjected principle only applies to decisions that do intend to impose rules that are binding, it follows that claims to democratic inclusion cannot be made in response to private decisions, even if others are affected by them.

The fourth and final limitation of the all-subjected principle appears in relation to rules made by normative systems that are radically immoral. The principle of democratic inclusion advanced here applies to the subjects of claims of *legitimate* authority. Though such claims are not premised on the possession of legitimate authority, the pretense of legitimate authority is undermined by radically immoral decisions. Tyranny is inconsistent with the claim to legitimate authority. Hence, no tyrannical political order is able to secure de facto authority over the population. Since rights to democratic participation are premised on subjection to de facto authority, such a system does not allow for claims to democratic participation. This conclusion makes the all-subjected principle vulnerable to the 'naked tyranny' objection (Wilson 2022: 185) that will be considered in the final section.

Social Norms

Social life is rife with social norms that provide standards for social conduct in everyday situations and that regulate, albeit informally, how people eat, salute, dress, and so on. Moreover, rules of etiquette, codes of conduct, and other social norms, frequently supplement the formal rules established by normative systems. Trade and commerce are not just regulated by the legal system but also by a variety of social norms that establish limits to acceptable conduct. The attempt to push your way forward in the bus queue is likely to be disapproved of by others, not because your behavior is illegal, but because it violates social norms about queuing. A similar negative reactive attitude is to be expected in response to offering your neighbor money in return for mowing your lawn. There is nothing illegal about the offer, of course. Yet, it is likely to violate norms of equal respect among the residents of neighborhoods (Elster 1989: 101).

In a similar vein, government institutions are not just regulated by the law. A wealth of social norms applies to public institutions and their representatives. Some of them are presumably of critical importance to a democratic political system. There are social norms to the effect that the government should not use executive power to stifle political opposition and there are social norms according to which it is wrongful to depict members of the opposition in ways that delegitimize them. When these norms are either absent or undermined, democracy tends to deteriorate. Systematic attacks on the informal norms that sustain democratic political competition tend to spell its demise (Levitsky and Ziblatt 2018).

Social norms are 'practice dependent' normative standards that are reflected in more or less stable and shared attitudes among the participants of social clusters (Brennan et al. 2013: 59). The fact that a social norm exists such that some conduct is either permissible or impermissible implies the existence of a practical reason that should be complied with. Yet, social norms are not enacted by bodies that claim the authority to regulate the behavior of others. Rules of etiquette that regulate eating and drinking in public spaces is a case in point. They are standards for behavior that vary between social and cultural contexts and that are manifested in either normative attitudes or expectations (Bicchieri 2005: 8). The norm that you should not burp or drool while eating in public spaces is an informal norm as it does not depend on any normative system; nobody decided that this behavior is wrongful, yet most people accept it as a norm and consider it as binding. Given that norms against burping and drooling in public spaces are binding, they provide reasons for action that should be complied with. We are, in effect, subjected to binding social norms of etiquette.

Does the principle of democratic inclusion apply to social norms? Given that social norms are binding, and that people should presumptively be included in rules regulating their behavior, it appears that the all-subjected principle does apply to social norms. Yet, social norms are not established by decisions. No one decided the norm that burping in public is rude; no one decided the norm that pushing your way forward in the queue is demeaning to others. Hence, there is no decision-making procedure in which people subject to social norms can be included.

The subjects of social norms are subject to binding reasons for action, yet not subject to bodies with the authority to regulate conduct. Social norms and etiquette are informal precisely in the sense that they are not established by normative powers conferred by a normative system (Brennan et al. 2013). Authority is a normative power to make decisions that depend on the existence of a normative system with de facto authority. Hence, authority can be claimed only by appeal to a normative system. Since social norms are not part of normative systems, the subjects of social norms are not subject to authority-claims. While social norms are binding, they are not claims for compliance made by an authority.

The implication is that the assertion that you are wrongly excluded from decisions on the norms of etiquette to which you are subjected is akin to a category mistake. The assertion is premised on the mistaken assumption that norms of etiquette belong to normative systems and not to the category of social norms.

Of course, it is possible to create normative systems that regulate social norms and that eventually provide the conditions for democratic participation in their creation. Perhaps the guests at a dinner party discover that they comply with different and conflicting norms of etiquette.[1] They may consequently agree to coordinate themselves and reduce confusion by taking a collective decision on which norms of etiquette to follow. Once they have agreed to make a collective decision about norms of etiquette, matters of inclusion and exclusion apply because they have now established an (informal) normative system that claims legitimate authority. Perhaps the host is away from the table at the moment when the guests are making the decision. Upon returning, the host might complain that she is excluded from the decision, although the decision is recognized as de facto regulative and the the host is expected to comply with it. The host could legitimately object to being subject to regulative claims made by the others, and yet refused a say in making the decision. The point is that the all-subjected principle applies only once such a claim to authority appears.

Epistemic Authority

Epistemic authority is the capacity to make decisions on matters of belief. An epistemic authority deciding that A is true, is providing a reason for others to believe that A is true. As we already know, the all-subjected principle holds that anyone subjected to a decision that claims to be binding should presumptively be included. It may consequently seem as if the all-subjected principle calls for democratic inclusion in relation to decisions made by epistemic authorities. Or does it really?

A conspicuous feature of epistemic reasons is that they apply to everyone. Reasons to believe are not person-relative; reasons to believe in the truth of a proposition apply irrespective of the goals and circumstances of any particular person. If the question is whether the president has lied to the public and the procedure adopted to decide the matter is trustworthy, the resultant decision provides an epistemic reason for belief that applies to everyone. Thus, an epistemic authority that is able to establish reasons to believe in P effectively gives everyone a reason to believe in P.

In the case that the all-subjected principle applies to epistemic decisions, the implication would be very radical indeed. The all-subjected principle holds that the subjects of claimed authority should presumptively be included in the decision. If everyone is subject to claims of epistemic authority, it follows that everyone should be included in the decisions made by epistemic authorities. It would arguably be undemocratic to exclude anyone from decisions that intend to determine reasons for belief.

To illustrate, consider a scientific council that evaluates the effectiveness of different public policies launched by governments in response to the COVID 19 pandemic. If the council is sufficiently qualified, there is reason to recognize it as an epistemic authority. The conclusions reached by the council are then reasons for belief that apply to all of us. Now, if I am excluded from participating in the decision of the scientific council, I am denied the opportunity to participate in a decision that claims to provide me with reasons for belief. This seems problematic given the current reading of the principle of democratic inclusion. The council gives me reasons for belief and, therefore, I should presumptively be included in the decision-making procedures of the council.

Now, there is clearly something strange about this argument. The all-subjected principle of democratic inclusion does not simply say that people should presumptively be included in decisions that apply to them. Rather, the all-subjected principle says that people should presumptively be included in decisions that claim to be *binding* for them. The question then is if the decisions made by an epistemic authority claim to be binding.

A reason is binding only if it should be complied with. Hence, to say that you should comply with epistemic reasons is to say that there are epistemic duties. The notion of epistemic duties is unusual but not at all mysterious. According to Feldman (2005) the most basic epistemological duty is to have justified beliefs. The epistemic duty to have justified belief is the duty to form beliefs according to certain methodological principles and to reject beliefs that do not comply with these principles.

Provided that there is such an epistemic duty, it appears that we should accept all decisions made by epistemic authorities. If A has an epistemic duty to form beliefs that are justified, and if epistemic authority B makes a justified decision on the truth of a proposition, it seems that A has a duty to form beliefs in accordance with B's decision. Yet, it is noteworthy that A's duty is not established *by* B's decision. The fact that A should comply because there is an epistemic duty to that effect is not equal to the claim that B claims the right to make decisions that are binding for A. Though there can be epistemic duties that provide reasons to comply with epistemic decisions, it remains uncertain that epistemic authorities claim the right to provide epistemic reasons that others should comply with.

The point is that it is widely accepted that epistemic authority is capable neither of de facto authority nor of legitimate authority. Epistemic authority does not claim to be legitimate since epistemic authority does not depend on moral justification. A subject of epistemic authority is, in other words, placed in a fundamentally different relationship to authority compared to the subjects of practical authority (Lamond 2016). As explained by Raz (2009b: 155) some people 'may or may not be experts in or authorities on eighteenth-century farming methods. But they cannot be de facto authorities or legitimate authorities on the subject'. The notions of either de facto or legitimate authority apply exclusively to the realm of practical reason. Only de facto and legitimate authority seek to establish what people should do. Therefore, only practical authority has the capacity to make decisions that are or claim to be binding in the sense of providing reasons that others should comply with. If only practical reasons can be binding, it follows that epistemic authorities are unable to make binding decisions – since they only make decisions about beliefs. In sum, the subjects of epistemic authority are not subject to binding decisions (Christiano 2004; Estlund 2007: 3; Himma 2018).[2]

For example, I may consider the Department of Physics to be an epistemic authority with respect to quantum-mechanics. Since I do, I take its statements on quantum-mechanics to be authoritative on the subject. But even though I do recognize the epistemic authority of the Department of Physics, I am not thereby placed under a duty to *comply* with the decisions it makes. The all-subjected principle is triggered only when subjected to claims for compliance.

It may be objected that epistemic authorities sometimes do intend to provide practical reasons for action. If there is a truth about how something 'is best done', and there is an epistemic authority that is able to identify this truth, it seems as if this authority is invested with the capacity to provide reasons for belief and action at the same time (Simmons 2016: 4).

Yet, it is misleading to assert that epistemic authority provides reasons for action by identifying reasons for how something is best done. Reasons for *how* to do things are not reasons for *doing* things. A recipe for how to best make muffins, is authoritative with respect to *how* muffins are best made, not with respect to the question if anyone should make muffins. Analogously, experts on public health may be able to give authoritative reasons on how to best combat the pandemic caused by the coronavirus. If these experts qualify as epistemic authorities, they are able to provide authoritative reasons for belief. Yet, these authoritative reasons are not reasons for action that others should comply with. Reasons to believe how something is best done are not reasons for action.

It is of course conceivable that a body with epistemic authority also wields practical authority. A body that claims both epistemic and practical authority, intends to be authoritative with respect to belief as well as with respect to action. Perhaps the Department of Public Health is authorized to decide public policy in response to the spread of the coronavirus. The decisions taken are no longer mere authoritative reasons for belief as they are also intended to regulate the conduct of others. The Department of Public Health now wields practical authority with 'epistemic content' (Simion 2018). The all-subjected principle of democratic inclusion evidently applies in that case and consequently applies to bodies with epistemic authority only if they also claim practical authority. The main conclusion, though, is that the all-subjected principle does not apply to purely epistemic authorities, as they do not claim to regulate behavior.

Private Decisions

Claims to legitimate authority presuppose the existence of a normative system that regulates and defines the normative power to make decisions. Associations and informal groups can be normative systems and thus potential sources of claims to authority. But what about decisions made by individuals? Surely, it is possible for individuals to make decisions that impinge on the interests of others, even though no normative system in the required sense is in place.

Consider, for example, the decision about whom to marry. The example is well-known from the work of Robert Nozick where he invites us to imagine a woman about to decide whether to marry any of the four men who have just proposed to her (Nozick 1974: 269).[3] Apparently, the woman's decision will affect each of the men in important ways. Hence, if you subscribe to the view that people should be able to influence decisions relevantly affecting their interests, you must either conclude that the four men should be included in the woman's decision, or explain why they are not relevantly affected by it.

Nozick uses the example to argue that the all-affected principle is absurd. He explains the alleged absurdity of the principle by the fact that it conflicts with the basic moral right of individuals. For Nozick, all human beings have 'property in themselves' such that they 'own' their bodies and the actions undertaken by moving their bodies in space (including goods and resources that are 'mixed' with their labor). From the basic moral right to 'self-ownership', Nozick believes that each person is entitled to decide without interference from others, subject only to side-constraints (Nozick 1974: 171). The moral right to self-ownership grounds the woman's right to decide whom to marry and to exclude others from participating in the decision.

Advocates of the all-affected principle have responded to Nozick's objection by redefining the relevant 'affected interests'. According to Valentini, only interests that do not fall under the umbrella of constitutional protection are grounds for rights to political participation. Given that marriage is 'a personal freedom that the law ought to protect', decisions about marriage do not provide grounds for rights to participation for others, even if they are significantly affected (Valentini 2014: 793). Others concur and insist that the all-affected is limited to matters of public morality (Owen 2011: 135; Warren 2017).

These attempts to rescue the all-affected principle are questionable, however. Similar to the position taken by Nozick, they presume that public and private interests can be separated without resort to democratic procedures. Their claim is that democracy belongs to the sphere of public concerns, but not to the sphere of private concerns. But the decision that some issues are public while other are private is itself of public concern as it matters immensely to the members of society. Since that decision is affecting them, they should all be able to participate in its making, according to the logic propounded by the all-affected principle. No pre-political definition of interests to be excluded from public regulation is available (Waldron 1999). Any decision that identifies the interests that should not trigger the democratic inclusion of others is itself a decision that should be made by all relevantly affected.

The all-subjected principle offers a more promising explanation of why some decisions are private in the sense of not triggering claims for the inclusion of others that are affected. Following the all-subjected principle, only claims to legitimate authority are presumptive grounds for democratic inclusion. But a private decision does not claim legitimate authority over others. My decision to cut my hair, go shopping, or eat a snack does not intend to regulate the conduct of anyone but myself. The distinction between private and public decisions can consequently be accounted for in terms of the authority claimed. Decisions are private if they only intend to regulate the conduct of the agent making the decision. This then is why the woman's decision in the above example is personal. In deciding to marry one of the four men, or none of them, she is not providing anyone but herself with reasons for action. The reason why the four men should not be included in her decision is consequently that they are not subject to it – they are not subject to claims of legitimate authority.

A possible objection against this argument is that authority over others *can* be claimed by individuals. There is nothing that prevents one of the men from making the decision that the women should marry her. In thus deciding, that man is 'claiming' the authority to regulate the woman's behavior. But this objection ignores the point – rehearsed many times in this book – that authority can be claimed only by de facto authorities. Unless a body or person is recognized as authoritative, the claims made by that body or person is no more than empty talk. The man's 'decision' that she should pick him for marriage is authoritative only if she recognizes his authority in that domain.

That is of course unlikely but not impossible. Hence, the fact that decisions about marriage are private in the sense just explained does not entail that they must be. Normative systems can be created that possess the authority to regulate what would otherwise be personal decisions. Consider, again, the four men and the woman and imagine that they agree to resolve the issue by a collective decision. In order for such a decision to be authoritative, they need to establish a normative system with the power to regulate decisions about marriage. Once that normative system is created, it appears that whom the woman should marry can be decided collectively. By implication, they are now subject to a normative system with the claimed authority to regulate conduct such that the all-subjected principle applies. In the case that the decision should be democratic, there are now grounds for the inclusion of all subjects in the making of the decision. Nevertheless, as people do not usually agree to regulate marriage collectively, these decisions tend to be personal. The all-subjected principle supplies the conceptual resources to explain why decisions about marriage usually do not trigger claims to the participation of others.

On the other hand, the authority claimed by legal systems does not recognize any limits with respect to the issues that they can regulate in the relevant domain. In contrast to the decisions made by individuals, legal systems make decisions on the premise that they are entitled to comprehensive authority (Raz 1979). Accordingly, most jurisdictions regulate the terms of marriage as illustrated by widespread laws against polygamy, incestuous marriage, and marriages between human and non-human animals. Of course, these laws can be, and often are, objected to on various grounds, as testified by political opposition to laws that prevent same-sex marriage. The point though is that laws regulating marriage are rules claiming the authority to regulate behavior and that is why people subject to them should be allowed to participate in their making.

Failures of De Facto Authority

Does the all-subjected principle apply to every system of governance, irrespective of its moral qualities? To put the question thus is to contemplate the possibility that there are limits to the kind of political units to which democratic principles apply. In fact, political scientist Philippe Schmitter has made an argument that at first glance seems to suggest that such limits do obtain. According to Schmitter, the 'one overriding political requisite for democracy' is that the political unit is legitimate (Schmitter 1994). If democracy is premised on the legitimacy of the political unit, the implication seems to be that illegitimate political units are not fit for democracy. A similar proposition is also found in the work of Robert Dahl. According to Dahl, 'the criteria of the democratic process presuppose the rightfulness of the unit itself' (Dahl 1989: 207). In the case that the rightfulness of the political unit is a 'presupposition' for the democratic process, it appears that democracy is not possible in a wrongful political unit.

How these statements are to be understood is not entirely clear, however. An obvious and quite innocuous reading is that they mean to establish the social and political conditions for well-functioning democracy. Democracy cannot flourish unless there is extant agreement on the boundaries of the political unit. But although there may be some truth in that view, it does not adequately reflect the statement that the rightfulness of the political unit is a 'presupposition' for a democratic process. The conditions that are conducive to well-functioning democracy are not *presuppositions* in the sense of being necessary preconditions for valid claims to democratic inclusion.[4]

A different possibility is that these statements mean to convey the view that democracy and associated claims for inclusion are justified only in political units that are morally legitimate. That would essentially amount to the moralized conception of the all-subjected principle that has been examined in previous chapter. If so, we should reject that view for the reasons given earlier. The notion that only the subjects of morally legitimate authorities should presumptively be included in the democratic process runs contrary to the precept that inclusion is among the requirements of legitimate authority. Furthermore, we should acknowledge the fact that a political unit need not be morally legitimate in order to *claim* the moral right to regulate behavior. The principle of democratic inclusion applies to any normative system that makes such a claim and hence applies also to institutions that are not morally legitimate.

There is a better way to understand the statements made by Schmitter and Dahl that is also congruent with the thesis defended here. The claim that the rightfulness of the political unit is a presupposition for a democratic process can be read to imply that claims to legitimate authority are subject to moral limitations. Not every normative system can claim the moral authority to rule. Indeed, that understanding is already implicit in the present reading of the all-subjected principle since only institutions with de facto authority can pretend to make decisions that are binding. As already emphasized, this implies that a purely coercive system of governance is not a de facto authority. Rule by coercion is basically no different from a terrorist group that uses threats of violence to achieve its ends. By comparison, a state with de facto authority is pretending to be something more due to its claimed moral authority. A de facto authority is widely perceived as legitimate and claims to be legitimate. But the actual system of rule that is practiced is arguably a constraint on the claims that can be made by it and the extent to which it is recognized as legitimate.

The fact that de facto authorities are widely recognized as legitimate might sound reassuring but is certainly no reason to conclude that the regime is morally legitimate. It is not difficult to find examples of public institutions that profess to be legitimate and where large sections of the population perceive them to be, despite acting contrary to minimal moral standards (Galligan 2006: 128). As pessimistically observed by Klosko (1992: 69) 'the fact that most citizens…believe that…their governments are legitimate indicates that their standards of legitimacy are rather low.'

This is of course just to confirm that institutions with de facto authority are not necessarily morally legitimate. But it does not follow that an institution with de facto authority can be radically immoral. The moral limits of de facto authority are helpfully explained by Horatio Spector.[5] According to him, claims to legitimate authority should be read as 'pragmatic presuppositions' applicable to all legal systems that are in force. Legal systems that claim to impose duties on subjects intend these duties to be received as moral and not merely legal duties. But in order for legal officials to form the intention that subjects are morally required to comply with the law, they must identify themselves as vested with the moral authority to create moral duties in others. That is the essence of the argument that legal practices pragmatically presuppose the legitimate authority of the legal system (Spector 2019: 35ff.).

Now, the point is that the 'presupposition' of moral authority cannot reasonably be attributed to officials in all circumstances. Officials that pursue 'blatantly immoral' laws or policies cannot think of themselves as vested with moral authority (Spector 2019: 45). If the law's claim to legitimate authority is conditioned by pragmatic reasons to think that officials are moral authorities, it follows that blatantly immoral laws undermine the claim to legitimate authority. Since the claim to legitimate authority is a defining element of de facto authority, we are compelled to conclude that legal systems that enact blatantly immoral laws cannot be de facto authorities.

The implication is that the principle of democratic inclusion may not apply to all states. Systems of governance that for moral reasons fail to achieve de facto authority are unable to subject the population to claims for legitimate authority. Since the all-subjected principle only applies to the subjects of putatively binding rules of conduct, it does not apply to the subjects of states that for moral reasons fail to achieve de facto authority. No demand for democratic inclusion can be made in relation to states that are radically immoral. Tyranny effectively eliminates the necessary presuppositions of democracy.

In reality it is of course often difficult to determine if some particular state satisfies the moral preconditions for de facto authority. Yet, recent history offers some likely candidates of public institutions that did fail in that regard. A plausible case is the *Generalgouvernement für die besetzten polnischen Gebiete* that was created by the German forces of occupation after the surrender of Poland in September 1939. The *Generalgouvernement* included those remaining parts of Poland that were not annexed by either the German Reich or its allies.[6] The territory was ruled by decree, issued by the general governor, Hans Frank, with the aim to exterminate all 'undesirable elements' of the population and exploit the rest for the benefits of the Reich. The administration made few efforts to rule by law or even to enforce the 'law' consistently. No legal machinery that applied and enforced rules in a predictable manner was created (Gross 1979).

The *Generalgouvernement* is perhaps the strongest candidate for a tyrannical political order in the 20th century. It is, therefore, safe to assume that it lacked public support and that few if any residents accepted the authority claimed by it. However, the more fundamental question is that – if we accept Spector's argument – the *Generalgouvernement* could not claim to be a legitimate authority because of the blatant immorality of the aims pursued and means employed. There is no basis for the pragmatic presupposition of moral authority among officials that willingly engage in policies of extermination and exploitation by means of arbitrary exercises of coercion.

The fact that the *Generalgouvernement* could not claim legitimate authority has implications for the prospect of democratic rule. According to the all-subjected principle, only the subjects of de facto authority are presumptively entitled to democratic inclusion. If the *Generalgouvernement* did not qualify as a de facto authority, the population that lived (and died) under its rule were not 'subjects' in the sense relevant for the all-subjected principle to apply. Thus, the system of terror that was introduced by the German forces of occupation *could not* have been democratic.

The case of the *Generalgouvernement* illustrates the practical significance of the notion that claims for democratic participation are conditioned by the minimal legitimacy of the political unit. The demand to participate in the making of rules that claim the authority to regulate conduct is irrelevant in a tyrannical order. For the people to be co-authors of decisions that claim the authority to rule them, they must first be subject to a system of rule that claims authority.

The conclusion may appear depressing or even misconceived. The obvious counter-argument is that authority-based conceptions of democratic inclusion are perverse exactly because they undermine claims for democratic inclusion in brutal or otherwise wrongful regimes. Surely people who are the victims of tyranny are as entitled to democratic rule as anyone else? (Wilson 2022: 185).

In responding to this final objection, it is necessary to return to the reflections introduced in the first chapter on the nature of principles of democratic inclusion. The thesis that the boundaries of the demos should be devised in accordance with the prescriptions of the all-subjected principle, is a normative claim that applies to associations that should be democratic. If there is an association that makes decisions that claim to regulate the behavior of others, and if there is reason to believe that this association should be ruled by democratic standards, the all-subjected principle tells us to presumptively include everyone subject to the decisions of that association.

Accordingly, the all-subjected principle does not provide a complete repertoire of normative reasons for democratic government. The all-subjected principle does not offer a full justification for the claim that any particular association and state should be governed by democratic procedures. More fundamentally, the all-subjected principle is not an account that supplies reasons for the creation of associations and states. Though there is reason to think that people should usually be granted the opportunity to participate in decisions that claim the authority to regulate them, this is not a reason for the creation of a system of governance that claims the authority to regulate conduct. Hence, neither the claim that tyranny should be replaced by a rule-based system of governance, nor the claim that such a rule-based system should be democratic, can be justified by the principle of democratic inclusion.

'Principles' are systematic condensates of reasons that should inform judgments of particular kinds. The reasons that ought to inform judgments about democratic inclusion are meant to inform judgments on the extent of the demos in associations that should be democratic. The reasons that should inform judgments on the creation of associations – whether they are states or other systems of governance at other levels – are different and consequently not provided by the principle of democratic inclusion. Furthermore, the reasons that should inform judgments about the governance of associations – whether they should be democratic or not – are also somewhat different and therefore at least not fully explicated by an account of democratic inclusion.

The final response the objection that the all-subjected principle fails to apply to tyrannies is accordingly as follows. Though there are obvious reasons for replacing tyranny with legal order, and though reasons for why legal orders should be democratic are powerful and convincing, these reasons cannot be inferred from an account of democratic inclusion alone. The account offered in this book seeks to articulate where the boundaries for participation in democratic associations should be drawn and why they should be drawn somewhere rather than elsewhere. Reasons for the creation of rule-based associations and reasons for how to govern them are important but distinct questions that are not answered by a theory of democratic inclusion.

Notes

1 For a discussion of the difference between manners and etiquette, see Kaplan (2021).
2 Cf. Marmor (2011: 126) who argues that epistemic authority generates exclusionary reasons but that subjects do not have duties to comply with them.
3 See also Kolodny (2014: 222) for a similar example.
4 Following Miller (2008: 34), presuppositional grounding refers to statements that are necessary preconditions for the validity of a conclusion even though they do not entail the validity of that conclusion.
5 Soper (1989: 224) defends a similar conclusion on different grounds. According to Soper, claims to legitimate authority depend on the law being enacted 'in good faith in the interest of the general welfare or justice'. Where legal officials either act in bad faith or do not aim to promote the general welfare, they are unable to claim title to legitimate authority.
6 Small pieces of Poland were also annexed by Slovakia, a German ally at the time.

REFERENCES

Abizadeh, Arash. 2008. 'Democratic theory and border coercion: No right to unilaterally control your own borders', *Political Theory*, 36: 37–65.
Abizadeh, Arash. 2010. 'Democratic legitimacy and state coercion: A reply to david Miller', *Political Theory*, 38: 121–130.
Abizadeh, Arash. 2021. 'The scope of the all-subjected principle: On the logical structure of coercive laws', *Analysis*, 81(4): 603–610.
Agné, Hans. 2006. 'A dogma of democratic theory and globalization: Why politics need not include everyone it affects', *European Journal of International Relations*, 12(3): 433–458.
Agnew, John. 2015. 'Revisiting the territorial trap', *Nordica Geographical Publications*, 44(4): 43–48.
Åkermark, Sia Spiliopoulou. 2009. 'The Åland Islands question in the league of nations: The ideal minority case?', *Redescriptions: Political Thought, Conceptual History and Feminist Theory*, 13(1): 195–205.
Alesina, Alberto, William Easterly, and Janina Matuszeski. 2011. 'Artificial states', *Journal of the European Economic Association*, 9: 246–277.
Alexander, Larry. 1990. 'Exclusionary reasons', *Philosophical Topics*, 18(1): 5–22.
Alexander, Larry. 2014. 'The ontology of consent', *Analytic Philosophy*, 55(1): 102–113.
Alexander, Larry and Frederic Schauer. 2009. 'Rules of recognition, constitutional controversies, and the dizzying dependence of law on acceptance', in Matthew Adler and Kenneth Einar Himma (eds.), *The Rule of Recognition and the U.S. Constitution*, pp. 175–192. Oxford: Oxford University Press.
Alexy, Robert. 1992. 'A discourse-theoretical conception of practical reason', *Ratio Juris* 5(3): 231–251.
Alston, William P. 2012. 'Reference and meaning', in Richard Schantz (ed.), *Prospects for Meaning*, pp. 35–60. Berlin/Boston: de Gruyter.
Alvarez, María. 2010. *Kinds of Reasons. An Essay in the Philosophy of Action*. Oxford: Oxford University Press.
Amariles, David Restrepo and Matteo Winkler. 2018. 'U.S. economic sanctions and the corporate compliance of foreign banks', *The International Lawyer*, 51(3): 497–536.

Angell, Kim. 2020. 'A life plan principle of voting rights', *Ethical Theory and Moral Practice*, 23: 125–139.
Armstrong, Chris. 2010. 'National self-determination, global equality and moral arbitrariness', *Journal of Political Philosophy*, 18(3): 313–334.
Arrhenius, Gustaf. 2018. 'The democratic boundary problem reconsidered', *Ethics, Politics and Society*, 1(1): 89–122.
Asp, Petter. 2017. 'Extraterritorial ambit and extraterritorial jurisdiction', in Antje du Bois-Pedain, Magnus Ulväng, and Petter Asp (eds.), *Criminal Law and the Authority of the State*, pp. 33–46. Oxford: Hart Publishing.
Axelrod, Robert. 1986. 'An evolutionary approach to norms', *American Political Science Review*, 80(4): 1095–1111.
Bader, Veit. 2018. 'Democratic inclusion in polities and governance arrangements', *Constellations*, 25: 570–585.
Bartelson, Jens. 2004. 'Facing Europe: Is globalization a threat to democracy?', *Distinktion: Scandinavian Journal of Social Theory*, 5(1): 47–60.
Bassiouni, M. Cherif. 2010. 'The history of universal jurisdiction and its place in international law', in Stephen Macedo (ed.), *Universal Jurisdiction*, pp. 334–346. Philadelphia: The University of Pennsylvania Press.
Bauböck, Rainer. 2018a. 'Democratic inclusion: A pluralist theory of citizenship', in Rainer Bauböck (ed.), *Democratic Inclusion: Rainer Bauböck in Dialogue*, Manchester: Manchester University Press.
Bauböck, Rainer. 2018b. 'Political membership and democratic boundaries', in Ayelet Shachar, Rainer Bauböck, Irene Bloemraad, and Maarten Vink (eds.), *The Oxford Handbook of Citizenship*, pp. 60–82. Oxford: Oxford University Press.
Beckman, Ludvig. 2006. 'Citizenship and voting rights: Should resident aliens vote?', *Citizenship Studies*, 10(2): 153–165.
Beckman, Ludvig. 2009. *The Frontiers of Democracy. The Right to Vote and Its Limits*. London: Palgrave Macmillan.
Beckman, Ludvig. 2013. 'Irregular migration and democracy: The case for inclusion', *Citizenship Studies*, 17(1): 48–60.
Beckman, Ludvig. 2018. 'Personhood and legal status: Reflections on the democratic rights of corporations', *Netherlands Journal of Legal Philosophy*, 47(1): 13–28.
Beckman, Ludvig. 2020. 'Is weak popular sovereignty possible', in André Campos and Susana Cadilha (eds.), *Sovereignty as Value*, pp. 35–52. Lanham: Rowman & Littlefield.
Beitz, Charles. 1989. *Political Equality*. Princeton: Princeton University Press.
Beitz, Charles. 1999. 'Social and cosmopolitan liberalism', *International Affairs*, 75(3): 515–529.
Beitz, Charles. 2011. 'Global political justice and the "democratic deficit"', in Jay Wallace, Rahul Kumar and Samuel Freeman (eds.), *Reasons and Recognition: Essays on the Philosophy of T.M. Scanlon*, pp. 231–248. Oxford: Oxford University Press.
Ben-Menahem, Yemima. 1997. 'Historical contingency', *Ratio*, 10: 99–107.
Beran, Harry. 1977. 'In defense of the consent theory of political obligation and authority', *Ethics*, 87(3): 260–271.
Berman, P.S. 2007. 'Global legal pluralism', *Southern California Law Review*, 80: 1155–1237.
Bertea, Stefano. 2004. 'On law's claim to authority', *Northern Ireland Legal Quarterly*, 55(4): 396–413.
Bertea, Stefano. 2021. 'Contemporary theories of legal obligation. A tentative critical map', in Stefano Bertea (ed.), *Contemporary Perspectives on Legal Obligation*, pp. 1–17. London: Routledge.

Besson, Samantha. 2019. 'Why and what (state) jurisdiction: Legal plurality, individual equality and territorial legitimacy', in Jan Klabbers and Gianluigi Palombella (eds.), *The Challenge of Inter-Legality*, pp. 91–132. Cambridge: Cambridge University Press.

Bicchieri, Cristina. 2005. *The Grammar of Society. The Nature and Dynamics of Social Norms*. Cambridge: Cambridge University Press.

Biersteker, T. 2013. 'State, sovereignty, and territory', in Walter Carlsnaes, Thomas Risse, and Beth Simmons (eds.), *Handbook of International Relations*, pp. 245–272. London: SAGE Publications Ltd.

Bix, Brian. 2001. 'John Austin', in Edward N. Zalta (ed.), *Stanford Encyclopedia of Philosophy* (Fall 2021 Edition), URL = https://plato.stanford.edu/entries/austin-john/Austin.

Bix, Brian. 2015. 'Rules and normativity in law', in M. Araszkiewics et al. (eds.), *Problems of Normativity, Rules and Rule-following*, Law and Philosophy Library 111, pp. 125–156. New York: Springer.

Blake, Michael. 2001. 'Distributive justice, state coercion, and autonomy', *Philosophy and Public Affairs*, 30: 257–296.

Blake, Michael. 2005. 'Immigration', in Raymond Gillespie Frey and Christopher Wellman (eds.), *A Companion to Applied Ethics*, pp. 224–237. Oxford: Blackwell.

Blake, Michael. 2008. 'Immigration and political equality', *San Diego Law Review*, 45: 963–979.

Blake, Michael. 2016. 'Agency, coercion, and global justice: A reply to my critics', *Law and Philosophy* 35(3), 313–335.

Bobbio, Norberto. 1965. 'Law and force', *The Monist*, 49(3): 321–341.

Bobbio, Norberto. 1998. 'Kelsen and legal power', in Stanley L. Paulson and Bonnie Litschewski Paulson (eds.), *Normativity and Norms: Critical Perspectives on Kelsenian Themes*, pp. 435–449. Oxford: Oxford University Press.

Bollen, Kenneth. and Robert W. Jackman. 1989. 'Democracy, stability and dichotomies', *American Sociological Review*, 54(4): 612–621.

Bongiovanni, Giorgio. 2018. 'Reasons (and reasons in philosophy of law)', in Giorgio Bongiovanni et al. (eds.), *Handbook of Legal Reasoning and Argumentation*, pp. 3–33. Dordrecht: Springer.

Brennan, Geoffrey, et al. 2013. *Explaining Norms*. Oxford: Oxford University Press.

Briffault, Richard. 1992. 'Voting rights, home rule and metropolitan governance: The secession of Staten Island as a case study in the dilemmas of local self-determination', *Columbia Law Review*, 92: 775–850.

Brubaker, Rogers. 1992. *Citizenship and Nationhood in France and Germany*. Cambridge: Harvard University Press.

Brun, Georg. 2016. 'Explication as a method of conceptual re-engineering', *Erkenntnis*, 81: 1211–1241.

Buchanan, Allen. 2003. 'The making and unmaking of boundaries: What liberalism has to say', in Allen Buchanan and Margaret Moore (eds.), *States, Nations and Borders: The Ethics of Making Boundaries*, pp. 231–261. Cambridge: Cambridge University Press.

Caney, Simon. 2005. *Justice beyond Borders*. Oxford: Oxford University Press.

Caney, Simon. 2008. 'Global distributive justice and the state', *Political Studies*, 56: 487–518.

Canovan, Margaret. 2005. *The People*. Cambridge: Polity.

Caporaso, James A. 2000. 'Changes in the westphalian order: Territory, public authority, and sovereignty', *International Studies Review*, 2(2): 1–28.

Cassidy, Julie. 2017. 'The international tax implications of New Zealand taxation of real property owned by non-residents (offshore persons)', *New Zealand Law Review*, 2017(2): 235–255.

Ceva, Emanuela and Valeria Ottonelli. 2021. 'Second-personal authority and the practice of democracy', *Constellations*. https://doi.org/10.1111/1467-8675.12575
Chang, Ruth. 2010. 'Voluntarist reasons and the sources of normativity', in David Sobel and Steven Wall (eds.), *Reasons for Action*, pp. 243–271. Cambridge: Cambridge University Press.
Christiano, Tom. 2004. 'Authority', in Edward N. Zalta (ed.), *The Stanford Encyclopedia of Philosophy* (Summer 2020 Edition), URL = https://plato.stanford.edu/archives/sum2020/entries/authority/
Ciepley, David. 2020. 'The Anglo-American misconception of stockholders as "owners" and "members": Its origins and consequences', *Journal of Institutional Economics*, 16(5): 623–642.
Cobbing, Andrew. 2018. 'A Victorian embarrassment: Consular jurisdiction and the evils of extraterritoriality', *The International History Review*, 402: 273–291.
Coleman, Jules. 1999. 'Authority and reason', in Robert P. George (ed.), *The Autonomy of Law: Essays on Legal Positivism*, pp. 287–319. Oxford: Oxford University Press.
Cooreman, Barbara. 2016. 'Addressing environmental concerns through trade: A case for extraterritoriality?', *International and Comparative Law Quarterly*, 65(1): 229–248.
Copp, David. 1999. 'The idea of a legitimate state', *Philosophy and Public Affairs*, 28: 3–45.
Crowe, Jonathan and Lucy Agnew. 2020. 'Legal obligation and social norms', *Adelaide Law Review*, 41(1): 217–241.
Dagger, Richard. 2018. 'Authority, legitimacy, and the obligation to obey the law', *Legal Theory*, 24(2): 1–26.
Dahl, Robert. 1985. *A Preface to Economic Democracy*. Cambridge: Polity Press.
Dahl, Robert. 1989. *Democracy and Its Critics*. New Haven: Yale University Press.
Davidson, Donald. 1967. 'Causal relations', *The Journal of Philosophy*, 64: 691–703.
Deakin, Simon. 2021. 'What is a firm? A reply to Jean-Philippe Robé', *Journal of Institutional Economics*, 17: 861–871.
Delacroix, Sylvie. 2004. 'Hart's and Kelsen's concepts of normativity contrasted', *Ratio Juris*, 17(4): 501–520.
Dorsett, Shaunnagh. 2006. 'Mapping territories', in Shaun McVeigh (ed.), *Jurisprudence of Jurisdiction*, pp. 137–158. London: Routledge.
Dorsett, Shaunnagh and Shaun McVeigh. 2012. *Jurisdiction*. London: Routledge.
Duff, Anthony. 1980. 'Legal obligation and the moral nature of law', *Juridical Review*, 25: 61–87.
Dworkin, Ronald. 1986. *Law's Empire*. London: Fontana.
Dworkin, Ronald. 2012. *Justice for Hedgehogs*. Cambridge: Harvard University Press.
Dyzenhaus, David. 2011. 'Austin, Hobbes, and Dicey', *Canadian Journal of Law and Jurisprudence*, 24(2): 409–430.
Eckersley, Robyn. 2020. 'Ecological democracy and the rise and decline of liberal democracy: Looking back, looking forward', *Environmental Politics*, 292: 214–234.
Edmundson, William. 1993. 'Rethinking exclusionary reasons: A second edition of Joseph Raz's Practical reasons and norms', *Law and Philosophy*, 12: 329–343.
Edmundson, William. 2004. 'State of the art: The duty to obey the law', *Legal Theory*, 10(4): 215–259.
Edmundson, William. 2010. 'Political authority, moral powers and the intrinsic value of obedience', *Oxford Journal of Legal Studies*, 30(1): 179–191.
Edmundson, William. 2012. 'Coercion', in Andrei Marmor (ed.), *The Routledge Companion to the Philosophy of Law*, pp. 451–466. London: Routledge.
Eekelaar, John. 2002. 'Judges and citizens: Two conceptions of law', *Oxford Journal of Legal Studies*, 22(3): 497–516.

Ehrenberg, Kenneth. 2011, 'Joseph Raz's theory of authority', *Philosophy Compass*, 6(12): 884–894.
Elden, Stuart. 2006. 'Contingent sovereignty, territorial integrity and the sanctity of borders', *SAIS Review of International Affairs*, 26(1): 11–24.
Eleftheriadis, Pavlos. 2010. 'Law and sovereignty', *Law and Philosophy*, 29: 535–569.
Elster, Jon. 1989. 'Social norms and economic theory', *Journal of Economic Perspectives*, 4(4): 99–117.
Enoch, David. 2014. 'Authority and reason-giving', *Philosophy and Phenomenological Research*, 89(2): 296–332.
Erman, Eva. 2022. 'The boundary problem of democracy: A function-sensitive view', *Contemporary Political Theory*, 21: 240–261.
Essert, Christopher. 2012. 'A dilemma for protected reasons', *Law and Philosophy*, 31: 49–75.
Estlund, David. 2007. *Democratic Authority*. Princeton: Princeton University Press.
Fabry, Mikulas. 2010. *Recognizing States: International Society and the Establishment of New States since 1776*. Oxford: Oxford University Press.
Feldman, Richard. 2005. 'Epistemological duties', in Paul K. Moser (ed.), *The Oxford Handbook of Epistemology*, pp. 362–384. Oxford: Oxford University Press.
Finneron-Burns, Elizabeth. 2016. 'Contractualism and the non-identity problem', *Ethical Theory and Moral Practice*, 19(5): 1151–1163.
Ford, Richard. 1999. 'Law's territory (A history of jurisdiction)', *Michigan Law Review*, 97: 843–930.
Florey, Katherine. 2019. 'Resituating territoriality', *George Mason Law Review*, 27: 141–204.
Fraser, Nancy. 2010. 'Who counts? Dilemmas of justice in a postwestphalian world', *Antipode*, 41: 281–297.
Galligan, Denis. 2006. *Law in Modern Society*. Oxford: Clarendon.
Gans, Chaim. 1986. 'Mandatory rules and exclusionary reasons', *Philosophia*, 15: 33–57.
Gardner, John. 2012. *Law as a Leap of Faith*. Oxford: Oxford University Press.
Gerring, John. 1999. 'What makes a concept good?: An integrated framework for understanding concept formation in the social sciences', *Polity*, 31(3): 357–393.
Golding, M.P. 1961. 'Kelsen and the concept of "legal system"', *Archiv für Rechts- und Sozialphilosophie*, 47: 355–386.
Goldsmith, M.M. 1996 'Hobbes on law', in Tom Sorell (ed.), *The Cambridge Companion to Hobbes*, pp. 274–305. Cambridge: Cambridge University Press.
Goodin, Robert. 2007. 'Enfranchising all affected interests, and it's alternatives', *Philosophy and Public Affairs*, 35: 40–68.
Goodin, Robert. 2013. 'Disgorging the fruits of historical wrongdoing', *American Political Science Review*, 107(3): 478–491.
Goodin, Robert. 2016. 'Enfranchising all-subjected, worldwide', *International Theory*, 8: 365–389.
Gould, Carol C. 2018. 'Democracy and global governance', in Chris Brown and Robyn Eckersley (eds.), *The Oxford Handbook of International Political Theory*, pp. 48–59. Oxford: Oxford University Press.
Gould, Stephen Jay. 1994. 'The evolution of life on the earth', *Scientific American*, 271(4): 84–91.
Grant, James. 2017. 'Reason and authority in administrative law', *Cambridge Law Journal*, 76(3): 507–536.
Green, Leslie. 1988. *The Authority of the State*. Oxford: Clarendon Press.
Green, Leslie. 1989. 'Law, legitimacy, and consent', *Southern California Law Review*, 62(4): 795–826.

Green, Leslie. 1996. 'The concept of law', *Michigan Law Review*, 94: 1687–1717.
Green, Leslie. 1999. 'Positivism and conventionalism', *Canadian Journal of Law and Jurisprudence*, 12(1): 35–52.
Green, Leslie. 2016. 'The forces of law: Duty, coercion, and power', *Ratio Juris*, 29: 164–181.
Green, Leslie and Thomas Adams. 2003. 'Legal positivism', in Edward N. Zalta (ed.), *The Stanford Encyclopedia of Philosophy* (Winter 2019 Edition), URL = https://plato.stanford.edu/archives/win2019/entries/legal-positivism/.
Gross, Jan Tomasz. 1979. *Polish Society under German Occupation: The Generalgouvernement, 1939–1944*. Princeton: Princeton University Press.
Hacker, P.M.S. 1973. 'Sanction theories of duty', in A.W.B. Simpson (ed.), *Oxford Essays in Jurisprudence*, pp. 131–170. Oxford: Clarendon Press.
Hage, Jaap. 2018. 'Of norms', in Gerald Postema et al. (eds.), *Handbook of Legal Reasoning and Argumentation*, pp. 103–138. Dordrecht: Springer.
Hage, Jaap. 2020. 'Two kinds of Normativity', in Stefano Bertea (ed.), *Contemporary Perspectives on Legal Obligation*, pp. 18–33. London: Routledge.
Halpin, Andre. 1996. 'The concept of a legal power', *Oxford Journal of Legal Studies*, 16: 129–152.
Hampton, Jean 1994. 'Democracy and the rule of law', in Ian Shapiro (ed.), *The Rule of Law*, NOMOS XXXVI, pp. 13–45. New York: New York University Press.
Hansen, Mogens Herman. 2010. 'Concepts of demos, Ekklesia and dikasterion in classical athens', *Greek, Roman and Byzantine Studies*, 50: 499–536.
Harmer, Nichola. 2020. 'Territory, identity and the UK overseas territory', in David Storey (ed.), *A Research Agenda for Territory and Territoriality*, pp. 83–102. Cheltenham: Edwar Elgar.
Hart, H.L.A. 1962. *The Concept of Law*. Oxford: Clarendon Press.
Hershovitz, Scott. 2003. 'Legitimacy, democracy and Razian authority', *Legal Theory*, 9: 201–220.
Hershovitz, Scott. 2012. 'The authority of law', in Andrei Marmor (ed.), *Routledge Companions to Philosophy of Law*, pp. 65–75. London: Routledge.
Hestermeyer, Holger P. 2009. 'Vienna convention on diplomatic relations (1961)', in Rüdiger Wolfrum (ed.), *Max Planck Encyclopedia of Public International Law*. Oxford Public International Law.
Himma, Kenneth Einar. 2001a. 'Law's claim of legitimate authority', in Jules Coleman (ed.), *Hart's Postscript*, pp. 271–309. Oxford: Oxford University Press.
Himma, Kenneth Einar. 2001b. 'The instantiation thesis and Raz's critique of inclusive positivism', *Law and Philosophy*, 20(1): 61–79.
Himma, Kenneth Einar. 2005. 'Final authority to bind with moral mistakes: On the explanatory potential of inclusive legal positivism', *Law and Philosophy*, 24: 1–45.
Himma, Kenneth Einar. 2007. 'Revisiting Raz: Inclusive positivism and the concept of authority', *APA Newsletter*, 6: 2.
Himma, Kenneth Einar. 2013a. 'A comprehensive Hartian theory of legal obligation: Social pressure, coercive enforcement, and the legal obligations of citizens', in Wil Waluchow and Stefan Sciaraffa (eds.), *Philosophical Foundations of the Nature of Law*, pp. 152–182. Oxford: Oxford University Press.
Himma, Kenneth Einar. 2013b. 'The ties that bind: An analysis of the concept of obligation', *Ratio Juris*, 26(1): 16–46.
Himma, Kenneth Einar. 2018. 'The problems of legal normativity and legal obligation', in Kenneth Einar Himma, Miodrag Jovanovic, and Bovan Spaic (eds.), *Unpacking Normativity: Conceptual, Normative, and Descriptive Issues*, pp. 135–154. London: Bloomsbury.

References

Hirt, Nicole and Abdulkader Saleh Mohammad. 2018. 'By way of patriotism, coercion, or instrumentalization: How the Eritrean regime makes use of the diaspora to stabilize its rule', *Globalizations*, 15(2): 232–247.

Hoefer, Carl. 2016. 'Causal determinism', in Edward N. Zalta (ed.), *The Stanford Encyclopedia of Philosophy* (Spring 2016 Edition), URL = https://plato.stanford.edu/archives/spr2016/entries/determinism-causal/.

Hohfeld, W.N. 1917. 'Fundamental legal conceptions as applied in judicial reasoning', *The Yale Law Journal*, 26(8): 710–770.

Honoré, Tony. 1987. *Making Law Bind*. Oxford: Clarendon Press.

Horty, John. 2003. 'Reasoning with moral conflicts', *Noûs*, 37(4): 557–605.

Hovell, Devika. 2018. 'The authority of universal jurisdiction', *European Journal of International Law*, 29(2): 427–456.

Hurd, Heidi. 1996. 'The moral magic of consent', *Legal Theory*, 2: 121–146.

Hurd, Heidi. 1999. *Moral Combat: The Dilemma of Legal Perspectivalism*. Cambridge: Cambridge University Press.

Hurd, Heidi. 2018. 'The normative force of consent', in Andreas Müller and Peter Schaber (eds.), *The Routledge Handbook of the Ethics of Consent*, pp. 44–54. London: Routledge.

Ireland-Piper, Danielle. 2017. *Accountability in Extraterritoriality: A Comparative and International Law Perspective*. Cheltenham: Edwar Elgar.

Ivison, Duncan. 2009. 'Historical injustice', in John Dryzek, Bonnie Honig, and Anne Philips (eds.), *The Oxford Handbook of Political Theory*, pp. 507–525. Oxford: Oxford University Press.

Jessop, Bon. 2015. *The State. Past, Present, Future*. Cambridge: Polity.

Joas, Hans. 2004. 'Morality in an age of contingency', *Acta Sociologica*, 47(4): 392–399.

Jurkevics, Anna. 2019. 'Democracy in contested territory: On the legitimacy of global legal pluralism', *Critical Review of International Social and Political Philosophy*, 25(2): 187–210.

Kaczmarek, Sarah C. and Abraham L. Newman. 2011. 'The long arm of the law: Extraterritoriality and the national implementation of foreign bribery legislation', *International Organization*, 65: 745–770.

Kaltwasser, Cristóbal 2014. 'The responses of populism to Dahl's democratic dilemmas', *Political Studies*, 62(3): 470–487.

Kamminga, M.T. 2012. 'Extraterritoriality', in Rudiger Wolfrum (ed.), *Max Planck Encyclopedia of Public International Law*, pp. 1070–1077. Oxford: Oxford University Press.

Kaplan, Jeffrey. 2017. 'Attitude and the normativity of law', *Law and Philosophy*, 36(5): 469–493.

Kaplan, Jeffrey. 2021. 'Attitude and social rules, or why it's okay to slurp your soup', *Philosopher's Imprint*, 21(28): 1–19.

Kayaoğlu, Turan. 2013. *Legal Imperialism: Sovereignty and Extraterritoriality in Japan, the Ottoman Empire, and China*. New York: Cambridge University Press.

Kelsen, Hans. 1945. *A General Theory of Law and State*. Berkeley: The University of California.

Kelsen, Hans. 1959. 'On the *basic norm*', *California Law Review*, 47: 107–110.

Kelsen, Hans. 1991. *General Theory of Norms*. Oxford: Oxford University Press.

Keyssar, Alexander. 2000. *The Right to Vote. The Contested History of Democracy in the United States*. New York: Basic Books.

Kleinig, John. 2009. 'The nature of consent', in Franklin Miller and Alan Wertheimer (eds.), *The Ethics of Consent: Theory and Practice*, pp. 3–24. Oxford: Oxford University Press.

Klosko, George. 1991. 'Reformist consent and political obligation', *Political Studies*, 39: 676–690.

Klosko, George. 1992. *The Principle of Fairness and Political Obligation*. Lanham: Rowman & Littlefield.

Koller, Peter 2014. 'On the nature of norms', *Ratio Juris*, 27(2): 155–175.
Kolodny, Nick. 2014. 'Rule over none I: What justifies democracy?', *Philosophy and Public Affairs*, 42(3): 195–229.
Kornhauser, Lewis. 1999. 'The normativity of law', *American Law and Economics Review*, 1(1/2): 3–25.
Korsgaard, Christine M. 2008. *The Constitution of Agency: Essays on Practical Reason and Moral Psychology*. Oxford: Oxford University Press.
Kramer, Matthew. 1999. 'Requirements, reasons and Raz: Legal positivism and legal duties', *Ethics*, 109: 375–407.
Kramer, Matthew. 2005. 'Of final things: Morality as one of the ultimate determinants of legal validity', *Law and Philosophy*, 24(1): 47–97.
Kramer, Matthew. 2018. *H.L.A. Hart*. Cambridge: Polity.
Krasner, Stephen. 1995. 'Compromising westphalia', *International Security*, 20(3): 115–151.
Kurki, Visa A.J. 2017. 'Legal competence and legal power', in Mark McBride (ed.), *New Essays on the Nature of Rights*, pp. 31–48. London: Hart Publishing.
Lahr, Mirazón et al. 2016. 'Inter-group violence among early Holocene hunter-gatherers of West Turkana, Kenya', *Nature*, 529: 394–398.
Lamond, Grant. 2001. 'Coercion and the nature of law', *Legal Theory*, 7(1): 35–57.
Lamond, Grant. 2014. 'Legal sources, the rule of recognition, and customary law', *American Journal of Jurisprudence*, 59: 25–48.
Lamond, Grant. 2016. 'Persuasive authority and the law', *The Harvard Review of Philosophy*, 17: 16–35.
Laponce, J.A. 2004. 'Turning votes into territories: Boundary referendums in theory and practice', *Political Geography*, 23(2): 169–183.
Layton, Alexander and Angharad Parry. 2004. 'Extraterritorial jurisdiction — European responses', *Houston Journal of International Law*, 26: 319–320.
Le Roux, Wessel. 2015. 'Residence, representative democracy and the voting rights of migrant workers in post-Apartheid South Africa and postunification Germany (1990–2015)', *Verfassung in Recht und Übersee*, 48(3): 284–304.
Lepsius, Oliver. 2020. 'Georg Jellinek's theory of the two sides of the state ('Zwei-Seiten-Lehre des Staates')', in Nicoletta Bersier Ladavac, Christoph Bezemek, and Frederick Schauer (eds.), *The Normative Force of the Factual*, Law and Philosophy Library book series 130, pp. 5–28. Dordrecht: Springer.
Levitsky, Steven and Daniel Ziblatt. 2018. *How Democracies Die: What History Reveals About Our Future*. New York: Crown.
Lindahl, Hans. 2001. 'Sovereignty and the institutionalization of normative order', *Oxford Journal of Legal Studies*, 21: 165–180.
Lindahl, Hans. 2007. 'The paradox of constituent power. The ambiguous self-constitution of the European Union', *Ratio Juris*, 20: 485–505.
List, Christian and Laura Valentini 2016. 'The methodology of political theory', in Herman Cappelen, Tamar Szabó Gendler, and John Hawthorne (eds.), *Oxford Handbook of Philosophical Methodology*, pp. 525–554. Oxford: Oxford University Press.
Little, Adrian. 2015. 'The complex temporality of borders: Contingency and normativity', *European Journal of Political Theory*, 14(4): 429–447.
López, Jaume and Marc Sanjaume-Calvet. 2020. 'The political use of de facto referendums of independence: The case of Catalonia', *Representation*, 56(4): 501–519.
Lopéz-Guerra, Claudio. 2005. 'Should expatriates vote?', *Journal of Political Philosophy*, 13: 216–234.
Lovett, Frank. 2012. 'What counts as arbitrary power?', *Journal of Political Power*, 5(1): 137–152.

Lovett, Frank. 2019. 'In defense of the practice theory', *Ratio Juris*, 32(3): 320–338.
Lowe, Vaughan and Christopher Staker. 2003. 'Jurisdiction', in M.D. Evans (ed.), *International Law*, pp. 289–315. Oxford: Oxford University Press.
Lyons, David. 1993. *Moral Aspects of Legal Theory*. Cambridge: Cambridge University Press.
MacCormick, Neil. 1997. 'Institutional normative order: A conception of law', *Cornell Law Review*, 82: 1051–1070.
MacCormick, Neil. 1998. 'Powers and power-conferring norms', in Stanley L. Paulson and Bonnie Litschewski Paulson (eds.), *Normativity and Norms: Critical Perspectives on Kelsenian Themes*, pp. 435–449. Oxford: Oxford University Press.
MacCormick, Neil. 2007. 'Why law makes no claims', in George Pavlakos (ed.), *Law, Rights and Discourse: The Legal. Philosophy of Robert Alexy*, pp. 59–67. Oxford: Oxford University Press.
MacIsaac, Samuel and Buck C. Duclos. 2020. 'Trade and conflict: Trends in economic nationalism, unilateralism and protectionism', *Canadian Foreign Policy Journal*, 26(1): 1–7.
Maltais, Aaron, Jonas Hultin Rosenberg, and Ludvig Beckman. 2019. 'The demos and its critics', *The Review of Politics*, 81(3): 435–457.
Mann, Michael. 1984. 'The autonomous power of the state : Its origins, mechanisms and results', *European Journal of Sociology*, 25: 185–213.
Marmor, Andrei. 2005. 'Authority, equality and democracy', *Ratio Juris*, 18(3): 315–345.
Marmor, Andrei. 2009. *Social Conventions: From Language to Law*. Princeton: Princeton University Press.
Marmor, Andrei. 2011. 'The dilemma of authority', *Jurisprudence*, 2(1): 121–141.
Martí, José L. 2021. 'The democratic legitimacy of secession and the demos problem', *Politics and Governance*, 9(4): 465–474.
Martin, Rex. 2003. 'Political obligation', in Richard Bellamy and Andrew Mason (eds.), *Political Concepts*, pp. 41–51. Manchester: Manchester University Press.
Meisels, Tamar. 2005. *Territorial Rights*. Dordrecht: Springer.
Mendonca, Daniel. 1998. 'Presumptions', *Ratio Juris*, 11(4): 399–412.
Mian, Emran. 2002. 'The curious case of exclusionary reasons', *Canadian Journal of Law and Jurisprudence*, 15(1): 99–124.
Mikhail, John. 2009. 'Is the prohibition of Homicide Universal? Evidence from comparative criminal law', *Brooklyn Law Review*, 75: 497–515.
Miklosi, Zoltan. 2012. 'Against the principle of all-affected interests', *Social Theory and Practice*, 38(3): 483–503.
Miller, David. 2008. 'Political theory for earthlings', in David Leopold and Marc Stears (eds.), *Political Theory: Methods and Approaches*, pp. 29–48. Oxford: Oxford University Press.
Miller, David 2009. 'Justice and boundaries', *Politics, Philosophy and Economics*, 8(3): 291–309.
Miller, David. 2010. 'Why immigration controls are not coercive: A reply to Arash Abizadeh', *Political Theory*, 38(1): 111–120.
Miller, David. 2014. 'Debatable lands', *International Theory*, 6: 104–121.
Miller, David. 2018. 'What makes a democratic people?', in *Democratic Inclusion: Rainer Bauböck in Dialogue*. Manchester: Manchester University Press.
Miller, David. 2020. 'Reconceiving the democratic boundary problem', *Philosophy Compass*, 15: 1–9.
Mindus, Patricia. 2013. 'Austin and scandinavian realism', in Michael Freeman and Patricia Mindus (eds.), *The Legacy of John Austin's Jurisprudence*, pp. 73–106. Dordrecht: Springer.
Mollendorf, Darrel. 2009. *Global Inequality Matters*. Basingstoke: Palgrave.
Moore, Margaret. 2015. *A Political Theory of Territory*. Oxford: Oxford University Press.

Moreono-Lax, Violeta. 2017. *Accessing Asylum in Europe: Extraterritorial Border Control*. Oxford: Oxford University Press.
Morris, Christopher. 2012. 'State coercion and force', *Social Philosophy and Policy*, 29(1): 28–49.
Murphy, Alexander B. 1996. 'The sovereign state system as political-territorial ideal: Historical and contemporary considerations', in Thomas J. Biersteker (ed.), *State Sovereignty as Social Construct*, pp. 81–120. Cambridge: Cambridge University Press.
Murphy, Liam. 2018. 'The normative force of law', in John Gardner, Leslie Green, and Brian Leiter (eds.), *Oxford Studies in Philosophy of Law Volume 3*, pp. 88–123. Oxford: Oxford University Press.
Nagel, Thomas. 2005. 'The problem of global justice', *Philosophy and Public Affairs*, 33(2): 113–147.
Näsström, Sofia. 2007. 'The legitimacy of the people', *Political Theory*, 35: 624–658.
Näsström, Sofia. 2011. 'The challenge of the all-affected principle', *Political Studies*, 59(1): 116–134.
Neuman, Gerald L. 1992. 'We are the people': Alien suffrage in German and American perspective', *Michigan Journal of International Law*, 13: 259–335.
Nili, Shmuel. 2017. 'Democratic theory, the boundary problem, and global reform', *The Review of Politics*, 79(1): 99–123.
Nine, Cara. 2008. 'The moral arbitrariness of state borders: Against Beitz', *Contemporary Political Theory*, 7(3): 259–279.
Noah Smith, Matthew. 2006. 'The law as a social practice', *Legal Theory*, 12: 265–292.
Nowell-Smith, Patrick. 1976. 'What is authority?', *Philosophic Exchange*, 7(1): 3–15.
Nozick, Robert. 1974. *Anarchy, State and Utopia*. Oxford: Blackwells.
O'Beirne, Brian H. 'Does legal philosophy need a theory of the state?', (October 26, 2011). Available at: SSRN: https://ssrn.com/abstract=1949858.
Ober, Josiah. 1989. *Mass and Elite in Democratic Athens: Rhetoric, Ideology, and the Power of the People*. Princeton: Princeton University Press.
Oberdiek, Hans. 1976. 'The role of sanctions and coercion in understanding law and legal systems', *American Journal of Jurisprudence*, 21(1): 71–94.
Ochoa, Espejo Paulina. 2011. *The Time of Popular Sovereignty*. Philadelphia: Pennsylvania University Press.
Ochoa, Espejo Paulina. 2014. 'People, territory, and legitimacy in democratic states', *American Journal of Political Science*, 58: 466–478.
Orentlicher, Diane. 2004. 'Who's justice? Reconciling universal jurisdiction with democratic principles', *Georgetown Law Journal*, 92: 1057–1134.
Östbring, Björn. 2019. *Migrationspolitiska dilemman: Om idealism och realism i liberal politisk teori*. Lund: Lund University.
Owen, David. 2011. 'Constituting the polity, constituting the demos: On the place of the all affected interests principle in democratic theory and in resolving the democratic boundary problem', *Ethics and Global Affairs*, 5(3): 129–151.
Oxman, Bernard H. 2007. 'Jurisdiction of states', in Rüdiger Wolfrum (ed.), *Max Planck Encyclopedia of Public International Law*. Oxford: Oxford University Press.
Paasi, Anssi. 2009. 'Bounded spaces in a 'borderless world': Border studies, power and the anatomy of territory', *Journal of Power*, 2(2): 213–234.
Page, Edward. 1999. 'Intergenerational justice and climate change', *Political Studies*, 47: 53–66.
Van Parijs, Philippe. 2007. 'International distributive justice', in Robert E. Goodin, Philip Pettit, and Thomas Pogge (eds.), *A Companion to Contemporary Political Philosophy*, pp. 638–652. Oxford: Blackwell.

Parker, Noel and Rebecca Adler-Nissen. 2012. 'Picking and choosing the "sovereign" border: A theory of changing state bordering practices', *Geopolitics*, 174: 773–796.

Parker, Noel, Nick Vaughan-Williams et al. 2009. 'Lines in the sand? Towards an agenda for critical border studies', *Geopolitics*, 14(3): 582–587.

Parrish, Austen. 2008. 'The effects test: Extraterritoriality's fifth business', *Vanderbilt Law Review*, 61(5): 1455–1506.

Parvu, Alexandre. 2015. 'The boundary problem in democratic theory: Cosmopolitan implications', in Tamara Caraus and Dan Lazea (eds.), *Cosmopolitanism without Foundations?* pp. 89–110. Bucharest: Zeta Books.

Pavel, Carmen E. 2018. 'Boundaries, subjection to laws, and affected interests', in David Schmidtz and Carmen E. Pavel (eds.), *The Oxford Handbook of Freedom*, pp. 319–340. Oxford: Oxford University Press.

Perry, Stephen. 2005. 'Law and obligation', *The American Journal of Jurisprudence*, 50(1): 263–295.

Perry, Stephen. 2006. 'Hart on social rules and the foundations of law: Liberating the internal point of view', *Fordham Law Review*, 75: 1171–1209.

Philpott, Daniel. 2002. *Revolutions in Sovereignty*. Princeton: Princeton University Press.

Piirimäe, Pärtel. 2010. 'The westphalian myth of sovereignty and the idea of external sovereignty', in Kent Kalmo and Quentin Skinner (eds.), *Sovereignty in Fragments*, pp. 48–80. Cambridge: Cambridge University Press.

Pogge, Thomas. 2002. *World Poverty and Human Rights: Cosmopolitan Responsibilities and Reforms*. Cambridge: Polity.

Pogonyi, Szabolcs. 2014. 'Four patterns of non-resident voting rights', *Ethnopolitics*, 13(2): 122–140.

Postema, Gerald J. 1998. 'Norms, reasons, and law', *Current Legal Problems*, 51(1): 149–179.

Przeworski, Adam. 2009. 'Conquered or granted? A history of suffrage extensions', *British Journal of Political Science*, 39: 291–321.

Putnam, Tonya. 2016. *Courts without Borders: Law, Politics, and US Extraterritoriality*. Cambridge: Cambridge University Press.

Qvortrup, Matt. 2014. 'Referendums on independence, 1860–2011', *The Political Quarterly*, 85: 57–64.

Raustiala, Kal. 2005. 'The geography of justice', *Fordham Law Review*, 73(6): 2501–2560.

Rawls, John 1955. 'Two concepts of rules', *The Philosophical Review*, 64(1): 3–32.

Rawls, John. 1993. *Political Liberalism*. New York: Columbia University Press.

Raz, Joseph. 1970. *The Concept of a Legal System*. Oxford: Clarendon.

Raz, Joseph. 1975. 'Reasons for action, decisions and norms', *Mind*, 84(336): 481–499.

Raz, Joseph. 1985. 'Authority and justification', *Philosophy and Public Affairs*, 14(1): 3–29.

Raz, Joseph. 1986. *The Morality of Freedom*. Oxford: Clarendon.

Raz, Joseph. 1990. 'Introduction', in Joseph Raz (ed.), *Authority*, pp. 1–19. New York: New York University Press.

Raz, Joseph. 1994. *Ethics in the Public Domain*. Oxford: Clarendon Press.

Raz, Joseph. 1999. *Practical Reason and Norms*. Oxford: Oxford University Press.

Raz, Joseph. 2004. 'Can there be a theory of law?', in Martin Golding and William Edmundson (eds.), *Blackwell Guide to Philosophy of Law and Legal Theory*, pp. 324–342. Oxford: Blackwell.

Raz, Joseph. 2009a. *The Authority of Law*. 2nd ed. Oxford: Oxford University Press.

Raz, Joseph. 2009b. *Between Authority and Interpretation*. Oxford: Oxford University Press.

Raz, Joseph. 2017. 'Why the *state*?', in Nicole Roughan and Andrew Halpin (eds.), *Pursuit of Pluralist Jurisprudence*, pp.136–162. Cambridge: Cambridge University Press.

Regan, D.H. 1990. 'Reasons, authority, and the meaning of obey: Further thoughts on Raz and obedience to law', *Canadian Journal of Law and Jurisprudence*, 3(1): 3–28.
Reinikainen, Jouni. 2022. 'What is the justifiable *demos* of a referendum on state secession?', *Ethics, Politics and Society*, 5(1): 47–70.
Ripstein, Arthur. 2004. 'Authority and coercion', *Philosophy and Public Affairs*, 32(1): 2–35.
Robé, Jean-Philippe. 2011. 'The legal structure of the firm', *Accounting, Economics and Law*, 1(1): 1–86.
Roht-Arriaza, Naomi. 2004. 'Universal jurisdiction: Steps forward, steps back', *Leiden Journal of International Law*, 17(2): 375–389.
Rose, Richard. 1982. 'Is the United Kingdom a state? Northern Ireland as a test case', in Peter Madgwick and Richard Rose (eds.), *The Territorial Dimension in United Kingdom Politics*, pp. 100–137. London: Palgrave Macmillan.
Ross, Alf. 1952. *Why Democracy?* Cambridge: Harvard University Press.
Ross, Michael. 2004. 'Does taxation lead to representation?', *British Journal of Political Science*, 34(2): 229–249.
Roughan, Nicole. 2018. 'The official point of view and the official claim to authority', *Oxford Journal of Legal Studies*, 38(2): 191–216.
Ryngaert, Cedric. 2008. *Jurisdiction in International Law*. Oxford: Oxford University Press.
Sandage, John Byron. 1985. 'Forum non conveniens and the extraterritorial application of United States antitrust law', *Yale Law Journal*, 94(7): 1693–1714.
Sangiovanni, Andrea. 2007. 'Global justice, reciprocity, and the state', *Philosophy and Public Affairs*, 35: 3–39.
Sassen, Saskia. 2006. *Territory, Authority, Rights: From Medieval to Global Assemblages*. Princeton: Princeton University Press.
Sassen, Saskia. 2013. 'When territory deborders territoriality', *Territory, Politics, Governance*, 1(1): 21–45.
Schauer, Frederic. 2015. 'Are officials above the law?', in *The Force of Law*, pp. 75–92. Cambridge: Harvard University Press.
Schedler, Andreas. 2007. 'Mapping contingency', in Ian Shapiro and Sonu Bedi (eds.), *Political Contingency*, pp. 54–78. New York: New York University Press.
Scheffler, Samuel. 2018. 'Membership and political obligation', *Journal of Political Philosophy*, 26(1): 3–23.
Scherz, Antoinette. 2013. 'The legitimacy of the demos: Who should be included in the demos and on what grounds?', *Living Reviews in Democracy*, 4: 1–14.
Schmitter, Philippe C. 1994. 'Dangers and dilemmas of democracy', *Journal of Democracy*, 5(2): 57–74.
Schneider, Bernard. 2012. 'The end of taxation without end: New tax regime for U.S. expatriates', *Virginia Tax Review*, 32(1): 1–76.
Sevel, Michael. 2018. 'Obeying the law', *Legal Theory*, 24(3): 191–215.
Shachar, Ayelet. 2009. *The Birthright Lottery: Citizenship and Global Inequality*. Cambridge: Harvard University Press.
Shapiro, Scott. 2002. 'Authority', in John Coleman and Scott Shapiro (eds.), *The Oxford Handbook of Jurisprudence and Philosophy of Law*, pp. 382–440. Oxford: Oxford University Press.
Shapiro, Scott. 2005. 'The rationality of rule-guided behaviour: A statement of the problem', *San Diego Law Review*, 42: 55–60.
Shapiro, Scott. 2006. 'What is the internal point of view?', *Fordham Law Review*, 75: 1157–1170.
Shaw, Jo. 2018. 'Citizenship and the franchise', in Ayelet Shachar, Rainer Bauböck, Irene Bloemraad, and Maarten Vink (eds.), *The Oxford Handbook of Citizenship*, pp. 290–315. Oxford: Oxford University Press.

Shaw, Malcolm N. 1982. 'Territory in international law', *Netherlands Yearbook of International Law*, XIII: 73–91.
Shaw, Malcolm N. 1996. 'The heritage of states: The principle of Uti Possidetis Juris today', *British Yearbook of International Law*, 67: 75–154.
Sheinman, Hanoch (ed.). 2011. *Promises and Agreements: Philosophical Essays*. Oxford: Oxford University Press.
Sher, George. 1981, 'Ancient wrongs and modern rights', *Philosophy and Public Affairs*, 10(1): 3–17.
Shiner Roger A. 1990. 'The acceptance of a legal system', *Canadian Journal of Law and Jurisprudence*, 3(2): 81–107.
Simion, Mona. 2018. 'No epistemic norm for action', *American Philosophical Quarterly*, 55(3): 231–238.
Simmons, A.J. 1995. 'Historical rights and fair shares', *Law and Philosophy*, 14: 149–184.
Simmons, A.J. 2016. *Boundaries of Authority*. Oxford: Oxford University Press.
Singer, Abraham. 2018. *The Form of the Firm: A Normative Political Theory of the Corporation*. Oxford: Oxford university Press.
Slys, Mariya Tait. 2014. *Exporting Legality. The Rise and Fall of Extraterritorial Jurisdiction in the Ottoman Empire and China*. Geneve: Graduate Institute Publications.
Sofier, Sasson. 2009. 'The prominence of historical demarcations: Westphalia and the New World order', *Diplomacy and Statecraft*, 20(1): 1–19.
Soifer, Hillel. 2008. 'State infrastructural power: Approaches to conceptualization and measurement', *Studies in Comparative International Development*, 43: 231–251.
Song, Sarah, 2012. 'The boundary problem in democratic theory: Why the demos should be bounded by the state', *International Theory*, 4(1): 39–68.
Soper, Philip. 1989. 'Legal theory and the claim of authority', *Philosophy and Public Affairs*, 18(3): 209–237.
Soper, Philip. 1996. 'Law's normative claims', in Robert P. George (ed.), *The Autonomy of Law*, pp. 215–248. Oxford: Oxford University Press.
Southwood, Nicholas. 2019. 'Contractualism for us as we are', *Philosophy and Phenomenological Research*, 99(3): 529–547.
Spaak, Torben. 2003. 'Legal positivism, law's normativity, and the normative force of legal justification', *Ratio Juris*, 16(4): 469–485.
Spector, Horatio. 2019. 'A pragmatic reconstruction of law's claim to authority', *Ratio Juris*, 32: 21–48.
Stevenson, Drury. 2003. 'To whom is the law addressed?', *Yale Law and Policy Review*, 21(1): 105–167.
Stilz, Anne. 2018. 'Territorial boundaries and history', *Politics, Philosophy and Economics*, 18(4): 374–385.
Suber, Peter. 1990. *The Paradox of Self-Amendment: A Study of Law, Logic, Omnipotence, and Change*. Bern: Peter Lang.
Tapper, Colin. 1965. 'Austin on sanctions', *The Cambridge Law Journal*, 23(2): 271–287.
Taylor, Charles. 1998. 'The dynamics of democratic exclusion', *Journal of Democracy*, 9: 143–156.
Taylor, P.J. 1994. 'The state as container: Territoriality in the modern world-system', *Progress in Human Geography*, 18: 151–162.
Tierney, Stephen. 2012. *Constitutional Referendums: The Theory and Practice of Republican Deliberation*. Oxford: Oxford University Press.
Torpey, John. 2009. *The Invention of the Passport. Surveillance, Citizenship and the State*. Cambridge: Cambridge University Press.
Troper, Michel. 2020. 'The structure of the legal system and the emergence of the state', in Baudouin Dupret, Julie Colemans, and Max Travers (eds.), *Legal Rules in Practice In the Midst of Law's Life*, pp. 44–88. London: Routledge.

Tuori, Kaarlo. 2018. 'Whose voluntas, what ratio? Law in the state tradition', *International Journal of Constitutional Law*, 16: 1164–1175.
Turner, Derek and Joyce C. Havstad. 2019 'Philosophy of Macroevolution', in Edward N. Zalta (ed.), *The Stanford Encyclopedia of Philosophy* (Summer 2019 Edition), URL = https://plato.stanford.edu/archives/sum2019/entries/macroevolution/
Ullman-Margalit, Edna. 1977. 'Coordination norms and social choice', *Erkenntnis*, 11(2): 143–155.
United Nations. 2014. *Report of the Monitoring Group on Somalia and Eritrea pursuant to Security Council resolution 2111 (2013)*, Security Council, S/2014/727.
Valentini, Laura. 2014. 'No global demos, no global democracy? A systematization and critique', *Perspectives on Politics*, 12(4): 789–807.
Valentini, Laura. 2018. 'The content-independence of political obligation: What it is and how to test it', *Legal Theory*, 24(2): 135–157.
van Inwagen, Peter and Meghan Sullivan. 2018. 'Metaphysics', in Edward N. Zalta (ed.), *The Stanford Encyclopedia of Philosophy* (Spring 2018 Edition), URL = https://plato.stanford.edu/archives/spr2018/entries/metaphysics/
Venezia, Luciano. 2014. 'Hobbes' two accounts of law and the structure of reasons for political obedience', *European Journal of Political Theory*, 13(3): 282–292.
Venezia, Luciano. 2020. 'Mistaken authority and obligation', *Legal Theory*, 26(4): 338–351.
Viehoff, Daniel. 2011. 'Procedure and outcome in the justification of authority', *Journal of Political Philosophy*, 19(2): 248–259.
Vinx, Lars. 2007. *Hans Kelsen's Pure Theory of Law: Legality and Legitimacy*. Oxford: Oxford University Press.
Waldron, Jeremy. 1999. 'All we like sheep', *Canadian Journal of Law and Jurisprudence*, 21(1): 169–190.
Waldron, Jeremy. 2002. 'Redressing historic injustice', *University of Toronto Law Journal*, 52(1): 135–160.
Waldron, Jeremy. 2006. 'Kant's theory of the state', in Pauline Kleingeld (ed.), *Toward Perpetual Peace and Other Writings on Politics, Peace, and History*, pp. 477–504. Yale: Yale University Press.
Warren, Mark E. 2017. 'The all affected interests principle in democratic theory and practice', Institute for Advanced Studies (IHS), Working paper 145.
Wendel, Bradley. 2006. 'Lawyers, citizens and the internal point of view', *Fordham Law Review*, 75: 1473–1499.
Westlund, Andrea. 2013. 'Voluntary associations and authority. Deference as a normative power', *Philosophical Studies*, 166(3): 455–474.
Whelan, Frederick G. 1983. 'Prologue: Democratic theory and the boundary problem', in J. Roland Pennock and John W. Chapman (eds.), *Liberal Democracy*, pp. 13–47. New York: New York University Press.
Whitt, Matt. 2014. 'Democracy's sovereign enclosures: Territory and the all-affected principle', *Constellations*, 21: 560–574.
Wijffelman, Anne. 2017. 'Child marriage and family reunification: An analysis under the European Convention on Human Rights of the Dutch Forced Marriage Prevention Act', *Netherlands Quarterly of Human Rights*, 35(2): 104–121.
Wiland, Eric. 2002. 'Theories of practical reason', *Metaphilosophy*, 33: 450–467.
Wilson, James L. 2022. 'Making the all-affected principle safe for democracy', *Philosophy and Public Affairs*, 50: 169–201.
Wolff, R.P. 1990. 'The conflict between authority and autonomy', in Joseph Raz (ed.), *Authority*, pp. 20–32. New York: New York University Press.

Worsnip, Alex. 2018. 'Eliminating prudential reasons', in Mark Timmons (ed.), *Oxford Studies in Normative Ethics 8*, pp. 236–257. Oxford: Oxford University Press.

Wright, G.R. 2010. 'Arbitrariness: Why the most important idea in administrative law can't be defined, and what this means for the law in general', *University of Richmond Law Review*, 44: 839–865.

Yack, Bernard. 2001. 'Popular sovereignty and nationalism', *Political Theory*, 29(4): 517–536.

Yankah, Ekow N. 2008. 'The force of law: The role of coercion in legal norms', *University of Richmond Law Review*, 42: 1195–1256.

Yaser Ziaee, Seyed. 2016. 'Countermeasures versus extraterritoriality in international law', *Russian Law Journal*, 4(4): 27–45.

Zion, James W. and Robert Yazzie. 1997. 'Indigenous law in North America in the wake of conquest', *British Columbia International and Comparative Law Review*, 20: 55–84.

Zipursky, Benjamin. 2006. 'Legal obligations and the internal aspect of rules', *Fordham Law Review*, 75: 1229–1252.

INDEX

Pages followed by n refer notes.

Abizadeh, Arash 73
acquiescence 57–58
all-affected principle 15, 102, 135
all-subjected principle 5–6, 10–11, 14–15, 17–18, 30–35, 44, 52, 87, 93, 100–102, 130, 134; and border conflicts 104–110; moralized conception of 20–22, 44–46, 137; objections to 98, 103–104, 107, 112, 123, 126, 130–140
apartheid 8
arbitrariness 111; moral 112, 117–119
Arrhenius, Gustaf 12, 103
associations 3, 5, 6, 11, 12, 18, 28; bylaws of 32, 34; chess 64, 67; political 28; sport 28
Austin, John 43, 75, 76, 81
authority thesis 47–48, 52, 69, 79
authority: claim to legitimate 28–29, 34, 47–48, 76, 87–88, 94, 124, 126, 137; comprehensive 79–80, 136; exclusive claim to 73, 79–80, 92, 100; de facto 28–33, 51, 65–66, 137–140; legal 45, 48, 53–54, 84; moral 138; practical v epistemic 133; systemic 45
autonomy 7–9, 99

Bauböck, Rainer 8–9, 114–115
Beran, Harry 19
Bertea, Stefano 65, 68
binding decisions 3–4, 17–22, 24–26
birthplace 116–117

border conflicts 104–110
border controls 98–101
Brennan, Geoffrey 57, 58

Caney, Simon 117
Catalonia referendum 107, 110
Catholic Church 32
causal explanation 113, 127
citizenship 2, 6–9, 117
climate change 70
coercion 6, 11, 14, 18, 22, 28, 41–43, 47–48, 56, 70–71, 75, 138; account of legal authority 74–77; defined 81n1; and state borders 99–101, 109
commands 43
commerical law 90–92
compliance, reasons for 22, 38, 42
consent 18–19
constitutions 32, 60, 135
content-independent reasons 27, 44
contingency 112; of borders 113–114; of peoples 114–117
corporations 5, 35, 37, 71, 82, 90–92
Crimea referendum 97, 108
crimes against humanity 87, 89

Dahl, Robert 3, 137
definitions 48
democracy: ideal of 5–6, 17; as ideal-type 11; and inclusion 1, 5, 25, 30, 46, 101; justification of 21, 127,

140; as justification of authority 46; presuppositions of 137; principles of 90, 100; procedural, 5, 12; rule-governed 33; in the workplace 29–30
democratic inclusion, principles of 10–13; and stability 9
democratic legitimacy 115–116
demos 1–2, 6–7, 93, 101, 139
diaspora tax 93–94

economic sanctions 90–92
effects doctrine 90–92, 96
epistemic decisions 15
Erman, Eva 12
Estlund, David 28
etiquette, rules of 67, 131–132
European Court of Human Rights 109n6
evolutionary process 113
exclusionary reasons 24, 27, 73, 74, 79, 130
extradiction 89
extraterritorial border policy 109n1
extraterritorial law 71, 84

Frank, Hans 139
Fuller, Lon 49n13

games, rules of 64, 66–67
genocide 87–88
Grundnorm 57–58, 75

Hart H.L.A. 4, 32, 36, 39, 43, 54–57, 62–67
Himma, Kenneth 58
Hobbes, Thomas 74, 76
Honoré, Tony 63
human rights 124

imperatives 41, 49, 75
independence referendums 104–110
internal point of view 55–59, 61–62, 68
International Chess Frederation, 4, 5, 102
international law 49, 80, 83–85, 90, 96, 98, 109–109
international taxation 71, 82, 93–95

jurisdiction 74, 82, 84, 92, 95; defined 82–83; extraterritorial 82, 84–87, 90–92; and territory 82–85, 95
justice: global 124–127; historical 113–124, 127

Kelsen, Hans 49n2, 57, 58, 75–78, 81

law: concept 40, 42–43, 48; dead-letter 77–78; substantive account of 72–74,

88–89; sources of 52–53; validity of 52, 54, 56–59, 81; *see also* international law
legal pluralism 80
legal spatiality 83
legal system 38–39, 48, 51, 53, 56–58, 73–78; dead 78–79; existence conditions of 76–77; indigenous 42; and territory 83; religious 42; and the state 71
legitimacy 27, 28, 29, 40, 31, 105, 109, 115–117, 137–138
Little, David 113

MacCormick, Neil 81
marriage, laws of 80, 135
Marti, José 107
membership principle of democratic inclusion 6–10, 18–21, 33–35
migration 7, 70, 99–100
Miller, David 9, 97–98
Montevideo Convention (1933) 70

national identity 102–103
nationalism 70, 101–103
Neanderthal species 122
non-identity problem 127
non-intervention principle 83, 124
normative power *see* power
normative system 4–5, 32, 42, 79, 130, 136
norms, concept of 39–41
Nozick, Robert 135
Nüremberg laws 7–8

obligation to obey the law 75; legal 41–43; moral 18–20, 43–47
Ochoa Espejo, Paulina 115
Ottoman Empire 86, 95

Parrish, Austen 90–91
Parvel, Carmen 111
Permanent Court of International Justice 84
Pinochet, Augusto 89–90
piracy 87–88
Pope Francis 32
Postema, Gerald 56
power: coercive 74; brute 28–29, 36, 39, 42, 48; causal 39, 71; normative power 32, 36, 38–39, 42, 43, 48, 71, 131
power-conferring norms 33, 36, 39, 54
practical reason 25–27, 36, 40, 76, 131
presumptions 12–13
promises 18–19
public/private distinction 130, 135

Raustiala, Kal 83, 85
Rawls, John 49n4
Raz, Joseph 5, 18, 24, 29, 36, 44–49, 53, 62–63, 67, 76, 78, 92
reasons for action 23, 36, 40–41, 43–45, 47, 49, 72–73, 90–92
rectificatory duties 122, 127

Scherz, Antoinette 111
Schleswig-Holstein referendum 107–108, 124
Schmitter, Philippe 137
Scottish independence referendum 109
secession 105, 107
self-constitution 116–117
self-determination 102
Shachar, Ayelet 117
Sheffler, Samuel 20
slavery 88
social norms 15, 39, 57, 63, 66, 130–132
social practices 52, 54, 58–62, 67
Song, Sarah 9
sovereignty 43, 75, 107, 108, 124
Soviet Union, referendum 107
Spector, Horatio 138
state: concept of 38–39, 42, 69–70, 83; and de facto authority 52, 137–140

taxation 93; of property 94–95; *see also* international taxation
Taylor, Peter J. 83
territorial borders 69–70, 82–83, 97–100; arbitrary 111–114, 117; and authority 100; contingency of 113–114; justice of 119–127; legitimacy of 123–124
territorial rights 121, 126–127
torture 88
Treaty of Lausanne (1923) 95
Treaty of Versailles (1919) 108, 109
Treaty of Westphalia (1648) 83, 95
Truss, Liz 32
tyranny 130, 139

unequal treaties 86
Union between Sweden and Norway, dissolution of 109, 115
universal jurisdiction 82, 86–90
universal suffrage 2
uti possidetis principle 121

Viehoff, Daniel 46
Vienna Convention of Diplomatic Relations (1961) 85, 95
vote, right to 1, 7–9, 15n3, 21, 87, 103, 109, 115

Waldron, Jeremy 56
Weber, Max 49n4
well-being 7–9, 99, 117, 125
Wendel, Bradley 59
Whelan, Frederic 104
Wolff, Robert 28

Yack, Bernard 113

Zipursky, Benjamin 59

Printed in the United States
by Baker & Taylor Publisher Services